Books by Lester R. Brown

SEEDS OF CHANGE
WORLD WITHOUT BORDERS

WORLD WITHOUT BORDERS

WORLD WITHOUT BORDERS

Lester R. Brown

RANDOM HOUSE

New York

9 8 7 6 5 4 3

Copyright © 1972 by Lester R. Brown

All rights reserved under International and Pan-American Copyright
Conventions. Published in the United States by Random House, Inc.,
New York, and simultaneously in Canada by Random House of Canada
Limited, Toronto.

Library of Congress Cataloging in Publication Data

Brown, Lester Russell, 1934–
World without borders.

Bibliography: p.
1. Economic history—1945-   2. Social history—1945-
I. Title.
HC59.B765 1972b   330.9'046   72-5409
ISBN 0-394-48220-4
Manufactured in the United States of America

*This book is dedicated to a world order in which conflict and compe-
tition among nations will be replaced with cooperation and a sense
of community*

The cult of sovereignty has become mankind's major religion. Its god demands human sacrifice.

ARNOLD J. TOYNBEE

. . . the fundamental problem of our time is not the struggle between the socialists and them [capitalists]. The plans for nuclearizing the world must stop, and large-scale investments and technical aid must be given to underdeveloped regions. The fate of the world depends on the answer that is given to that question.

FRANTZ FANON

The strategy of peaceful coexistence and collaboration must be deepened in every way.

ANDREI SAKHAROV

. . . the Members of the U.N. have perhaps ten years left in which to subordinate their ancient quarrels and launch a global partnership to curb the arms race, to improve the human environment, to defuse the population explosion, and to supply the required momentum to development efforts . . . [or the problems] will have reached such staggering proportions that they will be beyond our capacity to control.

U THANT

All that is necessary to create the psychological foundations of a world society is that people in Maine should feel the same degree of responsibility toward the people of Japan or Chile or Indo-China as they feel toward California. This is pretty small, really, but it is apparently enough to create the United States.

KENNETH BOULDING

. . . there is a need for a revolution in mankind's thinking as basic as the one introduced by Copernicus who first pointed out that the earth was not the center of the universe.

LESTER PEARSON

PREFACE

No one I know possesses the credentials for writing a book with as wide a scope as this one. Certainly I do not. But such an overview is sorely needed. In simplest terms, its purpose is to provide a global perspective for considering the future. It is a backdrop for decision makers, from voters to corporate executives, from prospective parents to national leaders. Although occasional sections are directed specifically at Americans, its audience is all mankind.

The issues addressed are not solely the property of economists, ecologists or political scientists, but of everyone. *World Without Borders* is an integrated global overview for educators in all disciplines wishing to put their specific subject matter into a socially relevant global context. It is written particularly for students whose careers will span the final quarter of this century and who will be wrestling with these issues.

There is risky thinking afoot in the United States, particularly in the wake of Vietnam, that we can in fact be isolationist, that we can consume a third of the world's resources but not concern ourselves with its problems of poverty and social injustice. This book argues, however, that the question is not whether the United States should be involved internationally, for we know that it must, but what the nature of that involvement should be. How will we relate to the 94 percent of mankind living outside our borders?

That the world of the late twentieth century is changing rapidly is not an original observation. But our world is so complex that it is difficult to ask the right questions, much less come up with the right answers. The pace of change forces a person undertaking a project such as this book to do research from daily newspapers, magazines and journals. Many of the dominant issues, the major emerging threats to human well-being, are not yet on library shelves.

This book attempts to both document the growing interdependence among nations and examine its meaning for the values we hold, for how we manage technology, establish priorities and relate to other countries. The picture is painted with a broad brush, otherwise it could not be contained in a single volume. Others will analyze the world's specific ills more thoroughly and prescribe remedies in more detail. This book is designed not so much to provide specific answers as to put various issues in perspective by revealing their relationships to each other, removing them from the narrow confines in which they are generally treated.

As is often the case, the book is merely the tip of an iceberg of material assembled and analyzed in its preparation. I regret the lack of detail but nonetheless rest comfortably with the book's central thrust and general conclusions. Hopefully it does give a sense of the inhumanity of our present ordering of global priorities and of the ways in which we must redirect our energies and change direction if the quality of human existence is to improve rather than deteriorate in the decades ahead.

ACKNOWLEDGMENTS

Let me first thank someone, whose name I do not know, for inadvertently supplying the title of this book and for sharing its vision. In March of 1969, a nineteen-year-old Czech college student was describing for Haynes Johnson of the Washington *Evening Star* the sort of world she and her contemporaries in Prague wanted: "We would like to build a common world, a *world without borders*." If by chance this book should make its way into her hands I would like to hear from her.

Few authors could be indebted to more people in the production of a book than I. In a very real sense, *World Without Borders* is a product of many individuals, only a few of whom can be cited here.

Prominent among these is James P. Grant, president of the Overseas Development Council, who shared my feeling of the need for a global overview and synthesis. His support, encouragement and advice all along the way are deeply appreciated. The intellectual and moral support of Frank Coffin have been of immeasurable value. He, too, has shared the vision of a new world order.

Friends and associates in this country and abroad have devoted several hundred hours to reading and criticizing various drafts of the manuscript. Among these are Douglas Bennet, I. M. Destler, Curt Farrar, Eric Ferguson, Gail Finsterbusch, Orville Freeman, Theodore Geiger, Edward Hamilton, Philip Handler, Peter Henriot, James Howe, Robert Hunter, William Jones, Lawrence Kegan, Charles Kiefer, Paul Laudicina, John Maddux, Richard Malow, Edward Mason, Dennis Meadows, Rufus Miles, James Perkins, Judd Polk, William Ryan, Martin Sattler, John Schnittker, John Sewell, Davidson Sommers, Lauren Soth, Graham Tayar, Richard Ullman, Leroy Wehrle. To Charles Elliott, Andrew Rice and Ted Thomas, I am particularly indebted because they twice read and commented on the manuscript as it evolved.

Several individuals have assisted in various phases of research. Among these are Mollie Iler, William Rich, Donald Swanson, Carol Whitaker and Susan Sammartano. For the typing of several drafts I am indebted to Mary Condeelis, Pat Neace and, most importantly, Blondeen Duhaney. Nancy Krekeler has generously proofread several drafts.

Albert Erskine, Jim Wilcox and Suzanne Beves have made my relationship with Random House a delightful one.

I am grateful to my wife, Shirley Ann, to our children, Brian and Brenda, and to my parents, who again and again sacrificed time together in order that this book might be written.

As the list of selected readings at the end of the book indicates, I've drawn on the work of hundreds of authors. But there are several to whom I owe a particular intellectual debt. Among these are Kenneth Boulding, Harrison Brown, Seyom Brown, Zbigniew Brzezinski, Norman Cousins, Rene Dubos, Paul Ehrlich, Richard Falk, Richard Gardner, Louis Halle, Joseph Kraft, Ezra Mishan, Gunnar Myrdal, Lester Pearson, Aurelio Peccei, John Platt, Charles Reich, James Reston, Jean Francois Revel, Andrei Sakharov, Frank Snowden-Hopkins, Arnold Toynbee and Barbara Ward.

CONTENTS

WORLD WITHOUT BORDERS

1

INTRODUCTION:
Overview of the Late Twentieth Century

At an early morning breakfast late in 1970 I asked an economist, a former president of the American Economic Association, whether he felt the quality of life throughout the world had improved or deteriorated during the sixties. "It has deteriorated," he quickly responded. This question, asked of literally hundreds of people at luncheons, on airplanes and in several countries over the past two years, has elicited a divergence of opinion. Many feel that the quality of life has improved, but many others respond as did the economist at breakfast.

After a decade which witnessed the most rapid global economic growth in history, one might have expected an overwhelmingly positive response, but such was not the case. Per capita income is becoming less and less satisfactory as an indicator of well-being. For many, the decline per person of natural amenities, ranging from mineral resources to fresh water and natural recreation areas, may offset completely any rise in incomes. Nor can we ignore the indirect effects of economic growth, such as air and water pollution, the increasing incidence of environmentally induced diseases and the lengthening list of animal species threatened with extinction.

Historically, well-being has been closely related to trends in the production of goods and services. But as the world has become crowded and the level of economic activity has begun to press against the earth's finite capacities, shrinking natural amenities per person and the indirect effects of economic growth have begun to markedly affect our daily lives. For a sizable segment of humanity they more than offset the positive contribution of such growth.

While our system of economic accounting measures rather well the goods and services produced by man, we have no comparable techniques for collectively measuring the amenities provided by nature or the indirect effects of growth. Nor, needless to say, can we combine these three factors into a single indicator to replace per capita income. The purpose of this book is more modest, namely, to identify a fresh, more comprehensive framework within which to examine the principal factors affecting human well-being in the late twentieth century. Here we focus on the physical factors affecting us, turning to other factors in later chapters.

As the global economic growth rate approached 5 percent yearly during the sixties, greatly outstripping population growth at 2 percent yearly, per capita income climbed steadily. In the rich countries these gains in productivity brought a wealth of new goods and services. New consumer appliances, wrinkle resistant fabrics and prepared foods removed much of the drudgery from housekeeping. Air conditioning in homes, offices and automobiles became a necessity rather than the luxury it once was. Television became commonplace in the Western countries and in Japan, bringing new forms of entertainment into the home. Advances in food preservation and marketing, making available a variety of fresh and frozen foods throughout the year, enlivened our diets. Reduced costs of air transport added richness to life, since now international travel was within the range of tens of millions who previously could not afford it.

In medicine, a new vaccine largely eliminated poliomyelitis. New contraceptive technologies such as the pill took apprehension out of the bedroom, permitting the fuller enjoyment of sex. Instead of one car in every garage as was promised by an American politician a generation ago, there are now often two or three, providing an unprecedented degree of mobility. The exploration of outer space has brought a certain excitement with it. In hundreds of thousands of villages in Asia, Africa and Latin America, electric lights, steel plows and transistor radios have become part of the local landscape. Life expectancy increased steadily in the poor countries during the sixties. The Green Revolution has expanded food supplies and improved nutrition for many. These are but a few of the many improvements in well-being associated with advancing technology and economic growth.

At an earlier point in history a 5 percent economic growth rate would have brought widespread and unquestioned improvements in the quality of life, but such was not the case during the sixties. While the per capita supply of goods and services produced by man was increasing at a record rate, that of those amenities provided by nature was declining, also at a record rate. The global population increase of nearly 700 million during the sixties was roughly the same as that occurring between 1800 and 1900. This increase of more than 20 percent brought a corresponding decline in the per capita natural amenities which are in fixed supply. For each of us there was nearly one fifth less fresh water, mineral reserves, arable land, energy fuels, living space, waste absorptive capacity, marine protein and natural recreation areas in 1970 than in 1960.

The significance of this dramatic decline in natural amenities during the sixties, which is continuing at an unabated rate during the seventies, goes far beyond the mere arithmetic of the decline itself. This changing relationship between man and the finite natural system within which he exists is not merely an ecological phenomenon. It has profound economic, social and political consequences, which we are only beginning to perceive. It is forcing us to re-examine some of our basic values and goals. It is altering traditional relationships between rich countries and poor, and it may eventually affect the organization of global society itself.

The growing scarcity of fossil fuels and minerals caused by rapidly expanding global consumption is generating growing competition for the control of mineral reserves. This competition exists among countries, among multinational corporations and between countries and corporations. Already, the terms on which countries are making some industrial raw materials available to the international community are stiffening.

As fossil fuel reserves decline and consumption climbs and the seemingly insatiable demands of the rich countries press against the earth's fixed reserves, the world energy market is being transformed from a buyer's market to a seller's market. The price of gasoline at the corner service station cannot be divorced from the aspirations of the forty million Arabs who control the major share of the world's exportable petroleum reserves.

Natural recreation areas are being steadily diminished throughout the world by agricultural expansion and industrial development. Thus, the decline in per capita terms is even more rapid than that resulting from population increase alone. Those Americans caught in traffic jams in Yellowstone National Park in recent summers can appreciate this.

In social terms, perhaps the most disturbing decline among the natural amenities is in arable land. As population has continued to grow rapidly in the densely populated poor countries with little new land to bring under the plow, the area of arable land per person has shrunk steadily over the past two decades. In parts of Asia, the Middle East, North Africa, Central America and the Andean countries this decline has reached the point where the area per person is often not sufficient to permit a person to earn a living with available technologies. Plots of land divided and subdivided over the generations cannot be divided any further. For many young people there is no means of earning a living in the rural communities where they are born and reared.

This is a unique situation in historical terms. For this group there is no longer a place in the countryside, no job waiting in the city and no New World to emigrate to. In short there is no meaningful economic role in society as currently organized. In economic terms, these are marginal men.

The third set of factors affecting our well-being is the indirect effects of economic growth. Some affect us positively, but the great majority do not. For example, the production and use of automobiles expand the gross national product and bring an unprecedented degree of individual mobility, but the automobile also brings air pollution, noise pollution and frequent personal tragedy. Each year 60,000 Americans are killed by automobiles, 170,000 are permanently maimed, and 3.5 million are injured.

As the level of economic activity continues to expand, the list of birds, fish and mammals threatened with extinction lengthens. The eutrophication of fresh water lakes is accelerating on every continent, converting them into putrid, algae-laden swamps unfit for bathing and in some cases even for boating. The discharge of industrial and other wastes has reached a level at which rivers are dying biologically, and even large bodies of water, such as the Baltic and Mediterranean, are threatened with the same fate. Hundreds of beaches are being closed to swimmers in California, Italy, Japan and elsewhere.

Air pollution has reached the point where it is literally unsafe to breathe in many urban centers. City leaders in Rotterdam were so concerned that they secretly prepared an evacuation plan in the event of an extended atmospheric inversion, which would concentrate air pollutants and bring about a widespread loss of life.

Environmentally induced illnesses are a major casualty of economic growth. Irrigation projects in tropical and subtropical countries expand the production of food, but they also create an ideal habitat for schistosomiasis, a rapidly spreading, debilitating disease, now afflicting an estimated 200 million people. The rising incidence of emphysema is a by-product of man's expanding energy consumption. Mercury poisoning comes from pesticides and industrial wastes. Lung cancer, bronchitis and reported cases of lead and cadmium poisoning occur with increasing frequency. As of 1970 the victims of environmentally induced diseases numbered in the hundreds of millions, substantially exceeding the population of North America or Western Europe.

Short of a massive survey addressing our question to a representative sample of the world's population, we have no way of knowing for certain whether the perceived quality of life for mankind as a whole improved or deteriorated during the sixties. While on balance it undoubtedly improved, it does seem clear that the gain in well-being was far less than gains in per capita income would indicate. Within many poor countries, scarcely perceptible gains in average income probably did not begin to compensate for the pronounced declines in arable land per person, the progressive deforestation, the declining supplies of irrigation water per person, the increased crowding in villages and cities, and the rising unemployment.

One consequence of the much more rapid growth in income per person in the rich countries than in the poor was that the economic gap steadily widened. An affluent global minority is overfed and overweight, but more than half of mankind is hungry and malnourished; some can afford heart transplants, but half of mankind receives no health care at all; a handful of Americans have journeyed to the moon, but much of mankind cannot afford a visit to the nearest city; several thousand dollars are spent on a college education for millions of young Americans, while much of mankind lacks the limited resources required to become literate. In a shrinking world these growing disparities place great stress on the international political fabric.

Adding to this stress is the growing realization that mankind may be on the brink of a new era, a transition from an era of accelerating global demographic and economic growth to one in which both are slowing. Although it is yet too early to be certain, there is a distinct possibility that global rates of demographic and economic growth—both at an all-time high during the sixties—may have peaked at some time during the late sixties. The costs of continuing on the demographic and economic paths we are now on are rising and becoming unacceptable for a growing number of people throughout the world. This is reflected in such things as the emergence of the strong zero-population-growth and technology-assessment movements in the United States. Within many communities in the United States, Europe and Japan there is already growing resistance to the further expansion of certain types of economic activity.

Coinciding with this approach to many of the earth's

finite limits is the increasing clamor for social justice. Indeed, the environmental crisis is bringing the issue of social justice to the fore on a global scale. As we press against the limits of the earth's capacity to absorb waste materials, to supply fresh water, to produce marine protein or to provide energy and certain scarce metals, we find ourselves confronting the issue of social justice within an entirely different framework. The issue is becoming less the traditional one of how charitable the rich countries should be toward the poor and more how to distribute the earth's finite resources and capacities equitably among its people.

In the late twentieth century, pleas for equal rights are becoming demands. Equal rights is the cry of black Americans, Soviet Jews, Western women and the Third World poor. This is the inevitable result of historical forces already in motion, the culmination of centuries of evolution in human rights.

The nation-state with its sacred borders brings with it a concept of territorial discrimination which is increasingly in conflict with both the emerging social values of modern man and the circumstances in which he finds himself. It says, for instance, that we can institutionalize the transfer of resources from rich to poor within national societies, but not among societies. The poor on the other side of a national border are somehow less needful or less deserving than those inside the border. If we consider ourselves as members of a human family, can we continue to justify territorial discrimination any more than religious or racial discrimination?

The dimensions of the problems confronting late twentieth century man are unique in their scale. Man has always experienced catastrophes—famines, floods, earthquakes and volcanic eruptions—but they were local and temporary. Over time, more and more crises have become global in character. Only in this century have wars been world wars; only in recent decades, with such scientific "breakthroughs" as the detonation of the first atom bomb, has man acquired the capacity to threaten the entire species.

We live in an age when problems are increasingly world-wide—the world food problem, threat of world inflation, world population problem, world environmental crisis, world monetary crisis, world drug problem, and so forth. Few, if any, of mankind's more pressing problems have purely national solutions. They can be solved only through multinational or global cooperation. No country can protect the value of its currency or the health of its people without the extensive cooperation of other countries. Even our daily weather can be influenced by man's activities elsewhere in the world. The earth's ecosystem will continue to support human life only if countries can cooperate to eventually limit the discharge of waste materials.

While the more perplexing problems man faces today are global in scope, the institutions to cope with them are largely national. New technologies are creating problems but not the institutions capable of solving them. Advances in transport, communications and managerial skills have spawned the multinational corporation, but no supranational institution has been created to ensure that the behavior of these corporations is consistent with the interests of society at large.

As rapid population growth in much of the world continues, mankind's backlog of unsolved problems is growing. Questions of global poverty, rising numbers of unemployed and massive rural-urban migration in the poor countries, and a global ecosystem showing signs of acute stress, emerge before our expanded consciousness. Each promises to worsen in the years immediately ahead.

Given the scale and complexity of these problems, the remainder of the twentieth century will at best be a traumatic period for mankind, even with a frontal attack on the principal threats to human well-being. At worst it will be catastrophic. At issue is whether we can grasp the nature and dimensions of the emerging threats to our well-being, whether we can create an integrated global economy and a workable world order, and whether we can reorder global priorities so that the quality of life will improve rather than deteriorate.

Inventory of Mankind's Problems

2

THE ENVIRONMENTAL CRISIS

Nothing has underlined the common dilemma of all mankind so clearly as the environmental crisis now unfolding. Signs of stress on the ecosystem are everywhere today, reported daily in the press. The life-support systems for man and the other living things with which we share our earthly habitat are being threatened. This crisis affects everyone, rich and poor, old and young, Asian and American, black and white, born and unborn. There are no ecological sanctuaries. And it is much more than just a crisis of physical dimensions, for it brings into question both many of the values now widely held by individuals and the principles by which global society is organized, most importantly those of national sovereignty and continuous economic growth.

As of 1970, the concepts of sustained economic growth and ever-rising living standards, originating in the industrial West, had become the global norm. But our finite biosphere cannot accommodate an infinitely expanding world economy, fueled both by increases in man's numbers and by his desire for continuously rising material affluence. In an effort to meet these growing demands, man is forced to intervene more and more in the natural system, attempting to alter it to suit his needs better. Unfortunately, the adverse effects of these interventions are becoming more costly.

Intervening in the Environment

The capacity of man the hunter for intervening in his environment was exceedingly limited, but man the tiller developed a seemingly unlimited capacity for altering his environment and shaping it to his ends. Initially quite simple and limited in scope, his interventions in the natural system became progressively more complex and widespread. Eventually some of their consequences were to exceed his understanding of them.

In simplest terms, agriculture was an effort by man to shape his environment to suit his needs better. Man selected and favored those species of animals and plants which were useful to him as a source of food or clothing, but in the process, the global composition and distribution of both plant and animal species were substantially altered. Over the past century or so, man developed thousands of chemical compounds to help protect these domesticated species from predators, especially insects, and from disease. He also learned to use chemicals to restore and enhance soil fertility. These chemical interventions designed to increase and protect man's food supply have had far-reaching consequences.

As the earth's food-producing capacity expanded, it permitted increases in population. This in turn exerted pressure on food supply, compelling man to further expand the food supply. Population growth and advances in food production have thus tended to be mutually reinforcing.

Agriculture set the stage for civilization, urbanization and, more recently, industrialization. The latter, with its capacity for large-scale organization and mass-production techniques, provides a greatly enhanced capacity to intervene in the environment, exploiting it and shaping it to man's ends. The industrial revolution enabled man to harness hidden reserves of energy, first in the form of coal to run the steam engine, and later in the form of petroleum for the internal-combustion engine, until today the mining of coal and pumping of petroleum are proceeding at record levels.

Man has harnessed these vast stores of energy to reshape the face of the earth, clearing and plowing land and building highways, airports, parking lots, homes and factories. In the process of consuming these vast amounts of energy and materials to raise living levels, waste products are being generated on an ever-expanding scale of variety. Since industrial man assumed that nature could dispose of the wastes which he generated, he depended on air and water to absorb the by-products of his industrial activities. Nature was expected to absorb the heat and the products of combustion in the factory and the automobile as well as the chemical wastes from manufacturing processes. The latter are being dumped into lakes, rivers and streams in an ever-swelling volume, most of them eventually ending up in the oceans. An estimated 500,000 compounds are being emptied into the environment as waste products of man's economic activity. Many of these disintegrate quickly into harmless components, but some, like DDT, methyl mercury and plastic containers, which are not biodegradable (not readily broken down by nature), do not. Unfortunately, little research has been done to determine the effect of these waste products on the ecosystem.

As population increases and consumption levels rise, man

is forced to alter the environment more and more to meet his needs, either directly, as in agricultural expansion, or indirectly, as in waste disposal. Efforts to satisfy increased consumption needs are eradicating numerous species of animal and plant life, destroying natural wonders such as fresh-water lakes, destroying recreational resources, altering the earth's climate at least locally, and, potentially, destroying the natural life-support systems on which man depends. Expanding economic activity is rendering air unfit for breathing, water unfit for drinking, beaches unfit for bathing, and fish unfit for eating. Eco-catastrophes are occurring with increasing frequency.

Environmentally Induced Illnesses

In Chapter 1 we noted that there are many negative effects of expanding economic activity. Among these are environmentally induced illnesses, those illnesses resulting from man's alteration of the environment. These changes take many forms, including such things as the introduction of toxic materials into our environment and the creation of conditions conducive to the rapid spread of certain infectious diseases.

Air pollution, now a problem in every major area of the world, has reached serious levels in some cities. Los Angeles schoolchildren are cautioned against vigorous play because of air pollution. Tokyo traffic policemen inhale pure oxygen from oxygen tanks every two hours to avoid carbon monoxide poisoning.

Lester Lave and Eugene Seskin, synthesizing the findings of scores of studies undertaken in several countries, found a strong relationship between the level of air pollution and the incidence of respiratory disease, particularly bronchitis, emphysema and lung cancer. In the United Kingdom, deaths due to bronchitis are twice as frequent in urban areas with heavily polluted air as in rural areas. A study in the United States based on data for forty-six states shows deaths due to lung cancer among lifelong urban residents to be double those of lifelong rural residents. A similar situation was found in England and Wales.

The incidence of emphysema in the United States is now increasing rapidly, doubling every seven years. Closely associated with rising levels of air pollution, it is reaching almost epidemic proportions in some cities. Post-mortem respiratory examinations of a group of forty-five-year-old men in St. Louis revealed evidence of emphysema in nearly half of them.

Lave and Seskin point to disturbing evidence of the relationship between air pollution and both stomach cancer and coronary disease. This alarming contribution of air pollution to the incidence of disease and death may at least partly explain why life expectancy among Americans did not increase significantly during the sixties despite impressive advances in medical technology and a vast rise in health service expenditures.

Another source of concern is the rapidly rising level of toxic compounds now circulating in the biosphere, including mercury, lead, arsenic and cadmium. Concentrations have reached the point in some localities where they are affecting human well-being, often causing discomfort, sickness and death. Once the mercury level in water, fish and other foods reaches a certain point, it begins to adversely affect the central nervous system of more complex organisms, particularly man. Deaths from mercury poisoning have occurred in such widely situated areas as Japan (89), West Pakistan (4), Iraq (300), and Guatemala (20). In Japan, 22 brain-damaged children were born to mothers who, though they did not have enough mercury in their bodies to exhibit symptoms of mercury poisoning, did have enough to affect the especially vulnerable fetus.

The mercury content of 89 percent of the swordfish

marketed in the United States in 1971 was above the tolerance level established by the Food and Drug Administration, causing the agency to advise against swordfish consumption by Americans. For similar reasons, the Swedish government recommends that Swedes limit fish consumption to once per week.

Adverse effects of lead on health are reported with mounting frequency as a result of the enormous quantities of lead now introduced into the biological system each year from underground reserves. An estimated 500 million pounds were discharged into the U.S. environment alone in 1970. Most lead absorbed by individuals comes from automobile exhaust fumes, plumbing systems and lead based paint.

New York City reported 2,600 cases of lead poisoning in 1970. Health officials in Washington, D.C., estimate that 5,000 children in that city have more lead in their blood than is safe, and that 500 are so seriously affected that they should be hospitalized immediately. The average level of lead in the blood of auto mechanics in the United States is very close to the danger level. A large proportion of the children living in urban areas in the United Kingdom, where the lead content of the air is twenty times that in the countryside, may have higher blood levels of lead than is safe. Professor D. Bryce Smith of the University of Reading indicates the gravity of the situation: "To my best knowledge, no other toxic chemical pollutant has accumulated in man to the average levels so close to the threshold for overt, clinical poisoning."

Other waste metals, such as arsenic, cadmium and selenium, have reached the point where concentrations are adversely affecting human health. A Japanese court has ruled on behalf of 400 victims of cadmium poisoning who are suing an industrial firm for damages. Farmers in the Chofu municipal region near Tokyo were not permitted to market their 1970 spinach crop because its cadmium content exceeded safety levels. Cadmium poses a particularly serious threat because it persists in the human body for decades after it is absorbed.

Analytical techniques and instruments sensitive enough to detect the presence of toxic materials at the levels which are injurious to health are only now being developed. As of mid-1971 the Food and Drug Administration, for example, has not yet been able to determine human tolerance levels for cadmium. As more information becomes available, we become more keenly aware of the seriousness of our plight. The levels of the great majority of toxic compounds in the biosphere are rising. Forms of life as we know them today, including man, evolved in an environment with very low concentrations of mercury, lead and cadmium. No one knows what the long-term consequences will be of increasing the amount of these persistent compounds in circulation in the ecosystem through the continuing mining of subterranean deposits.

Throughout the tropical, poorer countries an even greater threat to human well-being is the snail-borne disease schistosomiasis, or bilharziasis. Now that malaria has been curbed, it has become the world's leading infectious disease, afflicting some 200 million people, primarily in Africa, Asia, the Caribbean and the northeast coast of Latin America. Seldom immediately fatal, it dooms its victims to a debilitated existence with recurrent fever and diarrhea.

Labeled by some as "the poor man's emphysema," schistosomiasis is a persistent disease, which thrives in areas with perennial irrigation systems, riverside slums and shantytowns with open drains. The disease has spread rapidly in the developing world, where the expansion of irrigation systems has created an ideal environment for the alternate host of the parasite, a fresh-water snail. Most often contracted by workers in flooded rice fields or by children playing in fresh-water marshes or streams, the aquatic parasite penetrates the human skin on contact after having left its snail host. The schistosomes, or tiny worms, then migrate through the blood and lodge themselves in the liver, where they reproduce. The eggs are excreted with body wastes, often ending up in irrigation canals, open sewers and drainage ditches, where they hatch and are once again taken up by the snail, completing their life cycle. The disease is thus most prevalent in areas where human excrement is used as fertilizer, such as mainland China, and where there is frequent flooding or where a common lagoon serves as water supply for everything from washing animals to bathing.

Because it is a poor man's disease, schistosomiasis has received little of the pharmaceutical industry's research funds. Unless an international organization or national government takes the leadership in coping with schistosomiasis, this source of suffering for much of mankind will continue unabated.

As of 1971, the share of the world's population suffering from environmentally induced disease appears to be increasing steadily. Now numbering at least a few hundred million, these victims of mass alterations in the environment are bearing a disproportionately large share of the costs of continually expanding the global level of economic activity.

Endangered Species

Man is not the only species adversely affected by the deteriorating environment. Indeed, many animals have a much lower tolerance than man. Thus far during this century, an average of one species per year quietly made its exit somewhere in the world. As the number of human beings goes up, the number of extant species is going down.

The Department of Interior now maintains a list of endangered species within the United States. Totaling 79 in early 1970, this list was increased by 22 in October 1970, adding three mammals, eight birds and eleven fish. One world-wide list of endangered species, though obviously far from complete, given the lack of information for such areas as mainland China and the Amazon basin, now includes 275 species of mammals and 300 birds. As we move upward along the steeply inclined curve of population growth and pollution, new species are added to the list almost weekly.

Today there are no more than 2,500 wild elephants in Ceylon, fewer than half the number of twenty years ago. The source of subsistence for them is diminishing steadily as their forest and jungle habitat is cleared to produce food for the island's population, now doubling every twenty-three years.

In Denmark the return of the storks from wintering in North Africa has long been a national event, celebrated by young and old alike. At one time 10,000 storks arrived each year. Last year only 70 pairs came. The use of pesticides by farmers to control the locust in East Africa and the Nile River Valley is apparently eliminating the storks as well.

Pravda reports that the reckless use of chemical pesticides in agriculture is decimating many forms of wildlife in the Soviet Union, causing many species to become "zoological rarities." The duck-hunting season was canceled entirely in 1970 because of the declining number of ducks.

According to *Pravda,* now beginning to sound like Rachel Carson, "This question [the extinction of species] is worrying us more and more every year. Why do we see almost no flocks of geese and cranes in April? Almost all the partridges are gone. Our woods, gardens and fields are becoming quieter and quieter."

Numerous species of mammals, such as the Bengal tiger and the Indian rhinoceros, are endangered by the explosive population increase in Asia. The Washington *Evening Star* reports that fewer than 20 clouded leopards remain in East

Pakistan's Chittagong Hill Tracts. Fewer than 4,000 of man's close kin, the orangutan, remain in Indonesia.

The bald eagle, the U.S. national symbol, is now threatened with extinction by an intolerable level of nonbiodegradable pesticides, particularly dieldrin, in the biosphere. Should this majestic bird become extinct, the decision will have to be made whether to retain the bald eagle as a national symbol, basing future designs on photographs and other recorded information, or switch to some suitable living symbol. Perhaps Benjamin Franklin's proposal that our national symbol be the turkey, the only farmyard fowl domesticated in the New World, will be revived for reconsideration.

Once destroyed, those species of life now threatened by man cannot be re-created, however sophisticated modern technology might be. The irreversible loss of these species which evolved over hundreds of millions of years will diminish the variety and richness of life throughout the world. This trend can be reversed only by cooperation on a global scale. Failure to achieve the needed degree of cooperation will mean that in this area at least, the technologies created by man have become unmanageable, causing an irreversible decline in the quality of human life. The great difficulty here is attaching a price tag to the extinction of some species of wildlife. Presumably, since an extinct species is lost forever, any value at all, if calculated to infinity, would have to exceed any short-term gain from the activities causing extinction.

Altering the Earth's Climate

Perhaps the most dramatic but least understood effect of man's environmental intervention is the potential for altering the earth's climate, either intentionally or unintentionally. The desire for intentional climate modifications, such as rainmaking, is not new, but the technological capability for doing so, though still limited, is new.

The list of ways in which man is inadvertently affecting the earth's climate, at least locally, is much longer. Among these are the consumption of energy which can either warm local areas, as in urban heat centers which are measurably warmer than surrounding areas, or contribute to a cooling of the earth by discharging dust particles in the atmosphere which in turn reduces the inflow of solar energy. Agricultural activity, especially bringing marginal land under the plow resulting in dust-bowl conditions, could have the same effect.

Climatological data show that the earth's average temperature rose about 0.4 degrees Centigrade, or 1 degree Fahrenheit, between 1880 and 1940. Since 1940, however, it has begun to decline, dropping 0.5 degrees Fahrenheit. No one can say whether this observed temperature decline of the past twenty-five years was due to long-term natural cyclical changes, to increased particulate matter in the upper atmosphere from volcanic activity, from the expansion of agricultural dust-bowls in parts of Asia, especially the India-Pakistan subcontinent, from expanding industrial activity or from some entirely different factor. What is significant is that climatologists do agree that man's activities are now of such a scale that they can and may be affecting the earth's climate.

What is not so clear is what the specific climatic effects of various activities are. Some tend to warm the earth, others to cool it. What the net effect is we do not know. A report prepared for the United Nations in the summer of 1971 summed up the state of knowledge on the subject: "There can be little doubt that man, in the process of reshaping his environment in many ways, has changed the climate of large regions of the earth, and he has probably had some influences on global climate as well—exactly how much, we do not know."

Essential Unity of the Biosphere

Alterations of the earth's climate underline the essential unity of the biosphere. Unfortunately, the relationship between its functioning and man's activities is little understood by economic advisors, corporate leaders and political decision makers, even though decisions these individuals make bear directly on the health of the biosphere and its capacity to support life. They can influence the amount of solar energy entering the biosphere or the natural cycles of carbon, nitrogen, water or energy, in some cases accelerating the cycle, as with the fixation of nitrogen in fertilizer plants, or in others slowing it down, as with the damming of rivers to slow the return of water to the sea. The complex of natural cycles and systems and interdependent species of plant and animal life they support constitutes a very fragile structure, one easily upset by human intervention on the scale now occurring with modern technologies and levels of economic activity.

The continuing use of DDT, a nonbiodegradable compound used to protect human populations from the malaria-carrying anopheles mosquito and to protect crops from insects, is causing it to slowly accumulate in our biosphere. Circulating widely in the earth's biosphere, it is found in the tissues of penguins in Antarctica, in the bodies of children in villages in Thailand, and in mother's milk in Indiana. Levels in mother's milk in the United States, far higher than the "safe" level permitted by the Food and Drug Administration in foodstuffs entering interstate commerce, led biologist Charles Wurster to point out that mother's milk in any other containers would not be permitted to cross state boundaries!

Controlling the level of DDT in the biosphere requires a high degree of global cooperation. If most countries agreed that the use of DDT should be banned but a number continued to use it in heavy quantities, there would be no way to arrest the rising concentration of DDT in the environment. Our biosphere is a single unified system, one which bears no relationship to national boundaries as they appear on maps.

A Russian plan to reverse the direction of four rivers currently flowing northward and emptying into the Arctic Ocean might, if carried out, have far-reaching consequences for all mankind. These rivers would be diverted southward into the semiarid lands of southern Russia, greatly enlarging the irrigated area of the U.S.S.R. Some climatologists are concerned, however, that shutting off the flow of relatively warm water from these four rivers would alter not only the climate in the Arctic but that of the entire world as well. In the complex, continually interacting set of forces which determine climate—including the influx of solar energy, air currents, ocean currents and temperature exchanges between the two—an alteration such as that planned by the Russians could significantly change the global climatic system.

Levels of industrial activity in the United States are already affecting the food supply of the Soviet Union. The fish catch by Soviet trawlers off the Atlantic coast is being affected by declining fish stocks. Rivers in the eastern United States—the Charles, Delaware, Susquehanna and the Potomac—carry an ever-swelling load of industrial waste into the Atlantic coastal waters, destroying many of the fish once plentiful there. These are but a few examples of the ways in which human activity in one portion of the globe affects the well-being of people elsewhere. One could easily fill a volume with such illustrations.

The Knowledge Gap

One of the most disturbing dimensions of the environmental crisis we face today is the dearth of knowledge about it.

It is not what we know about it, but rather what we don't know about it that is of primary concern. Knowledgeable scientists, for instance, agree that man's economic activity is affecting the earth's climatic patterns, but they are not quite sure how.

One of the great difficulties associated with filling the knowledge gap is the cost of examining thoroughly the environmental impact of new products and activities. As a well-known professor of industrial hygiene in Sweden has pointed out, a clever chemist is able to devise just as many new chemical products every year as it will take a whole lifetime of an industrial hygienist to investigate from the point of view of occupational health. Because of this lack of understanding of what the effect of his consciously taken actions are, man is in effect using the earth's biosphere as a laboratory. Man, of course, is among the guinea pigs.

In 1948 Dr. Paul Herman Müller, a Swiss scientist, was awarded the Nobel Prize for his discovery of DDT. Just over two decades later several countries, including Sweden, the country awarding the prizes, were banning its use. This is not necessarily to say that the world would have been better off without DDT, but it does illustrate how little was understood about the environmental consequences of this potent insecticide when it was released.

Further dramatizing the extent of our ignorance concerning the impact of man's economic activities on the environment was the discovery by a Norwegian graduate student, Norvald Fimreite, that fish in Lake St. Claire, situated on the U.S.-Canadian border, contained seven times as much mercury as is considered safe in food by the U.S. Food and Drug Administration. Within months, quick checks elsewhere led to the banning of commercial fishing in literally hundreds of lakes and streams in thirty-three of our states. One wonders how many other widespread threats to human well-being await such a chance discovery.

Unfortunately, we do not know where the thresholds of

irreversibility are of many threatened alterations in the environment. There were no clear-cut warnings that Lake Erie was passing the point of no return a few years ago as advanced eutrophication set in. The demise of certain species of wildlife has occurred with little forewarning. The great danger is that the same thing could occur on a global scale where the climatic system, the oceans or some other portion of man's basic life-support system is concerned.

Economic Growth in a Finite System

Over the past two decades we have witnessed an explosion in human economic activity. The rate of global economic growth, averaging 4 to 5 percent annually since 1950, and encompassing both population growth and the near universal striving for higher incomes, is doubling the size of the world economy every eighteen years. Most of the world's current productive capacity has been created since 1950.

Economic activity depends on the earth's capacity to supply energy fuels, industrial raw materials and fresh water to produce forest products and marine protein, to provide living space and arable land, and to absorb waste products such as carbon dioxide, heat, nitrites, mercury, lead, phosphates and literally thousands of other compounds. The environmental crisis results from expanding economic activities until they exceed certain capacities of the natural system. Some of these capacities can continue to support the present rate of economic expansion for centuries to come. The supply of bauxite and other sources of aluminum is a case in point. But other finite capacities are already under stress either locally or globally.

The use of forest products for fuel in traditional societies, for newsprint in modern societies, and for lumber in both is now far outstripping the regenerative capacity of the world's forests. Combined with the continual clearing of new land for agriculture, this is resulting in the progressive deforestation of large areas of Asia, the Middle East and Africa.

Global demand for several commercial species of whales and fish now exceeds the annually renewable supply. The result is growing conflict among nations over fishing rights. The Russians and Japanese are continuously attempting to negotiate overlapping claims in the North Pacific. Several Latin American countries are extending their territorial limits as far as 200 miles offshore in an attempt to secure a larger share of the world's marine protein supplies.

As the discharge of nitrates and phosphates from the use of chemical fertilizers and household detergents increases, the eutrophication of fresh water bodies accelerates, destroying fish and converting lakes into swamps. Whatever the source of nutrients, the effect is the same. The additional nutrients cause a population explosion among the algae. As huge quantities of algae decompose, they reduce the level of free oxygen in the water to the point where fish can no longer survive. The swelling discharge of industrial waste into rivers and lakes can destroy all forms of life. Two tributaries of the Rhine, the Neckar and the Sieg, have been declared biologically dead.

The discharge of waste petroleum either from ocean-going vessels or from industrial processes and service stations, adversely affects the environment. Many Japanese and Mediterranean beaches have been declared unfit for bathing, while in California ninety-one beaches have been closed. News photos of volunteers attempting to rescue petroleum-saturated sea birds in the vicinity of oil spills or leaking offshore oil wells are becoming commonplace. Both Ohio's Cuyahoga River and the Soviet Union's Volga River have become so polluted with petroleum and other inflammable waste that they have caught fire, the former burning so vigorously as to damage low-lying bridges.

As more and more waste products are generated, we find the ecosystem beginning to deteriorate as a result of the overload. Minute quantities of chlorinated hydrocarbons such as DDT and dieldrin can irreversibly alter our natural environment. At four parts per million, certain species are threatened with extinction; at six parts per million, several more begin to drop out; at eight parts per million, the list of species threatened with extinction lengthens rapidly. As concentrations of sulfur dioxide in the air in urban areas begin to climb, so does the incidence of emphysema, bronchitis and lung cancer.

The recent explosion in economic activity has been so rapid that we have scarcely had time to examine its consequences. One way of putting the environmental crisis in perspective is to compare the situation in 1950 with that in 1970. In 1950 the gross world product (GWP) was just over $1 trillion. At that level of economic activity, the evident stresses on the system, the eco-catastrophes, were very few. In 1970 when the GWP was approaching $3 trillion, the list of eco-catastrophes seemed almost endless. Rapid eutrophication of lakes, oil spills, fish kills, devastating floods resulting from deforestation, particularly in Asia, are occurring more and more frequently. Each day the press reports new signs of environmental stress. Environmentally induced illnesses have become a prominent feature in the world health picture.

One must consider the historically recent explosive growth in global economic activity from two reference points. One is the magnitude of the increase itself. The other is the relationship of each incremental increase to the earth's various finite limits. It seems clear that addition of the third trillion dollars to the GWP has caused much more environmental stress than did the second trillion. How long will the list of eco-catastrophes be if the current GWP is doubled over the next eighteen years? If we assume a 4 percent annual rate of global economic growth by the year

2000 the result would be a GWP of nearly $10 trillion. What will be the state of the earth's ecosystem at that point?

Some of these alterations in the environment are reversible, but others are not. Once a lake eutrophies it can be reclaimed, but only at great cost. Once a species becomes extinct, there is no way of re-creating it. Because the threat to the ecosystem from expanding economic activity is so recent, we do not know what happens to the complex web of life as species begin to drop out in large numbers.

Our dilemma is that we do not have a very good idea of exactly what the limits are and how much slack remains in the system. We know that we can reduce the effect of some economic activities by such methods as recycling, but there are other stresses which we cannot ameliorate. We know there is a direct relationship between the amount of energy consumed and heat produced, and that as long as energy consumption goes up, thermal pollution worsens.

Future technological advances will push back some of the existing limits to growth. Cheap nuclear energy is often cited as a means of overcoming many constraints to growth such as the supply of fossil fuels and the rising cost of mining low content mineral ores. This will undoubtedly push back the limits, much as the Green Revolution has in agriculture, but it does not remove them.

Within agriculture some limits can be pushed back much more readily than others. The growing use of both pesticides and fertilizers is a source of environmental stress. For pesticides, there are now a number of promising biological controls in the experimental stage but there is no promising substitute in prospect for chemical fertilizers. All projections indicate use will soar in the decades ahead, bringing widespread eutrophication in its wake.

As a result of increasingly adverse effects of growth, there is growing resistance to the continuing expansion of certain types of economic activity, including the construction of new power plants, whether conventional or nuclear, paper mills, steel mills, and oil refineries. In some states within the United States, such as Oregon and Delaware, this resistance has taken the form of stringent regulations on the licensing of new plants. Resistance to construction of new power plants in some Northeastern communities threatens future power shortages. Californians are discussing future limitations on power generation as a way of limiting migration into California and the overall growth in economic activity in the state.

Growth in consumption of natural resources, both renewable and nonrenewable, is proceeding at an extraordinary rate. Petroleum consumption is expanding at 4 percent yearly, fresh water at 3 percent, marine protein at 4 percent and the use of chemical fertilizers at 7 percent. A 3 percent annual growth rate means a doubling in every twenty-four years; a 7 percent growth rate doubles every ten years. The exponential growth in consumption of finite resources, however large reserves may be, cannot continue indefinitely. In some cases substitutes will be found and in others it will be necessary to change the pattern of economic activity.

Another consequence of approaching some of the earth's finite limits in many cases is that costs of many resources are rising. Included in this category are seafood, energy fuels, forest products, fresh water, arable land, living space and several industrial raw materials. Rising costs are in part cancelling new efficiencies from technological advances. Discovering and exploiting new sources of petroleum are becoming more costly as the search spreads to remote desert and arctic areas and beneath the ocean floor. Expanding the supply of fresh water becomes increasingly costly in many parts of the world. As the ecosystem's capacity to absorb waste is overloaded either locally or globally, vast sums must be spent to reduce discharges of various wastes.

There is now reason to doubt whether the principal industrial economies, which account for the lion's share of global output, will grow as rapidly in real terms during the seventies as during the sixties. Economic growth in Western Europe has slowed measurably during the seventies. Japan, growing rapidly on imported technology and running up a sizable ecological debt during the sixties, will be hard pressed to match that performance during this decade. If the United States follows the recommendation of its Council on Environmental Quality for an expenditure of $105 billion by 1975 for a partial cleanup of air, water and solid waste, a sizable block of investment capital will surely be diverted from the production of new goods and services. The combination of growing resistance to continuing expansion of certain types of economic activity, the rising investments needed for pollution abatement and rising costs of industrial materials, particularly energy, is likely to slow growth in virtually all the industrial economies.

The long-term trend of accelerating economic growth, beginning with the discovery of agriculture and particularly in evidence since the industrial revolution, may have ended. In the rich countries, economic growth as we know it is beginning to slow, perhaps eventually to stabilize. Meanwhile, the poor countries must strive for even more rapid growth until such time as their consumption of food, energy and material goods reaches an acceptable level, whereupon they too may begin to move toward a steady-state economy. Hopefully, efforts to stabilize population will succeed before it becomes necessary to limit production of material goods.

Social Justice in a Finite System

Although we are approaching the limits of the ecosystem in some areas, we do not yet know what the population-sustaining capacity of the earth is at a given per capita income or life style. We do know that the earth cannot support nearly as many rich people as poor.

The rapid expansion of global economic activity until it strains some of the earth's finite capacities will force mankind to address the issue of social justice on a global scale, and against a backdrop far different from any which has existed in the past. Always before, the rich could urge the poor to wait, arguing that the benefits of growth would eventually trickle down. But when opportunities for further growth are limited or nonexistent, the dominant issue becomes not how to expand the pie, but *how to divide it*. The consequences of this latter point in terms of how countries relate to each other are only beginning to emerge.

Heretofore, the world's rich have always assumed that the economic gap between rich countries and poor would be reduced by raising incomes among the poor toward the level now enjoyed by the rich. But in our finite system it may be possible to narrow the gap satisfactorily only by slowing the rise in living levels among the rich; thus the stage is set for some revolutionary questions of distributive justice at the international level.

For purposes of discussion, let us assume that the earth's ecosystem will tolerate, on a sustained basis with a given technology, a level of economic activity of, say, $6 trillion yearly, or roughly double the current level. This then will accommodate any combination of population times income which does not exceed $6 trillion—say, 3 billion people with an average income level of $2,000 yearly (France in 1970), or alternatively, 6 billion people with an income of $1,000 (Japan in 1967). Any combination of people times income that does not yield more than $6 trillion yearly is tolerable. Any combination yielding more than this will result in unacceptable alterations of the system. That is, the cost incurred as the result of further growth in terms of environmentally induced illness, threatened species, climate modification and destruction of the natural habitat would become such that the forces opposing further growth would exceed those supporting it.

The crucial question then becomes, How do we distribute the earth's capacities for supplying certain natural amenities and raw materials, or for absorbing waste? One way, of course, would be to prorate everything equitably. Another would be simply to continue expanding population and raising incomes until the limit is reached and then attempt to prohibit further procreation and expansion of production. One might argue, and quite rightly, that this limit cannot be determined with any precision, but this does not mean that it is any less real. That the earth's biosphere is finite and can be disrupted and destroyed by man, there can no longer be any doubt.

What to do about the overload on the ecosystem's capacity to absorb DDT is already being debated in at least one international forum. In a Food and Agricultural Organization (FAO) assembly late in 1969, several rich countries proposed a ban on the use of DDT because of its adverse environmental effects. But it was rejected by the assembly, whose members were predominantly from the poor countries. Representatives from the rich countries supporting this proposal were concerned because the survival of several species of wildlife, including the bald eagle, the peregrine falcon, and other species of birds and fish at the top of the food chain, was threatened by the continuing use of DDT. Their loss would measurably diminish the quality of life for the rich. The poor countries, using DDT to control malaria and expand food output, were unwilling to limit its use. As yet there is not enough resistance to the use of DDT at the global level to ban its use, but it may eventually come. Perhaps the rich countries, unwilling to accept the adverse consequences of its continued use, will offer to assist the poor ones by bearing the expense of more costly alternatives to DDT in much the same way that the

United States has offered to bear some of the adjustment costs within Turkish agriculture as farmers switch from production of opium to less profitable alternatives.

Within the past few decades, as population pressure has increased, competition for the earth's limited fresh-water supply has become intense, and a source of contention in many regions. With world consumption increasing at 3.4 percent yearly and doubling every twenty-one years, competition is certain to become even more intense.

As world population has increased at an explosive rate since World War II, so too has the world fish catch. Each year from 1950 to 1968 it set a new record, more than doubling during the period. Then suddenly, in 1969, production dropped from the previous year, falling 5 percent per capita world-wide, largely because of a decline in the Peruvian catch.

The global fish catch readily divides into two types, those for table use and those for fish meal. Various projections for the latter indicate a potential expansion of several fold before reaching the limit. This assumes, of course, that oceanic pollution does not worsen measurably. For table-grade species, where the rate of increase in the catch slowed markedly in the late sixties, prospects for expanding the catch are not so bright. Many authorities share the assessment of marine biologists Lucien Sprague and John Arnold of the University of Rhode Island that "The exploitation of table-grade fishes worldwide is about at its sustainable yield."

If this analysis proves correct, it is likely that international competition for the limited supply of table-grade fish will become increasingly keen. It will bring into sharp focus the difficult issue of how to divide a finite global fish catch among an expanding population. Should the catch of table-grade fish be apportioned as at present, with the rich countries getting the dominant share of the total, or should it be equitably apportioned on a per capita basis in which case the poor countries would get three fourths of the total catch? What if the poor-country leaders recommend a formula which would give countries with protein-deficient diets first claim on the world's marine protein supplies, with the rich countries permitted to claim only the residual, if any?

Unhappily, we may have reached the point where such alternatives will have to be considered and negotiated. As we move ever closer to the various limits of our ecosystem, the question of how to divide its finite capacities will dominate international relations more and more.

Technology-Institution Gap

Nowhere does the gap between advancing technology and the institutions required to manage it seem so great as in the relationship between man and nature. Advances in technology expand man's intrusions into the natural system, often without safeguards to protect the system. It is widely recognized that man is placing growing stress on the ecosystem, but not that this is placing increasing stress on the international political system as well.

Between 1950 and 1970 the gross world product nearly tripled, greatly increasing the pressure man places on the ecosystem. Many of those suffering the consequences of overload on the earth's ecosystem, either individuals or nation-states, do not have effective political recourse outside their own boundaries under the existing system. Not only is the current system of largely independent, sovereign nation-states not designed to cope with the problem of apportioning the earth's finite capacities, but it actually aggravates it by inducing economic competition among nation-states. The competitive nature of the system actively thwarts efforts to alleviate the problem by forcing man to play brinksmanship with the destruction of his life-support system. For example, some species of whales are threatened with extinction because those countries involved in the whaling industry are unable to agree on how a sustainable annual catch should be divided among them. The same situation may shortly be reached with several commercial species of fish whose stocks are dwindling.

Not only are many of man's institutions incapable of resolving the problems he now faces, but his values, inherited largely from the past, are inconsistent with his survival. Values which are widely held, many of them built into the economic system, such as "growth is good," "planned obsolescence," "reverence for motherhood," and the nationalistic feelings which many of us hold, are becoming threats to our future well-being. Man must evolve a new social ethic, one which emphasizes economic and demographic stability and the recycling of raw materials. Such an ethic replaces international competition with global cooperation and sees man in harmony with nature rather than having dominion over nature.

We can no longer separate the health of the biosphere and our future well-being from our global mode of political organization. Man's prospects for coping successfully with the environmental crisis are directly related to his capacity to achieve a far higher level of international cooperation than currently prevails. A principal obstacle at present is the low priority accorded the global environmental crisis by the poor countries. The rich countries with their very high levels of material well-being are sensitive to the impact of environmental deterioration on the quality of life, but for those living in grinding poverty in the poor countries, worrying about the global environmental problem becomes something of a luxury.

The initial low level of interest by the poor countries in the United Nations Environment Conference held in Stockholm in 1972 should not have come as a surprise to the rich countries. Only when the rich countries demonstrate a concern over the quality of life for all of mankind, something now belied by their declining levels of aid and their discriminatory trade policies toward the poor countries, can the poor be expected to cooperate. In other words, global cooperation on the scale needed to preserve the ecosystem on which the quality of life in the rich countries depends must await a much more serious effort by the rich to reduce the widening rich-poor economic gap.

3

THE WIDENING RICH-POOR GAP

The world today is rapidly polarizing along economic lines into two camps, rich and poor. A line separating English-speaking North America, Europe, the Soviet Union and Japan from Latin America, Africa and Asia delineates these two camps. The majority of the human family lives south of this line, and except for scattered pockets of affluence, is desperately poor.

In effect, our world today is in reality two worlds, one rich, one poor; one literate, one largely illiterate; one industrial and urban, one agrarian and rural; one overfed and overweight, one hungry and malnourished; one affluent and consumption-oriented, one poverty-stricken and survival-oriented. North of this line, life expectancy at birth closely approaches the Biblical threescore and ten; south of it, many do not survive infancy. In the North, economic opportunities are plentiful and social mobility is high. In the South, economic opportunities are scarce and societies are rigidly stratified.

Unfortunately, poverty is not an economic abstraction, it is a human condition. It is despair, grief and pain. It is the despair of a father with a family of seven in a poor country when he joins the swelling ranks of unemployed with no prospect of unemployment compensation. Poverty is the longing of a young boy playing outside a village school but unable to enter because his parents lack a few dollars needed to buy textbooks. Poverty is the grief of parents watching a three-year-old child die of a routine childhood disease because, like half of mankind, they cannot afford any medical care. In this book we deal with poverty abstractly at the global level, but we are concerned with it because it affects people.

Emergence of the Gap

The gap between North and South is rather recent in historical terms. Prior to the industrial revolution there was little difference between the living standard of peasants in Western Europe and that in Egypt or China. They were all poor, illiterate, malnourished, and suffering from chronic and debilitating disease. They did not expect to live much more than thirty years. Except for a few ruling elites, both were destined to live in poverty and accepted it.

With the birth of the industrial revolution in Western Europe the living standard gradually began to rise, opening a gap, small and scarcely perceptible at first. By 1850 the ratio between incomes in the industrializing societies and those in the rest of the world was perhaps 2 to 1. In 1950 it had opened further, to about 10 to 1, in 1960 to nearly 15 to 1. If trends of the past decade continue, it may reach 30 to 1 by the end of the century. Even though the indicator used to measure levels of living—the per capita GNP—overstates on many accounts the current contrast between rich and poor, it does, nonetheless, accurately reflect the widening of the gap.

According to recent estimates, just over half of the human family lives in countries where per capita incomes average less than $100 per year. One fourth lives in countries where they exceeded $1,000. The remaining one fourth, the global middle class, lives in countries with incomes between $100 and $1,000.

DISTRIBUTION OF GLOBAL POPULATION
BY AVERAGE INCOME LEVEL

PER CAPITA INCOME (Dollars)	NUMBER (Million)	SHARE OF TOTAL (Percent)
Below 100	1,832	51
100–500	672	18
500–1000	212	6
Above 1,000	903	25
TOTAL	3,619	100

In 1970, income per person in the United States was $4,100, and in India $90. Three decades hence, they are projected to be $10,000 and $215, a ratio of nearly 50 to 1. The *annual increase* in the goods and services produced in the United States of $50 billion, assuming a 5 percent rate of economic growth, is equal to *all* the goods and services produced annually in India, a country of 550 million.

During the sixties, the gap between the rich and poor countries widened both absolutely and relatively. Overall economic growth rates were roughly the same, but population grew twice as rapidly in the poor countries. As a result of their lower economic base and more rapid population growth, these countries raised per capita incomes only $10 during the decade, compared with $300 in the rich countries.

With an income per person of $90 yearly, life is largely a struggle for survival. When nearly all income is required to purchase food, a pronounced rise in food prices, as occurred in India in 1966 and 1967 following two consecutive monsoon failures, seriously threatens survival. Expenditures on medical care for most of the population are virtually non-existent, since half of the world's people receive no health care whatsoever. Serious illness, seldom treated, is often fatal, and high infant mortality contributes to a low life expectancy. Expenditures on clothing, shelter and fuel are nominal. Textbooks required for school-age children are beyond the means of tens of millions of families, making it impossible for their children to attend school. Travel is largely limited to a twenty-five mile radius from home; that is, a distance which can be traversed on foot.

The widening gap between the rich countries and poor is much more than just a quantitative economic difference. It is increasingly a gap in values, in social organization, in contrasting life styles, in perceptions of the world in which we live and, ominously, a gap over which it may become increasingly difficult to communicate effectively.

Reasons for the Gap

A great deal has been written attempting to explain the historical economic divergence of the North and South. In the past, the subject has attracted an unusual number of theorists who have attempted to explain the entire phenomenon in terms of either climate, religion, natural resource endowments, child-rearing techniques, colonialism or any number of other factors. Individually, none of these explanations is satisfactory. The phenomenon is far too complex.

The origins of the gap might be better understood if it were defined. We customarily refer to it as an economic gap because it is most easily measured in economic terms, but it might also be described as a technological or educational gap. Perhaps the principal distinguishing characteristic of the rich societies is their capacity to develop and exploit technology to raise the material living standard and improve the quality of human life. Technology in this context is broadly defined to include not only manufacturing processes and agricultural production techniques but also such things as marketing skills and the capacity to organize production units and financial markets. This is not necessarily related to natural resource endowments, prevailing religion or climate.

For the first time anywhere, living standards for a large group began to rise significantly above the subsistence level in Great Britain during the decades immediately following the industrial revolution. This revolution, based on the creation and exploitation of new technologies, spread from Britain to a number of other countries, principally in Europe and North America. With the exception of Japan, these were countries that enjoyed certain cultural, linguistic and religious affinities with Britain. This undoubtedly facilitated the transmission and adoption of these new technologies, which enabled man to harness additional sources of energy augmenting his own.

Levels of productivity among the populations within these countries began to rise in a steady, sustained fashion, interrupted only by war and economic recession. Elsewhere productivity increased little, if at all. Once in existence, this gap has tended to perpetuate itself and to widen. In part, this is due to conscious actions by the rich countries to use their economic power, and the political influence springing from it, to protect their privileged position in the world.

Once the process of amassing economic and political power begins, it tends to feed upon itself with each advance in economic power, making possible a further concentration of political power. Initially the European countries which achieved a lead over the rest of the world in terms of technology and organizational capacity used it to establish their colonial empires throughout Asia, Africa and the New World. After the colonial era ended, a wide range of economic policies has been used by the industrial countries to preserve the favorable terms of exchange of their manufactures for industrial raw materials and foodstuffs. Policies affecting trade consistently discriminate against the export products of the poor countries. As pointed out recently by Arthur Lewis, the tariff structure in force today in the rich countries leads them to charge, in effect, twice as much duty on goods they import from the poor countries as from each other, thus tending to reinforce the existing economic stratification.

The tariff structure not only discriminates against imports from poor countries, but places an inordinate cost on value added by processing. Unprocessed commodities often enter duty-free, while tariffs are imposed on the same product if it has been processed. Juliet Clifford and Gavin Osmond from the Overseas Development Institute illustrate this with copper. Unprocessed copper is imported free of duty, while a duty is levied on copper wire. Essentially this duty is imposed on the value added by processing, which in this instance amounts to a stiff 12 percent. Hides and skins enter the United States duty-free, while leather is liable to a 4 to 5 percent tariff, and shoes to an 8 to 10 percent tariff. In the European Economic Community the tariff on cocoa beans from nonassociated countries is 3 percent, while cocoa products bear an 18 percent tariff. Not only does this eliminate the comparative advantage of lower labor costs in poor countries but it also discourages industrial growth and reinforces traditional patterns of raw-material exports from poor countries.

Also acting to widen the gap is a population growth rate in the poor countries which is easily double that of the rich ones. The related effects of malnutrition, retarded development, poor health and low worker productivity tend to perpetuate these trends from one generation to the next.

In the absence of external factors capable of breaking the cycle, these conditions will no doubt continue indefinitely into the future.

Gaps Within Societies

Despite traditional notions that income is less equitably distributed within traditional societies, data becoming available on several poor societies indicate a pattern of income distribution not too different from that of the rich countries. Using the ratio of pre-tax income received by the richest one fifth of population to that of the poorest one fifth as an indicator, we find ratios within the poor countries varying from a low of 5 in Taiwan and India to a high of 18 in the Philippines. This compares with a concentration within the rich countries between 9 in Japan and the United Kingdom to possibly 16 in the United States.

Perhaps more important than the actual distribution of income within a society is the change over time. Data spanning a decade ending in the early sixties show a disturbing worsening of income distribution in several poor countries. In 1950, income among the upper one fifth of the Mexican population was ten times that of the lower one fifth, but by 1963 it was seventeen times greater. Indeed the worsening of the relative position of the lower one fifth is so great that it suggests a possible decline in absolute terms as well. Of the half-dozen poor countries for which data are available, the three with the most rapid population growth—Mexico, Ceylon and the Philippines—experienced a worsening income distribution, indicating that runaway population growth rates may aggravate the income distribution problem.

Two poor countries, India and Taiwan, achieved a more equitable distribution of income during the decade under review. India managed only a very modest improvement, but Taiwan achieved a resounding improvement, reducing the ratio of income received by the highest quintile to that received by the lowest from 15 to 5, certainly one of the most dramatic short-term improvements in history. It could usefully serve as a model for other countries seeking the same end.

Changes in Distribution of Income in Poor Countries

COUNTRY	YEAR	RATIO OF INCOME RECEIVED BY TOP 20 PERCENT TO BOTTOM 20 PERCENT
Argentina	1953	6.7
	1961	7.4
Ceylon	1953	10.3
	1963	11.6
China (Taiwan)	1953	15.2
	1964	5.3
India	1952	6.1
	1960	5.2
Mexico	1950	9.8
	1963	17.0
Philippines	1957	12.2
	1965	15.8

Once a group gains a significant advantage in economic terms, whether it be within a national society or among societies, it invariably attempts to use the economic power associated with this advantage to further strengthen and preserve its position. Various techniques can be used to ensure this, including systems of taxation favoring the wealthy, educational systems catering to members of elitist groups, and economic systems shifting the terms on which goods are exchanged between the privileged and the poverty-stricken in favor of the former. This is particularly the case where urban elites and depressed rural masses are involved.

Territorial Discrimination

The current North-South polarization of human society along economic lines, and the associated failure of the rich North to demonstrate any meaningful concern for the poor, constitute a new form of discrimination, one based on place of residence. At issue is whether an accident of birth should deprive an individual of enough food to fully develop his physical and mental capacity, of the opportunity to become literate, or of any other basic amenities of life in a world where resources are more than adequate to meet these needs. As the world is now organized, national borders allow the world's rich to seek refuge from global problems, avoiding exposure to the suffering and need of the poor elsewhere.

Each of the rich countries accepts internally the principle of income redistribution through progressive taxation systems and a wide variety of welfare programs, including such things as free medical care or unemployment compensation. But internationally the rich nations only nominally accept this concept by providing token amounts of financial assistance to the poor countries. In terms of aggregate resources at the disposal of rich countries and in terms of pressing human needs, transfers of resources from rich countries to poor across national boundaries are only crumbs from the table. Total U.S. assistance to poor countries with 2 billion people is only moderately larger than the New York City welfare program, and most of the former is loans requiring repayment.

Recognition of this territorial discrimination, like many other forms of discrimination, is strong among the young. The older generation tends to take poverty and serious inequities in the distribution of income and wealth for granted because in the not too distant past it was not possible to seriously consider eliminating all poverty in the world. For those born into the postwar era of affluence and rapidly advancing technology, the realization that the resources to eradicate global poverty do exist is much stronger.

The Growing Awareness of Poverty

The seventies are almost certain to witness an emerging consciousness on the part of the majority of mankind that they live in desperate poverty relative to the affluent minority. The eventual consequences of this are difficult to foresee. Americans had first-hand experience in the sixties observing what happened when TV sets in the ghettos provided a window on the world beyond, showing ghetto residents just how badly they were faring *relative* to fellow Americans outside the ghetto. For much of mankind, the realization that they are not only poor but cut off from any possibility of advancement promises to engender a sense of futility and desperation. For many there will be little to lose from disrupting or even destroying the existing order.

Although the continued existence of widespread poverty is not conducive to political stability, we should recognize that the process of modernization itself is not likely to ensure political tranquillity. Rapid progress in a traditional society can be enormously destabilizing, as rapid change tears people loose from their traditional social moorings.

Most immediately, the destabilizing impact of severe poverty and *perceived* growing inequities either within or among societies is likely to cause violence. Over time it will become an international issue, if for no other reason than that national leaders may wish to create external crises to divert attention from seemingly insoluble internal problems. Such tactics were used by such national leaders as Sukarno, Nasser and Nkrumah.

Wide gaps between rich and poor within individual societies have been commonplace throughout recorded history, but the emergence of such gaps among societies is
rather recent. This is increasingly significant because of
the extent to which these gaps are now being perceived by
the poor through new forms of communication. A widening
economic gap in a shrinking world will exert growing stress
on the international political fabric

Poverty, Political Instability and Violence

The confrontation between rich and poor at the global level
is not temporary or accidental. It is too deeply rooted, too
fundamental to be stilled by ignoring it or by repressing
those who wish to make it an issue. As the world continues
to shrink through advances in communication and transportation, we face the prospect of a de facto single global
society in which the living levels of the richest one fourth
of society are perhaps twenty times those of the poorest
one half. At some point as stresses increase, social forces
assume a political dimension, often mobilizing the apoliti-
cal and sometimes assuming a revolutionary form and character.

Overwhelmed with the frustration and the futility of attempting to change things in an orderly fashion, the depressed resort to more desperate means of achieving
change, of redressing the imbalance of power and wealth.
As awareness of disparities in wealth rises among the poor
and as evolving concepts of social justice spread, new concepts of violence and of property rights are emerging.
Violence, once considered a physical act of injury or destruction, extralegal and punishable by law, is now being
redefined by many to include indirect harm to an individual
through, for example, the sale of defective automobiles or
worthless cereals, through excessive interest rates or

through discrimination by the rich countries against the textiles produced in the poor ones—actions which are often condoned or even sanctified by law. The traditional definition of violence having been broadened, those suffering from these injustices then feel justified in using traditional forms of violence to counter them.

The inviolability of property rights is also changing. Within some countries such as India and Chile, forcible expropriation of large land holdings by landless laborers or tenants is becoming commonplace. In Turkey and Peru, rural migrants lacking funds to buy land in urban fringe areas are simply occupying it and refusing to leave. At the national level, governments in poor countries such as Zambia or Ceylon are expropriating foreign investments, taking legal title to properties, sometimes without compensation. Diplomatic immunity, a time-honored code, is now being regularly violated by political dissidents in many countries, particularly in Latin America.

Redistributing Power and Wealth

In societies where the distribution of wealth is worsening, dissident groups are seeking to capitalize on social and political unrest. The result is civil strife, political instability, social disintegration, and in some cases, civil war and anarchy. This is most likely to occur first in areas where poverty is aggravated by severe crowding.

In some societies there is now emerging a "Robin Hood" phenomenon with small organized groups undertaking to redistribute wealth by forcibly taking from the rich and distributing among the poor. This activity is especially prominent in Mexico, where the distribution of income has worsened dramatically since 1950. A group calling itself the Movement for Revolutionary Action engineered a wave of bank robberies in the fall of 1971. In one instance, this group kidnapped a rich banker and distributed his ransom of $36,000 among the poor peasants in the area. In another, they robbed the Banco de Commercio near Mexico City of $14,000. Mexican President Luis Alvarez referred in his State of the Union message to this group as following "a deliberate plan to destroy social tranquillity" and "frequently connected with underground movements from abroad." A similar pattern is being followed in Iran, where sixteen guerrillas holding up a bank in Teheran told tellers money was "for the people." In Argentina a group proclaiming itself the People's Revolutionary Army kidnapped a part-time British consul who also represented a British meatpacking firm's investment interest, holding him for a ransom of foodstuffs and goods to be distributed "to the people."

Other techniques to embarrass and undermine governments and force them to make political concessions are evolving. Prominent among these is the kidnapping of diplomats as in Brazil, Argentina, Uruguay and Turkey, to mention a few from a steadily lengthening list. Dissident groups in Brazil first kidnapped the American ambassador and shortly thereafter the Swiss ambassador asking that a total of seventy political prisoners be freed in exchange for their release. During the fifteen months ending in December 1970, an average of one diplomat per month was kidnapped in Latin America, moving the U.S. State Department to request a supplemental appropriation of $1.25 million in mid-1970 to strengthen embassy guard forces and to provide additional cars to escort senior diplomats wherever they went.

Another technique commonly employed by dissident groups to gain political leverage is aerial hijacking. Palestinian guerrillas, Kashmiri independence advocates, Black Panthers in the United States and a range of dissident political groups in Latin America have employed this technique. Aerial hijacking invariably involves two countries—a country of origin and one of destination—and in some cases a country of registry for the aircraft as well. That this technique is hazardous, there can be little doubt. A South Korean airliner crashed, taking seventeen persons to their deaths following a battle with a hijacker in which the copilot's arms were blown off. Although the number of hijackings was virtually unchanged between 1969 and 1970, about 70 per year, the number of countries in which hijackings were attempted increased from 17 to 27, making the technique a more universal one.

Acute poverty combined with crowding in a situation where there is no prospect of improving one's lot can result in chronic political instability, sometimes bordering on anarchy, as in parts of the Philippines or in eastern India recently. During the ten months preceding national elections held in the spring of 1971 in India, the official police count for Calcutta listed 244 political murders, many of them candidates for office. The total is believed to be far greater, simply because many murders are committed in areas of the city no longer patrolled by police and, there fore, not reported.

The distribution of power and wealth within Nigeria and Pakistan was an issue underlying the devastating civil wars within those countries. In each case, major powers tended to align themselves with one of the two factions. With Nigeria, the major powers were involved only indirectly as arms suppliers, but in the case of the Pakistan civil war, India was eventually drawn in as well.

Political instability and social disintegration often go hand in hand. The worsening distribution of income, convincing many that the system is not working for them, will almost certainly contribute to this process. Where the system neither provides nor holds out the prospect for a better life, futility and despair will lead many to work outside the system, using whatever leverage they can command to alter or even overthrow the system.

Narrowing the Gap

The widening gap between rich countries and poor is creating pressures on governments in the latter to become more militant in international forums, to seek a redress of imbalances between rich and poor. The first large-scale organized effort focused on this specific issue was the formation in the early sixties of the United Nations Conference on Trade and Development, in effect a lobby representing the interests of the poor countries. Intended as a forum to air grievances of the poor countries with the rich, it now has a permanent secretariat headquartered in Geneva. Thus far, the richer countries have not been overly responsive to the UNCTAD initiatives, but the poor countries are becoming more militant, more demanding. The gathering of representatives of the twenty-one Latin American republics assembled at Viña del Mar in Chile in May 1969 produced a unanimous list of demands for American action to correct existing inequities in economic relationships with its sister republics. This list, presented to President Richard Nixon by the Chilean ambassador in Washington, was but the first salvo of a battle that promises to dominate international relations increasingly in the seventies.

A remark by President Suharto of Indonesia further indicates the growing tendency of poor countries to challenge the discrepancy between America's rhetoric and its actions in setting national priorities. As President Nixon and his entourage, basking in the light of the Apollo 11 moon landing, were leaving Indonesia in late summer of 1969, President Suharto, paraphrasing astronaut Neil Armstrong, commented, "A giant leap for whom?" He was clearly implying that conditions in Indonesia had not been improved by the accomplishments of the American space program.

In later chapters we will discuss detailed actions to narrow the economic gap between rich countries and poor, but essentially there are two ways. One is to raise consumption levels among the poor more rapidly than among the rich, initially narrowing the gap in relative terms and eventually in absolute terms as well. The other is to consciously slow the growth in consumption among the rich, transferring the resources made available to poor countries. Until recently, only the first was seriously considered, but now attention has begun to focus on the second in some circles. There are two reasons: the sheer inhumanity of the super-affluence enjoyed by many while much of mankind lacks even the basic amenities for a humane level of existence, and the growing stresses on the ecosystem from continually expanding levels of global economic activity.

This latter view is reflected in a recent statement to the Swedish people by Ernst Michanek, the highly respected Director General of the Swedish International Development Authority: "Anyone who advocates narrowing the gap between rich and poor nations, while at the same time envisioning, let us say, a continued three to five percent increase per year in real income for the bulk of the Swedish people, is supporting two irreconcilable policies. If he advocates both these and predicts that both can be carried out simultaneously, he is either ignorant or mendacious."

Raising the entire world to current American consumption levels would require an increase in the gross world product from the current $3 trillion to $18 trillion. Needless to say, a sixfold expansion in economic activity would be catastrophic. We must then, give serious thought both to alternative life styles which require fewer resources, and to an alternative means of reducing the global economic gap between rich and poor. The changing relationship between man and his natural environment dictates a new approach to the global poverty problem by the rich countries.

The total resources available from the rich countries for narrowing the gap must increase significantly over the next few years if significant progress in eliminating poverty is to occur during this decade. Unless the poverty problem can be effectively dealt with, the prospects of controlling population growth and alleviating stress on the environmental threat are nil, and the prospect of a deteriorating quality of life for all becomes very real.

The widening gap between the rich countries and the poor can no longer be viewed in economic terms alone. It must be viewed in the context of a shared ecosystem and mutual dependence on the earth's life-support systems. The focus must be on the creation of a world economic, social and political order in which the gap will narrow and the quality of life will everywhere be raised to human levels. The attraction of a unified global society for the newly independent, strongly nationalistic poor countries may be simply that this is the only hope for achieving any meaningful improvement in their quality of life.

4

MARGINAL MEN

Closely related to the worsening distribution of income in the poor countries is the continually growing number of people without jobs, a phenomenon which promises to become one of the world's gravest social ills during the seventies. In many of these countries, entrants into the job market outnumber new jobs being created by 2 to 1, creating levels of unemployment far in excess of any the rich countries have ever experienced. As w th the environmental crisis, the widening gap between rich countries and poor, and the depressing rate of rural-urban migration, the unemployment situation is likely to get much worse before it gets better.

Employment and employment-related issues are likely to dominate international development in the seventies much as the food issue did in the sixties. Stated differently, the food-population crisis of the past decade may become the employment-population crisis of the current decade. The population explosion, which began in most poor countries fifteen or twenty years ago, resulted in an almost immediate demand for additional food. But since babies do not require jobs, there is a grace period of fifteen or twenty years on the employment front that does not exist for food. As we enter the seventies we approach the end of this grace period, first in Latin America and soon thereafter in Asia and Africa.

Unemployment Trends

With the number of young people entering the job market swelling year by year, the day of reckoning with the impact of the population explosion on employment has arrived. In some poor countries the labor force is now growing at three times the rate of the industrialized countries. As a result, the number of potentially productive but unemployed people is rising. In Latin America the number of unemployed climbed from 2.9 million in 1950 to 8.8 million in 1965, tripling in fifteen years. The unemployment rate went from under 6 percent to over 11 percent during this period. Since 1965 the ranks of the unemployed have swelled still further.

The level of unemployment in India is estimated to have increased from 11 percent of the labor force in 1951 to 15 percent in 1961, a trend which continued through the sixties. During the 1970s, India's labor force is projected to increase from 210 million to 273 million, an increment of 63 million. Already plagued with widespread unemployment and underemployment, India is now confronted with 100,000 new entrants into the labor force *each week*. Fifteen percent or more of the labor force is now unemployed in Pakistan, Ceylon, Malaysia, the Philippines and probably Indonesia.

In Colombia, the one poor country where the employment situation has been examined in some detail, the outlook is bleak. A 500-page International Labor Organization (ILO) report describes the situation as follows: "At a conservative estimate one-half million Colombians out of an active urban labor force of some three million are seeking work but are unable to find it. Probably as many again would like to work but are not currently looking for it, having given up in frustration or having not even started to look with any seriousness, deterred by the knowledge that their chance of finding a job is slim."

As the full brunt of the population explosion, beginning a few decades ago, comes to bear on employment conditions in Colombia, the outlook worsens. The report assesses future trends by saying: "If we allow for both unemployment and urban under-employment, only about five million man years are being used in 1970 by comparison with an estimated labor capacity of six and one-half million. Yet the labor force in 1985 will be nearly 11 million. To reach a high level of employment, i.e., with only five percent unemployment, at least five million jobs need to be created in the meantime. If just the recent growth rate of 2 to 2.5 percent in employment continues, the number of jobs will rise by 40 percent between 1970 and 1985 to a total of seven million, leaving four million unemployed, or more than one-third of the labor force."

Adding to an already dismal prospect, the classical definition of unemployment—those seeking work at the prevailing wage rates—greatly understates the extent of unemployment because it does not measure the hidden unemployment or underemployment. According to Eric Thorbecke, who has examined the employment situation in Latin America in considerable detail, "If one considers unemployment as the ratio of available but unused labor hours to the total available labor hours, which is one way of measuring both unemployment and underemployment, the magnitude and the seriousness of the problem is magnified. For one continent, Latin America, this technique revealed unemployment equivalent rates ranging from 20 percent in some countries to over 50 percent in others. For the region as a whole it was 26 percent. This was based on data for 1960." If the same data were available for 1970 they would undoubtedly show an unemployment equivalent much higher.

As population pressure builds in rural areas and unemployment increases, the depression of living standards drives people out of the countryside into the cities, often converting rural underemployment into urban underemployment. The latter is usually concentrated in the urban service sector in such activities as vending postcards or chewing gum, shining shoes or providing domestic services.

Causes of Rising Unemployment

The sharp increase in the number of new entrants into the job market in the poor countries is a direct result of the acceleration of population growth which occurred following World War II, largely as a result of the decline in infant mortality. As the population multiplies in countries where there is little new land to be brought under the plow, we find that the changing relationship between man and his natural environment is spawning social problems of enormous proportions. In communities where parcels of land have been divided and subdivided over the generations, it becomes almost impossible to find gainful employment. Take Colombia again: "In the countryside open unemployment is less common but hundreds of thousands work for such low wages or receive so little on the holdings because they are so small that they must be considered unemployed."

Rural social structures further aggravate employment conditions in many countries. Farmland is concentrated in the hands of wealthy landowners. Land is farmed extensively and operations are often highly mechanized. This greatly reduces labor use below what it would be if land were distributed more equitably among rural populations in family-size units.

Within the global economy, discrimination by rich countries against labor-intensive products from poor countries, both agricultural (e.g., sugar) and industrial (textiles) further aggravate the unemployment problem. Other factors adversely affecting employment levels are overvalued exchange rates within the poor countries which in effect subsidize the import of equipment, artificially reducing the cost of capital relative to labor. The classic case of the latter is West Pakistan, where foreign exchange rates applied to the import of farm tractors make a tractor less costly in Pakistan than in the United States, thereby discouraging the use of farm labor in Pakistan. In a similar vein, imported equipment, both agricultural and industrial, is often based on technologies designed for countries where labor is scarce and capital is abundant.

Unemployment in Rich Countries and Poor

Whenever the number of entrants into the labor market significantly exceeded the number of jobs available for an extended period of time in European countries, the surplus was usually siphoned off by emigration. This was particularly true during the nineteenth century, when tens of millions of Swedish, Italian, German, Irish, Spanish, Portuguese, Polish, Greek, British and Dutch citizens migrated abroad, principally to the New World. Indeed, North America along with Australia and New Zealand was settled largely by this overflow from Europe.

In many of the countries to which Europeans migrated, such as the United States, the excess labor was often absorbed by pushing back the settlement frontier and bringing new land under the plow. This safety valve was of central importance in absorbing increases in the U.S. labor supply during the late nineteenth and early twentieth centuries, or from roughly the end of the Civil War until the beginning of World War I, when homesteading ceased.

At present, unemployment levels in the industrialized countries of the West and Japan range from near zero to about 6 percent, usually fluctuating with business cycles. Whenever unemployment begins to exceed 6 percent of the labor force, it becomes something of a national crisis. This contrasts sharply with the poor countries, where unemployment levels are high, chronic and rising. With growth of the labor force now being fueled by the population explosion, annual increases may approach or even exceed 3 percent per year. As population growth outstrips the finite supply of arable land, a growing share of the population is becoming redundant, creating the so-called marginal man.

On the other hand there are some rich countries where labor scarcities are becoming chronic. Several, including West Germany, Switzerland, Belgium, the Netherlands, Sweden and France, are importing labor from lower-income countries bordering the Mediterranean. An estimated 1.6 million foreign workers are employed in West Germany today, principally in manufacturing. Of this total, some 330,000, or 21 percent, are Italians, with Yugoslavs and Turks each making up just under one fifth. As incomes rise in Italy, the number of Italian workers residing in West Germany is declining. This decline is being offset by increases in the number of other nationalities, principally Yugoslavs and Turks. In tiny Switzerland, 600,000 foreign laborers constitute nearly one fourth of the total labor force of 2.5 million. The number of foreign workers has grown so large relative to the local population that it has created social tensions and become a national political issue. Several hundred thousand Algerians work in France. Other Mediterranean groups employed in large numbers in northwestern Europe as far north as Sweden include workers from Portugal, Spain and Greece, along with a scattering from several Arab countries.

This large-scale migration of labor illustrates two things: first, countries with low birth rates, slowly growing labor forces and rapidly growing economies can ensure full employment and even create a need for imported labor; second, this import demand in the richer countries can provide jobs for unemployed workers in the poor countries that are geographically nearby. But as a contribution to alleviating overall unemployment in the Third World, the worker migration is a small measure indeed.

Japan is now experiencing a decline in the number of young people entering the labor market as a result of the sharp drop in birth rates which occurred in the early 1950s. Combined with an economy expanding at 10 percent or more yearly, this decline created an acute labor shortage during the late sixties. This was partly offset by drawing upon the reservoir of rural labor, reducing the farm population from 31 percent of the total in 1960 to 16 percent at decade's end. With opportunities for drawing upon this reserve now limited, Japan is faced with the need to either import labor, as in northwestern Europe, or begin exporting some of its more labor-intensive industrial activities. Japan has opted almost entirely for the latter and is now exporting many labor-intensive assembly operations in the automotive and electronics industries, as well as in textiles.

Japanese industrial and business firms are aggressively recruiting new entrants into the job market, often beginning a year before they graduate from high school. The intensity of their efforts is reflected in their use of such recruiting devices as home visits by company representatives, elaborate gifts (such as wrist watches) to families of potential young recruits, and paid visits to plant sites for parents.

In the United States there has been a chronic shortage

of unskilled labor in agriculture since World War II. For some time this was offset by the importation of several hundred thousand Mexican *braceros* for seasonal work in fruit- and vegetable-producing areas. Following the cancellation of this program by the U.S. government in 1964, much fruit and vegetable production along with processing industries have moved south of the border, taking advantage of the low-cost labor in Mexico.

American firms in such industries as electronics and textiles have been following a similar path in recent years, establishing what is sometimes described as twin plants, i.e., a U.S. plant is paired with one just south of the border, where the more labor-intensive operations are undertaken. Within the past five years, 230 such plants have sprung up, providing direct employment for 30,000 Mexicans. In both agriculture and industry, the United States is now in effect exporting jobs to Mexico rather than importing labor, as was once the case.

Social Implications of Rising Unemployment

Perhaps the most disturbing single dimension of rising unemployment in poor countries is its adverse impact on the distribution of wealth within these societies. When the portion of the population that is effectively unemployed rises, the distribution of income among the population can only worsen. The ILO study of Colombia which examined this effect reports: "The bottom third of the rural population may be no better off today than in the 1930's." Further aggravating the situation is the effort by organized labor to use collective bargaining among those who already have jobs as a means of raising wages from 5 to 15 percent yearly. James P. Grant sums it up: "There will be a sizeable group in the developing countries whose standard of living will be rising rapidly while unemployment is increasing, thereby sharpening the contrast between those for whom the system is working and those for whom it is not."

In most situations there is no unemployment insurance, welfare payments or social security to cushion the impact of unemployment. For many, reduced to living on handouts from relatives or foraging through garbage cans, survival itself becomes a dismal prospect. This is the new "marginal man," created by the population explosion in conjunction with a lack of opportunity. Entirely without unemployment compensation or relief, living on occasional scraps of food, often without shelter and almost always without any semblance of medical care, the unemployed face sharply diminishing prospects for survival. Their life expectancy and that of their dependent children is of necessity far less than that of their employed counterparts.

From society's point of view the unemployed represent a wastage of human resources. In some instances the unemployment represents a social investment in education which cannot be recouped unless the nonworking are productively employed. The Pearson Commission Report, the review of international development and foreign aid initiated by the World Bank, identifies the growing underutilization of human resources in the poor countries as one of the real challenges to international development. In addition to aggravating the distribution of income within societies, the rising levels of unemployment in poor countries contribute to a further widening of the gap between the rich and the poor countries.

The swelling ranks of unemployed in poor countries create political as well as social problems. Joblessness is concentrated among the younger segments of the population, particularly those between fifteen and twenty-four. One of three males in this age group is unemployed in Ceylon and Guyana; in Ghana, the Philippines and Malaya, it is one out of every five. Young people are by nature restive and questioning, but idle, frustrated young people are even more so. The unemployment crisis, fueled by the relentless growth of population, is unquestionably raising the level of discontent among this group, creating a socially inflammable situation which threatens to disrupt the existing social and political order. Rising unemployment was a leading political issue in the election campaigns of Mrs. Gandhi in India and Salvador Allende, now President of Chile. It was largely unemployed youth who organized and led the near overthrow of the Ceylonese Government in early 1971.

Reversing Unemployment Trends

Arresting the rising unemployment of the past two decades is imperative if the quality of life for this expanding segment of humanity is not to deteriorate to an intolerable level. A successful strategy consists of many components. The most crucial action required is a reduction in births. After the birth rates have been reduced, the next need for these countries is rapid economic growth. Though necessary, it is not in itself sufficient. As former ILO Director David Morse has pointed out: "One of the most significant and sobering lessons of the world's development effort in the past 20 years has been the discovery that social progress and the rising levels of employment on which it depends do not automatically emerge from economic progress."

During the 1960s the poor countries as a group expanded their economies at an average rate of 5 percent yearly in real terms. The Pearson Commission Report recommended a target rate of growth for the 1970s of six percent yearly. But if the past is any guide to the future, this would not be sufficient to arrest the trend of rising unemployment. Raul Prebisch, in his report to the Inter-American Development

Bank on economic development in Latin America, pointed out that an 8 percent rate of economic growth would be essential to cope with the unemployment crisis in the years ahead. In most situations a 3 percent rate of economic growth is required to accommodate each 1 percent increase in the labor force.

It is instructive to examine the strategies employed in four poor contries which have had pronounced success in reducing unemployment—South Korea, Taiwan, Hong Kong and Singapore. South Korea reduced its unemployment level from 13 percent in 1964 to 6 percent in 1968. When data become available for 1970, they will undoubtedly show a still lower level, given the exceedingly rapid economic growth of 1969 and 1970. Singapore has reduced its unemployment level from 10 percent several years ago to perhaps 5 percent or less in 1970. Taiwan and Hong Kong, both plagued with widespread unemployment a decade ago, now have unemployment levels from 1 to 3 percent. These four economies with a total population of 52 million have two things in common: all have been steadily reducing birth rates for several years and all have achieved fantastically high economic growth rates, among the highest in the world. Beyond this, Taiwan and South Korea, the only two of the four with agricultural sectors, have each had land-reform programs. Taiwan's "land to the tiller" program in the early 1950s was a particularly thorough land redistribution effort.

Each of these four economies has been exceedingly successful in converting low wages into an asset to attract investment from abroad in labor-intensive manufacturing activities, especially by American and Japanese firms. Perhaps even more importantly, South Korea and Taiwan have avoided substituting capital for labor unnecessarily. Dr. M. M. Mehta of the International Labor Organization, using the rubber products industry in Asia, points out that investment per worker varies widely among countries. South

Korea and Taiwan ·invest $626 and $756 per worker, respectively, while India and the Philippines have tied up $1,272 and $2,645 per worker Rubber products produced in Taiwan are comparable in quality, price and profitability to those produced in India. By investing much less per worker, South Korea creates far more jobs with a given amount of investment capital than does the Philippines or India. Within any developing economy there is a broad scope of potential substitution between capital and labor as the above examples from the rubber industry indicate. How much employment is created with a given amount of capital depends on production technologies used, national economic policies and prevailing wage levels.

South Korea and Taiwan have benefited from a large inflow of capital from abroad, both for foreign investment and from the rapidly expanding exports this investment has helped make possible. In the case of South Korea, regarded by many economists as a "basket case" only a decade ago when imports exceeded exports by tenfold, exports expanded a fantastic *503 percent* from 1964 to 1969.

The combination of overpriced labor and underpriced capital has aggravated the employment situation in many countries. Overpriced labor, particularly industrial labor, resulting from strong union pressure for higher wages, discourages investment from abroad in labor-intensive activities. This means that the bargaining power of organized labor must be regulated in many poor countries if it is not to worsen an already grave situation. Governments in countries with overvalued foreign exchange rates can often correct this through administrative action, conserving foreign exchange in the process.

Land reform can also create additional jobs, since family farms invariably employ more labor per acre than do large landowners, who must hire virtually all their labor. But efforts to redistribute land have been nominal; although it is socially desirable, the internal power structure in most countries has thus far prevented any meaningful redistribution of land. In two countries which had effective land reform, Japan and Taiwan, sufficient economic progress has since been made so that it is now economically and socially desirable to begin consolidating small holdings into larger units.

Another possibility for ameliorating unemployment is public works programs. Mainland China has relied heavily on the use of underutilized labor to construct irrigation works and roads and for reforestation. In many countries, rural public works programs such as the construction of farm-to-market roads or the improvement and expansion of irrigation systems can expand employment in two ways: construction of the facilities themselves requires labor, and the new facilities create additional employment, either by linking isolated farmers with the market or through the more intensive cultivation of land, which the additional water makes possible. Urban public works projects, particularly the construction of low-income housing, can also help.

One of the great research voids as far as the poor countries are concerned is in the development of agricultural and industrial technologies which are appropriate to the relative availabilities of labor and capital. This is an area in which the establishment of an international research institute to examine the economics of intermediate technologies could be exceedingly helpful. Certainly the potential consequences of rising unemployment in poor countries is such that it more than justifies such an effort by the international community. As the magnitude and urgency of the unemployment crisis become clear, it is evident that an adequate response to the employment crisis is in many ways beyond the resources of the poor countries alone.

The projected 8 percent rate of economic growth required by the poor countries to solve their unemployment problems has many implications for the relationship between these countries and the rich ones. The close correlation between rates of economic growth and expansion in exports means the poor countries need to gain greater access to export markets. Labor-intensive products such as farm commodities and light industrial goods must be exported in growing quantities, since they both represent an export of labor and earn the foreign exchange needed to spur economic growth. This in turn requires the rich countries to open their highly protected markets to these products.

The expansion of agricultural and industrial exports is not likely to occur without the heavy investment in the infrastructure—power, transport and communications— needed to accommodate this growth. This in turn requires assistance from abroad on a much greater scale than at present. The target levels of assistance outlined by the Pearson Commission Report are not adequate to achieve this. A far greater flow of resources is needed. The poor countries lack not only capital but they also often lack as well the organizational capacity to create jobs on the scale required to reduce unemployment, nor do they have the technology to do so. This is not just a matter of manufacturing processes, but even more important, a matter of organization, marketing skills and know-how. It is in this area, as well as in the provision of capital, that the multinational corporation comes into the picture in a strategic way. Some poor countries such as Taiwan and South Korea have discovered this and are exploiting the resources of scores of multinational corporations based in Japan, Western Europe and North America to great advantage. Both countries, as a result of phenomenal rates of sustained export expansion and economic growth, are now facing labor scarcities.

As the unemployment crisis in the poor countries begins to unfold in the seventies, the world will be forced to take inventory of the means whereby rural employment can be expanded in these countries. When it does, protection of inefficient production of cereals and beet sugar in the rich countries is certain to be examined. The response to this crisis must be global in scope, involving rich countries as well as poor. Although rising levels of unemployment in the poor countries may seem rather remote to the rich countries, the political instability it will almost certainly generate if the unemployment trends of the past two decades continue is not. Our future well-being in an increasingly interdependent, interwoven world is tightly linked to that of the remainder of mankind.

5

FROM COUNTRYSIDE TO CITY

The continuous, swelling flow of people from countryside to city in the poor countries is creating a serious social crisis, the ramifications of which may eventually affect the quality of life of much of mankind. The returns from the 1970 world census are documenting what has seemed obvious, namely, that the populations of the poor countries are converging on the cities at a record pace.

Urban populations in the poor countries, now totalling 600 million, are expected to increase to 3 billion over the next three decades, a 500 percent increase in scarcely a generation. Since urban services and facilities are already overburdened, one can conclude that in the absence of massive external assistance, the level of services will deteriorate dramatically in principal urban centers. By future standards, the Calcutta of today may be a model city.

As things are now going, it appears that the twentieth century will be the one in which human society will be transformed from a primarily rural society to one which is primarily urban. The human habitat is being transformed from one in which most of mankind has lived close to the land and close to nature, to one which is primarily man-made, where most of mankind lives in intimate, continuous association with a vast number of other human beings.

Origins of Cities

To understand fully the significance of contemporary and projected rates of urban growth in the poor countries, it is helpful to examine both the circumstances under which the early cities were formed and the history of urban growth. The first urban centers emerged about 5,500 years ago in the Middle East around the Fertile Crescent. Although agriculture set the stage for urbanization, the first cities were not formed until several thousand years after agriculture began. With the invention of irrigation and the harnessing of draft animals it became possible to produce a consistent surplus of food, enough to support a small fraction of the population in cities engaged in nonagricultural pursuits.

These technological advances in agriculture permitted urban centers to emerge, but the rate of urbanization was exceedingly slow, indeed scarcely perceptible prior to 1800. It was the industrial revolution that made possible the urbanization of entire societies. According to Kingsley Davis, "Taking only the cities of 100,000 or more inhabitants, one finds that in 1600 their combined population in Europe was 1.6 percent of the estimated total population; in 1700, 1.9 percent; and 1800, 2.2 percent. On the eve of the industrial revolution, Europe was still overwhelmingly an agrarian region."

During the nineteenth century, however, urbanization progressed rapidly in Western Europe as the industrial revolution unfolded. In 1800 less than one tenth of the population of England and Wales lived in cities of 100,000 or larger, but by 1900 the majority of the population was urban. By 1960 one third of all mankind was living in urban areas, including cities and towns of all sizes.

Urbanization: Rich Countries and Poor

The process of urbanization is common to every poor country today. It is also common to most rich countries, though not all. Some such as the United Kingdom have reached "urban maturity," that is, the share of urban population has stabilized. Its experience and that of other countries which urbanized earlier indicates that once the urban share of the total population reaches 80 percent it tends not to increase further, stabilizing around that point. Several industrial societies of northern Europe, such as the Netherlands, Belgium and West Germany, appear very close to urban maturity.

Throughout most of history people have migrated from countryside to city largely in response to opportunities in the city. Urbanization served as an index of industrialization and modernization. Today urbanization in the poor countries results much more from uncontrolled population growth and declining opportunities in overpopulated rural areas. Urban pull has been replaced by rural push. Increasingly urbanization is serving as an index of frustration and as an indicator of the potential explosiveness in the urban slums (*bustees* in India, *favellas* in Brazil, or *gecekondu* in Turkey) being created.

This flow away from the countryside and the resulting urban unemployment problems are exacerbated by the uneven global development which finds preindustrial societies juxtaposed with others making the transition into the technetronic, or postindustrial, era. The transfer of inappropriate technologies from advanced nations can make the development process in poor ones even more disruptive than usual. In certain cases, overly rapid mechanization of the rural sector has displaced rural labor, forcing migration to the city at a rate far in excess of urban development opportunities. In the city, too, the application of industrial technology inappropriate to the stage of development has contributed to an imbalance between economic and employment growth.

The use of advanced technology in a country experiencing rapid urbanization may also render many of the new migrants not only unemployed, but unemployable. Migration has occurred primarily among the least skilled and least educated segment of rural workers. This creates an increasing divergence between the technical skills needed in industry and the supply of skilled labor.

Modernization as symbolized by the city fosters aspirations in excess of the real opportunities. The gap between rural and urban incomes, often as much as 300–400 percent, makes the city, despite its shantytowns and frustrations, attractive to displaced rural workers. The great gap between aspirations and opportunities is not yet perceptible enough to act as a deterrent to continued urban migration, nor should it necessarily. Despite the low productivity of migrant labor and the high rates of urban unemployment, urban income and productivity on a per capita basis are in most cases still far higher than in rural areas. As long as rural development continues at such a slow pace, and investment continues to be a primarily urban phenomenon, rapid urbanization will continue.

Dimensions of Urbanization in the Poor Countries

Urbanization as a process is proceeding much more rapidly in the poor countries than in those which industrialized earlier. Populations of urban centers in Asia, Africa and

Latin America are growing at 5 to 8 percent yearly, almost regardless of the existing degree of urbanization. Those with growth rates of 5 percent double in size in fifteen years; those growing 8 percent yearly double in nine years and quadruple in eighteen years. Kingsley Davis points out that "The change from a population with ten percent of its members in cities of 100,000 or larger to one in which 30 percent lived in such cities took about 79 years in England and Wales, 66 in the United States, 48 in Germany, 36 in Japan, and 26 in Australia." Although comparable data for poor countries are not yet available, it is clear they are compressing even more urbanization into a shorter period of time.

Growth in urban population can come either from a natural increase of the urban population or migration from rural areas. In those countries where birth rates are low and only modestly above death rates, as in Eastern Europe, and where rural and small-town birth rates are higher than in urban centers, we may deduce that the rate of natural increase in these centers is negligible, if not negative. Any growth of urban population in cities in these regions must come from rural migration. During the nineteenth century, growth in urban populations in Great Britain also depended almost entirely on rural migration, but for different reasons. In urban areas, lack of sanitation and health measures resulted in extremely high death rates, frequently exceeding birth rates. Growth in urban populations depended on migration from rural areas. In the poor countries, by contrast, both natural increase of the urban population and rural migration contribute to the growth in urban numbers.

Urbanization in the poor countries has certain distinctive features. One is the rate of transformation from rural to urban societies. Urban centers in Turkey and Ghana, growing at 7 percent yearly, are representative. Populations in these countries are doubling every twenty-five years or so.

The population of large cities in the poor countries is doubling every ten to fifteen years, but that of the urban slums or shantytowns is doubling in many cases in five to seven years.

The population of large cities in Latin America is doubling every fourteen years, a rate of growth without historical precedent anywhere in the world. The population of urban squatters in the Philippines is growing at 12 percent yearly. The population of Calcutta is projected by some to reach 40–50 million by the turn of the century. Projections for Lima indicate a population of 6 million by 1990, three fourths of which will be in what were originally squatter settlements.

Runaway urbanization is resulting in congested living conditions, with the great bulk of rural migrants to the cities ending up in squatter communities or shantytowns. The United Nations reports that the sheer magnitude of uncontrolled settlement is revealed in Mexico City, where *colonias proletarias* amount to one third of the capital's population of 4.5 million, and in Ankara's *gecekondu* ("builders of the night"), where one half of its 1.5 million people live. As the rate of growth in squatter settlements continues to exceed that of the city proper in most metropolitan areas in the Third World, often growing at twice the rate of the city itself, we face the prospect that much of mankind will be living in slums and shantytowns by the end of the century. With one third to one half of the inhabitants living in the shantytowns ringing the cities, as in several Latin American capitals, municipal and social services including health, education and welfare are greatly overburdened, to say the least. One can conclude that any increment in urban population will lead to a further deterioration in the quality of urban life as the gap between services available and those needed widens rapidly.

Social and Political Consequences

Perhaps more significant than the actual rate of rural-urban migration is the social situation which it is creating. The result of people piling up in the cities, spontaneously and unplanned, is that many of the basic amenities of life are lacking. According to Charles Abrams, "Armies of squatters are taking over every vacant place, not only on the outskirts but even in the centers of towns and putting up shacks of tin, wood, or cardboard . . . Most of the squatter camps have no services, no schools, no sewers, not even water, except what the squatters fetch in pails or oil drums, or buy at high cost from peddlers. Garbage piles up around their shacks. The settlements are fire and health hazards, but the city governments are almost helpless to enforce controls or do much to improve their condition."

The disproportionate need for social services due to rapid urbanization leads to many dangerous situations, particularly in sanitation. Calcutta, for example, has two water systems: one which distributes an intermittent and inadequate supply of filtered water, and the other a continuous supply of unfiltered water at hydrants. The latter is the primary source for the vast numbers of street dwellers for their cooking, drinking, bathing and laundering. Under such conditions the high potential for epidemics of waterborne disease becomes obvious. Contagious disease spreads under crowded conditions, and the stifling atmosphere within dwellings, particularly in cultures where women are confined to the home, leads to a high incidence of tuberculosis. Migrants from destitute, overcrowded rural areas are bearing the cost of society's failure to control human fertility.

While the need for improved and expanded services increases, the resources for providing them do not. Local tax scales may be adjusted, but little in additional funds can be squeezed from people who are already unemployed and virtually penniless. Expanded services may in fact do little to improve conditions, since they may simply attract even more migrants to the city. Even where services are not readily accessible to the new migrants, the fact that they exist at all and do not in the rural areas acts as a magnetic force.

These rural migrants are not being readily absorbed into the urban social and economic system. Unprepared for urban living, they remain villagers in an urban setting. The rate at which people make the transition from shanty-towns to the city proper or at which shantytowns are upgraded is very slow, only a trickle relative to the incoming flood.

Often the migrants arrive in groups or settle in enclaves of people of similar background, again inhibiting the adaptation to urban life. The single person who makes a permanent move to the city is perhaps potentially the most disruptive. Faced with the same lack of opportunity to enter the urban social and economic sector, he has no traditional ties to resort to. His destitution, frustrations and despair are more likely to translate into political and social instability than those of his migrant counterparts who are a part of a family or community.

In most cases the migrants in the newly erected shanty-towns are not the source of social and political discontent. So long as they are allowed to "establish" their property and home, be it ever so meager, hope remains. Rather than the miserable conditions, it is the frustration of not being able to build or provide for themselves which leads to despair. As long as they can hope for children, they do not usually resort to radical measures. The bitter alienation and explosive forces are often a second-generation phenomenon. When the hopes of the children are dashed, when their limited schooling opens the door to aspirations but offers no opportunity, when unemployment becomes a way of life rather than a temporary situation, when village ties are no longer a psychological support, then the social and political repercussions make themselves felt.

There is little in past human experience against which to assess the social repercussions of the massive rural-urban migration now under way in the poor countries. Among the rich countries, perhaps the closest parallel would be that of the blacks drawn from the rural South into the urban North of the United States. Employment on farms in the Mississippi Delta declined nearly 90 percent over the two-decade span from 1940 to 1960 as the mechanical cotton picker and chemical weed-killer replaced hand labor. For hundreds of thousands of blacks there was no alternative but to migrate to the urban areas in the North—Cleveland, Watts, Newark, Detroit, Harlem and Chicago. Unable to find work and confined to their ghettos, they became alienated, bitter and resentful. These feelings intensified among the second-generation ghetto dwellers, eventually reaching the explosion point as they rioted, burned and looted. Scarcely a city in the United States escaped their wrath. The feeling that they had been denied a rightful share of the economic opportunities and material abundance of the society of which they were ostensibly a part, combined with the feeling that they had little to lose, triggered the explosion.

Alienation and despair are common in both situations. The lack of steady employment for the great bulk of the shantytown dwellers will have a deep, psychological impact. The combination of the size of this group and its exposure to better living conditions elsewhere within the same city are creating a social tinderbox, a potentially disruptive force.

One of the consequences of the desperate plight of the ever-swelling ranks of disenfranchised in the poor countries is the alteration of traditional concepts of ownership and property rights. Hagmuller, for example, reports that, "The barriadas of Peru have become notorious for their elaborate planning as well as their clandestine organization whose large quasi-military groups are used in the sudden occupations of projected squatting settlements. More than 100 such innovations to set up barriadas have taken place in the Lima area in the past 20 years." Hagmuller then elaborates further: "Nonintegration and the marginal position of the urban poor with respect to the leading institutions of society are often paired with a remarkable capacity for self-help, leadership, and community organization, which is threatening legal sovereignty and established order in a less violent though perhaps more fundamental way: by their usurpation of land to which they have no legal title, uncontrolled urban settlements are proliferating throughout the third world. They have defied numerous police actions and bulldozer operations in past years. Millions of squatters are thus challenging a cherished symbol: the sanctity of property rights and the civil order on which it stands."

This phenomenon of large numbers of urban populations which are socially and economically alienated will affect not only the urban community itself, but inevitably the national political climate as well. Erich H. Jacoby describes another aspect of this: "It seems safe to say that the larger part of the turmoil and riots, almost of daily occurrence in the cities of Calcutta, Lima, and Caracas, must be viewed as a desperate protest by the semi-urbanized peasants for whom there is no room in either village or city."

The social conditions of the shantytowns are in many ways reminiscent of the Palestinian refugee settlements of two decades ago, settlements which were later to spawn numerous guerrilla movements among the youth. John Dyckman observes that "concentration in urban centers gives revolutionary cadres a position closer to the management of the society and the conduct of its political life."

One must also speculate on the contagious nature of the potentially volatile political movement given the increasing connections among cities both within and among countries. There is a likely prospect that massive protests and uprisings, once begun, will spread among cities. This was clearly the case with the protests by frustrated blacks in the urban communities of the United States during the mid-sixties.

The urbanization process creates yet another problem for developing countries. Since the creation of shantytowns reinforces the cleavage between modernized and traditional sectors, political integration becomes more difficult, as does economic integration. The move away from rural towns and villages to the primary capital cities may also inhibit the growth of marketing and communication channels between the two sectors. The favoring of the cities in the development process often leads to peasant resentment and may in part be responsible for their unwillingness to supply sufficient food for the cities, a situation apparently prevailing in Communist China in recent years. Peasants, wary of a national government of which they feel no part or benefit, are unwilling to give up scarce food supplies which may be needed in a poor crop year.

It would be unrealistic to regard urbanization in the poor countries in a totally negative light. Although it is less of an indicator of industrialization and development than it was in the West, certainly urbanization does act as a modernizing force. The pace at which it is occurring may lead to many frustrations, disruptions and even economic setbacks, but it does bring people out of the subsistence economy and eventually into the market economy. Certain traditional values which are counterproductive and detrimental to society as a whole in this era, such as a high desired rate of fertility, are more easily abandoned in an urban setting. Although urban growth has far outstripped industrialization in the poor countries, there is no reason to believe that the city cannot assume the same role of a dynamic center for social and cultural change as it did in the West

Cities in the International System

As urbanization proceeds, it is moving the world toward the day when most of mankind will be concentrated in several hundred sprawling urban centers or megapolises scattered throughout the world. In 1920, 28 percent of the world's population was located in such areas. By 1960 this had increased to 41 percent. In the year 2000 it is expected to be in excess of 60 percent.

As the world becomes increasingly urbanized, the character of the city is changing. Early cities related primarily to the surrounding rural regions, exchanging urban manufactured goods and services for agricultural food and fiber. Modern cities relate much less to adjacent rural areas and much more to each other, exchanging goods and services and often becoming highly specialized in the process. Thus today some cities are manufacturing centers, others centers of commerce or finance, and some, such as Washington, Rawalpindi and Brazília, provide primarily government services.

Traditionally, the greater urban concentrations have always been in the rich countries. But this is now changing. As of 1970, several urban centers in the poor countries have a population greater than 7 million each. Included among these are Shanghai, Peking and Calcutta in Asia, and Mexico City, Rio de Janeiro and São Paulo in Latin America.

Over time, economic and social activity is becoming increasingly centered around the cities, which are the nerve centers of human society, the nodes on the global systems of transportation and communication. The organization of global society into urban communities may make them a more relevant organizational unit than the nation-state.

This may increasingly generate overlaps and conflicts between the city and the nation-state in such functions of government as taxation, law enforcement and welfare, and so forth, some of which are already becoming evident.

In many ways the cities of the world are the victims of both the rampant militarism and international trade protectionism of the nation-states. The problems of the cities, and the claims for resources in their behalf, have increased dramatically during a period of rising global military expenditures. Cities in the rich countries and poor are paying dearly for the diversion of resources into armaments. Both are suffering the effects of wholesale mechanization in agriculture without regard for the consequences. Third World cities are paying dearly for the protectionist policies of the richer nation-states as well.

Coping with Urbanization

Coping with problems of urbanization in the poor countries is one of the most complex undertakings confronting modern man. It is a multifaceted problem, one with economic, social, political and ecological dimensions. Rural development must aim at increased production through expanded but more efficient labor utilization. With increased employment opportunities and higher incomes, rural living will become more competitive with the attraction of the city. Beyond this, the provision of better health services and education in rural areas would do much to stem the flow from countryside to city.

Internationally the liberalization of trade by the rich countries, particularly for agricultural and light industrial products, would both make conditions more attractive in the countryside and provide employment for those already in the cities. Unless population growth is curbed, there is no solution to the urbanization problem in the poor countries. One reason the rich countries have not faced urbanization crises on the same scale as the poor countries is that they have been spared the population explosion.

Governments in the poor countries must recognize the growing squatter settlements for what they are, a reality which must be confronted rather than being considered just an embarrassment which can be swept under the rug. Some governments still focus their attention on simply driving squatters away and pushing down their shacks with bulldozers. But bulldozers treat only the symptoms, not the causes of this social ill. Governments are being forced to seek solutions to this problem with exceedingly limited resources. A pilot project described in United Nations Social Situation Report provides an example: "At the Valdivieso project in Lima, 700 families were provided with lots (eight by twelve metres) with U-shaped permanent brick walls at the rear partly shared with neighbors, a provisional dwelling of cane matting and bamboo, and water spigots spaced at frequent intervals. The twelve year loans of $450 at six percent interest were within the means of most families. While the principle proved workable and successful, it was criticized for not providing maximum stimulus to the settlers."

One objective of governments must be to prevent settlement from taking place in a random fashion, with people locating themselves in an unimprovable pattern. Potential squatters should be guided into carefully designed settlement areas and assisted to locate there. Often this activity may be associated with the formation of new urban centers. Some governments, such as that in Mexico, are consciously redistributing new industrial investments, both domestic and foreign, away from the primary city, in this case Mexico City. Pakistan is coordinating the establishment of new settlement colonies with new private investments so as to ensure employment for the new settlers.

The science of human settlement is in its infancy, but it

must mature quickly if man is to cope with the problems emerging in the world's cities. Otherwise the process of urbanization may lead to a decline rather than an improvement in the quality of life. Already it is clear that the cities of the Third World are the social frontier of the future. It is also clear that a satisfactory and humane solution to the problem of massive and rapid urbanization cannot be solved in the absence of a major global shift in priorities, away from military activity and toward some of mankind's serious and worsening social ills.

6

THE HUNGRY MAJORITY

In the late twentieth century, an era of unprecedented affluence, hunger is still the common lot of a majority of the human race. For this hungry majority, the quality of life is influenced more by the lack of food than by any other single factor. For them, daily existence is circumscribed by the quest for food, reducing life to very fundamental biological terms. This is not new, but what distinguishes the current era from earlier ones is that hunger is unnecessary today. As it becomes less necessary it also becomes less tolerable.

Few of man's needs have resisted fulfillment so strenuously as has the need for food. Prior to the beginning of agriculture ten thousand years ago, the earth could not support more than 10 million people, fewer than live in London or Afghanistan today. Since then the earth's food-producing capacity has increased several hundredfold. But despite this enormous expansion, growth in population has consistently absorbed the increase, leaving two thirds of mankind still hungry and malnourished.

Dimensions of Hunger

Average calorie intake in countries containing close to two thirds of the world's people is below the nutritional minimum required for normal growth and activity. Much of this group suffers from chronic protein malnutrition as well. Where death certificates are issued for preschool infants in the poor countries, death is generally attributed to measles, pneumonia, dysentery or some other disease, when in fact these children were probably victims of malnutrition. Severely malnourished infants or children with low resistance frequently die of routine childhood diseases. If, as Paul Ehrlich has suggested, all the deaths that would not have occurred given adequate nutrition could be attributed to malnutrition with reasonable accuracy, it would bring the social costs of malnutrition into much sharper focus.

Malnutrition has many costs, both economic and social. The effect of low food intake on the productivity of labor is easy to see. American construction firms operating in developing countries and employing local labor often find that they get high returns in worker output by investing in a good company cafeteria that serves employees three meals a day.

The pervasive impact of undernourishment was dramatically illustrated during the summer of 1968, when India held its Olympic trials in New Delhi to select a track and field team to go to Mexico City. Despite its population of 535 million, not one of the contestants could meet minimum Olympic qualifying standards in any of the thirty-two track and field events. Outdated training techniques and the lack of public support were partly responsible, but widespread undernourishment undoubtedly contributed to this poor showing.

In contrast to India, the youth of Japan today are visible examples of the change that improved nutrition can bring.

Well nourished from infancy as a result of Japan's newly acquired affluence, teen-agers on the streets of Tokyo average perhaps two inches taller than their elders.

Protein is as crucial for children's mental development as for their physical development. This was strikingly shown in a recent study conducted over several years in Mexico; youngsters who had been severely undernourished before the age of five were found to average 13 points lower in IQ than a carefully selected control group that had not experienced severe malnutrition. Protein shortages in the early years of life impair development of the brain and central nervous system, permanently reducing learning capacity. Furthermore, this damage is irreversible. If widespread protein shortages are allowed to continue, we risk a loss which no amount of investment in education could correct. With this disturbing information we turn to an examination of man's historical quest for food.

Man's Quest for Food

Man's age-old quest for food was given a great boost by agriculture, which brought with it a steady increase in the earth's food-production capacity, and ultimately a capacity by man for intervening in the environment unmatched by any other sector of human activity. Following the discovery of agriculture, a series of technological advances which extended to the modern era further expanded the earth's food-production capacity. Prominent among these were irrigation, the harnessing of draft animals, invention of the internal-combustion engine, the discovery of genetics, and advances in agricultural biochemistry.

One of the first major innovations was irrigation, the obstruction by man of the flow of streams and rivers, diverting water onto the land he was cultivating. This intervention in the hydrological cycle, closely associated with the emergence of early civilizations, greatly boosted the productivity of land. It was not long, however, before some of man's technological intrusions began to exceed his understanding of them. He knew how to divert water onto land but he didn't understand the subterranean dynamics of rising water tables, resulting in the waterlogging and salinity problems which eventually beset most irrigation systems. The remains of civilizations buried in the sands of the Middle East bear witness to man's incomplete understanding of the consequences of intervening in the hydrological cycle.

In a world where water, not land, is often becoming the principal constraint on food production, and where competition for fresh water is increasing, man is being forced to consider far-reaching interventions in the hydrological cycle to expand the supply of fresh water. These include diverting the flow of rivers from the oceans to low-rainfall agricultural areas, commercial rainmaking and in extreme cases the costly desalination of sea water for agricultural purposes. Commercial rainmakers intervene in the global climatic system when they attempt to cause precipitation. Firms headquartered in the United States will contract their services to national governments, local governments, farmers' associations or any other concern willing to pay for their services. Often they attempt to shift precipitation patterns so that rainfall now occurring over the oceans will be shifted to land masses. Particular areas such as Baja California or parts of the Sahara could be made quite productive if sufficient water were available. The government of Florida, for example, recently contracted with a rainmaking firm to increase rainfall over the Florida peninsula, in an effort to relieve an extended drought there.

A thousand years or so after learning to irrigate, man discovered a way of intervening in still another cycle, this time the energy cycle. Harnessing draft animals enabled him to convert roughage, an otherwise unusable form of energy, into a form which could increase his food supply. The harnessing of draft animals greatly augmented man's own limited muscle power, raising the efficiency of his labor to the point where a small segment of the population could be spared from food-producing activities. Even today, perhaps half of the world's cropland is tilled with cattle, water buffalo, horses and camels.

The harnessing of draft animals affected man's relationship with nature in two important ways. First, it greatly enhanced his capacity for bringing new land under cultivation. In the New World, for instance, the pre-Columbian Indians had limited their farming largely to the rich alluvial soils of the river flood plains, but with the introduction of draft animals from Europe and invention of the steel plow, the tough, virgin sods of the Great Plains were opened for crop farming. Second, dependence on animals for draft power as well as for food meant an increase in their number closely paralleling those in human population. As livestock populations increased in the more densely populated areas of the world, their grazing needs came to exceed the rate of natural replenishment of vegetation, resulting in a gradual denuding of the countryside.

Much later, the next major intervention of man in the energy cycle came with the internal-combustion engine. Burning fossil fuels, these engines permitted man to tap the solar energy received by the earth eons ago and stored underground as petroleum. The productivity of labor employed in agriculture climbed sharply, for the first time in history permitting a minority to meet the food needs of the entire population.

Another advance occurred through alteration of the genetic composition of domesticated species of plants and animals. Through selective breeding over the millennia, man altered the germ plasm of domesticated species, gradually improving the productivity of his farmyard animals. With the discovery of the principles of genetics by Mendel and their refinement by others, efforts to breed crops and livestock for greater productivity were given a great boost.

The first domesticated cattle probably did not yield more than 600 pounds of milk per year, barely enough to support a calf to the point where it could forage for itself. The average cow in the United States produced nearly 8,000 pounds of milk last year. A Maryland cow, Rheinharts Ballad, produced a new world record of 42,000 pounds of milk in 1970. This productive animal could deliver 49 quarts of milk on one's doorstep every day, outperforming her early ancestors by a factor of 70 to 1.

The early ancestors of our current hen probably did not lay more than 15 eggs, or one clutch, per year. The average American hen last year laid 220 eggs. The world record is held by an industrious Japanese hen which laid 365 eggs in one year.

The high-yielding dwarf wheats developed in Mexico under the leadership of Dr. Norman Borlaug, recipient of the 1970 Nobel Peace Prize, represent the telescoping and packaging of several decades of genetic progress in the rich countries into a form widely adapted to conditions in the poor countries. Once the potential success of the Mexican wheats became evident in the early sixties, the Rockefeller Foundation, which sponsored this research, joined forces with the Ford Foundation in 1962 to establish the International Rice Research Institute at Los Baños in the Philippines. Building on the Mexican experience, scientists at IRRI, under the leadership of Dr. Robert Chandler, struck pay dirt quickly when one of their early crosses produced a prolific dwarf rice, IR-8, now known around the world as the "miracle rice." Like the Mexican wheats, IR-8 was capable of doubling yields over traditional varieties, given the appropriate water, fertilizer and management.

These advances in plant and animal genetics have environmental consequences in that their new genetic potentials can be realized only under very specific environmental conditions. In effect, they dictate to a substantial degree the character of world agriculture. For example, the genetic potential of the new wheats and rices can be realized only with heavy applications of fertilizer. Modern breeds of cattle and poultry supply vastly greater quantities of protein for human consumption than their ancestors, but they require large amounts of concentrated nutrients in the form of cereals and protein-rich commodities such as soybeans and fish meal, along with their traditional intake of roughage. In order to produce the necessary feedstuffs, a large proportion of the earth's agricultural land has been put under the plow, converting it from grassland to cropland. Much of the Peruvian fish catch is used to meet the protein needs of modern poultry flocks in the United States, where it is consumed indirectly in the form of poultry, meat and eggs.

The use of agricultural chemicals, both to improve soil fertility and to control pests, has enabled man to greatly expand the earth's food-producing capacity. Modern agriculture uses literally hundreds of chemical compounds to control pests of crops, livestock and poultry. As the global food-demand curve has climbed since World War II, the use of pesticides and chemical fertilizer has climbed even faster. In 1960 the world's farmers spread 29 million tons of chemical fertilizer—nitrates, phosphates, potash—on their land. A decade later they were pouring some 70 million tons of fertilizer into the earth's ecosystem. The use of chemical fertilizer today accounts for easily one fourth of the world's food supply, enough to feed a billion people. In countries where fertilizer is used intensively, as in the Netherlands or Japan, discontinuing its use could halve the food supply.

Population and Affluence

There are two forces expanding the global demand for food: increasing population and rising incomes. In some countries the former dominates, and in others, the latter. In Indonesia, where the population is growing rapidly and incomes are rising slowly, population growth accounts for nearly all the year-to-year increases in the demand for food. In West Germany, where the population has virtually stabilized and income per person is rising 5 percent annually, most of the additional demand for food is generated by rising affluence, even though only one fourth or so of additional income is spent for food. World-wide, population growth is currently responsible for two thirds to four fifths of the growth in demand for food of 2.5–3 percent yearly.

If the projected end-of-century world population of 6.5 billion were to materialize, food production would have to nearly double present levels merely to maintain current inadequate consumption levels. The increase in the earth's food-producing capacity over the next three decades would have to equal that achieved from the time agriculture originated to the present.

The relationship between rising incomes and food requirements can be readily visualized in per capita consumption of grain, which accounts for more than half of man's food energy intake when consumed directly, and a significant part of the remainder when consumed indirectly in the form of livestock products. The 2 billion people living in the poor countries consume an average of less than 400 pounds of grain per person yearly, or about a pound per day. With only one pound per day, nearly all must be consumed directly to meet minimal energy requirements; little remains for feeding livestock. Europeans, at intermediate levels of affluence, each consumes about one half ton of grain. The average North American, in contrast, requires nearly *one ton* of grain per year. Only 150 pounds is consumed directly as bread, breakfast cereals and pastries; the rest is consumed indirectly in the form of meat, milk and eggs.

Thus the average North American, enjoying the luxury of the highly inefficient animal conversion of grain into tastier and somewhat more nutritious proteins, exerts five times as much pressure on the earth's agricultural eco-system as someone living in a poor country. If income levels in these latter countries rise over the coming decades, so too will their demand for a richer diet of animal products Combined with the projected near doubling of population, this desired improvement in diets could easily expand world demand in food by 2.5 times over the next three decades. This is not a welcome prospect in ecological terms.

Two Sources of Production

Increased supplies of food to meet the projected food needs can come either from expanding the cultivated area or from raising yields on land already under cultivation. Over the ten millennia since the beginning of agriculture, increases in production have come largely from expanding the area. Man moved from valley to valley and from continent to continent, always bringing more land under the plow, always pushing back the frontiers. Within this century, however, the frontiers began to disappear. Homesteading had ceased in the United States by World War I. Mid-century marked the global turning point. Since 1950, most of the increase in the world's food supply has come from raising yields on the existing cultivated area. Only parts of sub-Saharan Africa and the interior Amazon basin contain significant areas of potentially cultivable land. Some countries such as the United States and the Soviet Union have reduced land under cultivation in recent decades as marginally productive land has been retired. In Europe and Japan farmland is being steadily lost to nonfarm uses such as roads, airports, industrial developments and urban spread.

While the rich countries with their advanced agricultural technologies have found it relatively easy to raise yields when it became necessary to do so, the poor countries have not. Lacking much new land to bring under cultivation and unable to raise yields appreciably, all but a handful of poor countries were converted into food importers between 1945 and 1965. For many the capacity to raise yields and reduce dependence on imported food awaited the Green Revolution, the shorthand expression used to describe the introduction and spread of the new high-yielding wheats and rices into the poor countries. This phenomenon, beginning in the mid-sixties, is based on the use of new cereals which are both extraordinarily responsive to chemical fertilizer and efficient in their use of resources. Given the necessary physical and management inputs, they are capable of doubling yields over the traditional varieties they replace, yielding not only far more per acre of land, but also much more per unit of fertilizer, water and labor.

Between 1965 and 1970, land planted to the new varieties of wheat and rice in the poor countries, principally in Asia, expanded as follows:

1965	200 acres
1966	41,000 "
1967	4,047,000 "
1968	16,660,000 "
1969	31,319,000 "
1970	43,914,000 "

By 1970, the acreage of Mexican wheats in Asia was seven times that in Mexico! Although scarcely one tenth of the region's grain acreage was seeded to the new wheats and rices in 1970, it had a disproportionate impact on production, since it was the most fertile, well-watered land.

In one of the most spectacular advances in cereal production ever recorded, West Pakistan increased its wheat harvest over 70 percent between 1967 and 1970, becoming a net exporter in the late sixties. India's production of wheat, a minor staple in the Indian diet, doubled in six years, bringing India to the brink of cereal self-sufficiency in early 1972. Ceylon's rice crop increased 34 percent in two years. The Philippines, with four consecutive record rice harvests, has at least temporarily ended a half-century of dependence on rice imports, actually exporting rice in some recent years. Among the other Asian countries that are beginning to benefit from the new seeds are Turkey, Burma, Malaysia, Indonesia and Vietnam. Even such remotely situated Asian countries as Afghanistan, Nepal and Laos are using the new seeds. The Mexican wheats, introduced recently in Tunisia and Morocco, are beginning to spread in both countries.

Even though the national economic deficits in cereals— the difference between what is produced domestically and what the market will absorb at prevailing prices—are being reduced or even eliminated, as in West Pakistan or India, the nutritional deficit remains, largely because incomes (read productivity for those not in the market economy) of most people are simply not high enough to permit adequate diets. The new seeds have at least temporarily arrested the deteriorating food situation in some of Asia's most populous countries—India, Pakistan, Indonesia, Turkey and the Philippines—but they do not of course provide an ultimate solution to the food-population problem.

Agricultural Stresses on the Ecosystem

New signs of agricultural stress on the earth's ecosystem appear almost daily as the growing demand for food presses against our ecosystem's finite capacities. Interventions by early agricultural man were local in effect, but the technological intrusions of modern agriculture often have global consequences. Efforts to expand the food supply, either by expanding the area under cultivation or by intensifying cultivation through the use of agricultural chemicals and irrigation, bring with them troublesome and disturbing ecological consequences.

As expanding population has increased the need for both new agricultural land and forest products for fuel, particularly in the poor countries, the countryside is being steadily denuded. Livestock populations, expanding to meet growing demands for food and draft power, are stripping the countryside of natural cover in many parts of the world. In areas where the demand for wood for fuel exceeds the rate of natural replenishment, the forested area is steadily shrinking, leaving much of the soil unprotected and resulting in the overall denudation of the countryside. As vast areas of the earth's surface are deforested, those living in countries such as India and Pakistan are forced to use cow dung for fuel, depriving the land of a natural source of fertility.

As a growing area of the earth's land surface is deprived of its original cover of grass and trees, soil is left bare to be eroded by wind and water. Millions of acres are abandoned each year in the poor countries, forcing rural people into already overcrowded cities. Nature requires centuries to create an inch of topsoil, but man can destroy it in a matter of years. The thin mantle of life-sustaining topsoil, measured in inches over most of the earth's surface, is being slowly destroyed in many areas.

As the demand for food expands, more and more land which is too steep or too dry to sustain cultivation is being brought under the plow. In the poor countries, where most of the level land is already cultivated, farmers are moving up the hillsides. In West Pakistan the recently completed $600-million Mangla irrigation reservoir, which originally had a life expectancy of one hundred years, is now expected to be nearly filled with silt in half that time. Clearing steep slopes for farming, deforestation and overgrazing in the reservoir's watershed are responsible for its declining life expectancy. Clearing new land for farming in one area is reducing the water for irrigation in another. Farmers moving up the hillsides in Java are causing irrigation canals to silt at an alarming rate.

Damming the Nile at Aswan expanded the irrigated area for producing cereals but largely eliminated the annual deposits of rich alluvial silt on fields in the Nile Valley, forcing farmers to rely more on chemical fertilizers. In addition, interrupting the flow of nutrients into the Nile estuary caused a precipitous decline in the fish catch there. Intensive farming in the Philippines with chemical fertilizers is expanding the rice supply but causing fresh-water lakes and streams to eutrophy, destroying fish and depriving local villagers of their principal source of animal protein.

The virgin-lands project in the Soviet Union, which was launched in the late fifties, involved plowing up an estimated 100 million acres of drylands. Only after the land was plowed was it realized that much of it lacked sufficient precipitation to sustain continuous cultivation. Eventually some of the land was returned to grass but not before it became known as the drylands fiasco.

A historic example of the effects of man's abuse of the soil is all too visible in North Africa, which once was the fertile granary of the Roman Empire and now is largely a desert or near-desert whose people are fed with the aid of food imports from the United States. Land once productive was eroded by continuous cropping and overgrazing until much of it would no longer sustain agriculture. Irrigation systems silted, depriving land of the water needed for cultivation. Similar situations are being created in parts of Asia experiencing a rapid build-up of population during this century.

Efforts to intensify agricultural production also have adverse environmental consequences. If the effect of chemical fertilizer could be confined to agriculture, it would be fine, but unfortunately it cannot. The water runoff from agricultural land carries chemical fertilizer with it, raising the nutrient content of streams and lakes throughout the world, causing them to eutrophy.

Lake Erie, the best-known victim of eutrophication, has received nutrients from agricultural, industrial and municipal sources. It would require an estimated $40 billion, equivalent to the Department of Interior budget for the next eighteen years at the current level, to restore Lake Erie to its original state as a fresh-water body. Tens of thousands of fresh-water lakes are threatened throughout North America, Europe, and increasingly, in the poor countries where fertilizer use is beginning to climb. No one has calculated the cost to mankind of losing these fresh-water lakes, but it is staggering.

Our preceding analysis shows that the market price of food represents only one of the costs associated with its production. Unfortunately, there is no complete inventory of what it costs to expand the world food supply continually to meet the ever-increasing needs. There is no calculation of the trade-off between increases in population and improvements in diet, a choice which we are now forced into making as we press against the finite limits of our ecosystem.

An unwillingness to bear at least some of the costs of expanding our food supply indefinitely is beginning to translate into constraints on food production. Many countries have banned or seriously delimited the use of DDT, dieldrin and other chlorinated hydrocarbons, a group of cheap, highly effective pesticides. Resistance to the construction of new irrigation reservoirs is rising in a lengthening list of countries. A seemingly endless number of local and state governments are banning the use of phosphates in detergents because of eutrophication. It may be only a matter of time until the use of phosphate fertilizer is regulated in some communities. Levels of nitrate in water supplies in Decatur and other Illinois communities, far exceeding FDA tolerance levels, have led the state government to hold hearings on the need to limit the use of nitrogen fertilizer, possibly at application rates well below those now used by many farmers. Problems associated with the vast quantities of waste generated by commercial feed lots in Kansas have led to state regulation of feed-lot size. The conflicts between economic efficiency and ecological soundness are myriad. DDT is a potent, low-cost pesticide; chemical fertilizer is far cheaper than organic fertilizer; and beef finished in large commercial feedlots is cheaper than that finished in family-farm-operated feed lots.

We do know that the costs associated with man's unending quest for food are high. They include the eutrophication of fresh-water lakes throughout the world. Many of these, once suitable for fish and for bathing, are now filling with algae. The costs of reclaiming eutrophied lakes is, as indicated earlier, fantastically high. We do not know how many species of birds, fish and mammals must be sacrificed in order to achieve a 5 percent increase in the world's food supply. We do know that as the number of people in the world goes up, the number of extant species goes down. Over time we can expect that willingness to pay all the costs for expanding our food supply will diminish. As resistance to continuing on our current path rises, pressure to reduce birth rates will also rise.

Alleviating Ecosystem Stresses

While striving to reduce the pressure of the growing demand for food on the earth's ecosystem, man must also seek to reduce the adverse impact of his agricultural interventions. One way of doing this for pesticides is to substitute "selective" pesticides for "broad range" pesticides. Another is to devise more biological controls, a few of which have been used quite successfully on minor pests. Among the more successful is the "sterile male" technique, which involves sterilizing large numbers of males of a given insect species. This technique, developed under the direction of Edward Knipling of the U.S. Department of Agriculture has been used successfully on the screwworm fly, a pest of cattle. A large number of male screwworm flies are sterilized by irradiation and then released. These bred with local females which laid eggs that were infertile. When a high ratio of sterile males is maintained, population of the screwworm fly decreases. In the United States, population of this pest has been held to negligible levels by releasing 125 million sterile flies weekly wherever the flies reappear, particularly a 300-mile zone along the Mexican border. The cost of this control program is estimated at one fifteenth that of the annual losses which would result from the screwworm fly in the absence of control. The USDA and the Mexican government are now considering pushing the control zone southward to the Isthmus of Panama in order to virtually eradicate the screwworm fly from North America. By the use of this technique, efforts are now under way in California to control the Mexican fruit fly and the pink bollworm on cotton.

Another approach which is expected to be successful with some pests is the breeding of pest-resistant strains. An example of this is the Hessian fly, pest of wheat. In areas where resistant strains of wheat have been used, the population of the Hessian fly has been so reduced that it is no longer a problem. Strains of corn resistant to the corn borer and to the corn earworm have also been released.

Perhaps the most difficult of agriculture's adverse ecological effects to cope with is eutrophication. Unfortunately there is no economical means to achieve massive increases in world food production without greatly increasing the use of chemical fertilizer. The present prospect, therefore, is for progressive eutrophication of fresh-water bodies in agricultural areas.

Action must also be taken to reduce the adverse effects of overextending the area under cultivation. The only possible way to stabilize the relationship between man and the land on which he lives in the densely populated poor countries is to introduce techniques to conserve the soil by reducing wind and water erosion. The dust-bowl era of the thirties in the United States did not end until the formation of the Soil Conservation Service as well as widespread adoption of conservation practices by farmers. An estimated 20 million acres of land were fallowed, alternating this land with strips of wheat (strip cropping) to reduce the blowing of soil on the idle land. In addition, thousands of miles of tree windbreaks were planted across the Great Plains perpendicular to the prevailing winds. The relationship between man and the land in the Great Plains has now been stabilized; erosion is negligible and productivity is high.

The world's more densely populated regions, however, are in no position to adopt such tactics. Their food needs are so pressing that they cannot afford to take large areas out of cultivation. Nor do they yet have the financial resources or the technical skills for the vast projects in reforestation, contour farming, fallowing, the regulated grazing of cattle and goats, and systematic management of watersheds that are required to prevent soil losses. Like many other problems confronting the poor countries, this one can be solved only with massive capital and technical assistance from the rich countries.

Down the Food Chain

One way to reduce agricultural stresses on the ecosystem, as earlier discussion implies, is to blunt the effect of rising incomes by lowering high-income man on the food chain through the use of vegetable-derived livestock-product substitutes. Some trends in the United States are already moving in this direction. Both milk and egg consumption per person have declined more than 20 percent since 1950 as Americans have adopted a more sedentary way of life. Substitution of a midmorning coffee break for breakfast, particularly by white-collar workers, has steadily lowered egg consumption. Vegetable oils are being substituted for animal fat, in part for dietary reasons. In 1940 the average American consumed 17 pounds of butter and 2 pounds of margarine. By 1971 butter had dropped to 5 pounds, and margarine had climbed to 11 pounds. This was closely paralleled by a decline in lard consumption, as lard was nearly pushed off the supermarket shelf by the hydrogenated vegetable shortenings. Recent data indicate that 65 percent of the whipped toppings and 35 percent of the "coffee whiteners" purchased by U.S. consumers are now of nondairy origin. These latter examples illustrate how economic and ecological forces can sometimes push in the same direction rather than in opposing directions, as is so often the case.

Countering these trends, however, is an increase in beef consumption in the United States from 55 pounds per person yearly in 1940 to 114 pounds in 1970. This may have more than offset the reduction in stress on the ecosystem by the decline in milk and egg consumption and the substitution of vegetable oils for animal fats.

If agricultural pressures on the earth's ecosystem become too severe, we may eventually be forced to replace meat and milk by soybean-derived substitutes, besides stabilizing population growth. An early breakthrough in this direction is the successful commercialization by General Mills of a soybean-derived baconlike product marketed under the trade name Bacos. A factory devoted entirely to the production of Bacos has been constructed near Cedar Rapids, Iowa. This plant procures soybeans from the surrounding countryside and converts them into Bacos, by-passing the livestock phase of the cycle. Bacos is then marketed in direct competition with bacon produced by farmers adjacent to the plant site who still rely on hogs to combine corn, soybeans and other products to produce bacon. As vegetable-derived meat substitutes are perfected, substitution for some meats could become extensive.

While new high-yielding cereals are helping overcome calorie deficits, they are not contributing as much to alleviating protein malnutrition. Historically, diets in the richer countries improved when cereal supplies began to exceed direct consumption needs, leaving large quantities to be converted into high-protein livestock products. But this conventional path to achieving high-quality diets is a costly one. If cereals could be re-engineered or fortified so that their protein quality approached that of livestock protein, this cost could be greatly reduced.

Corn, for example, is deficient in the protein building block lysine, and to a lesser extent tryptophan, both essential to human nutrition. Corn-consuming populations therefore suffer from a shortage of these amino acids in their diet. These deficiencies may be overcome either genetically or biochemically through fortification of the corn itself. The discovery of a high-lysine gene, Opaque-2, in a collection of corn germ plasm by Edwin T. Mertz and his associates at Purdue in 1963, opened a new front in man's efforts to combat malnutrition on a global scale. From this breakthrough, Rockefeller Foundation scientists developed commercial corn varieties with a high lysine content in Colombia which were released for general use in 1969.

High-lysine corn has a great potential for alleviating protein malnutrition in both Latin America and sub-Saharan Africa, where it is an important food staple. To the extent that both high-yield and high-protein content can be incorporated in the same varieties, the prospect for enlarging protein supplies is exciting. Seeds that double yields and raise protein content by one fourth will increase protein output per acre by 150 percent. Encouragingly, nearly all nutritional shortcuts which reduce the cost of attaining an adequate diet also reduce pressure on the ecosystem.

Scientists have invented ways of synthesizing amino acids economically, just as they had earlier synthesized vitamins, making it possible to upgrade the quality of protein in cereals, simply by adding the necessary amino acids. Adding four pounds of lysine to a ton of wheat costs only $4, but results in one third more usable protein. Additions of essential amino acids to plant protein can make it equal in quality to animal protein. Government bakeries in Bombay, India, are now fortifying wheat flour with lysine, as well as with vitamins and minerals. Bread made with this flour may be the most nutritious marketed anywhere.

Paradoxically, in many poor countries, widespread protein hunger coexists with vast quantities of unused protein meals, largely the product of local vegetable-oil-extraction industries. In India, Nigeria and several smaller countries, literally millions of tons of peanuts are produced for their oil, which is used in cooking. Other countries use coconut or soybean oil. After the seeds are crushed and the oil extracted, the meal remaining is largely protein. Unfortunately, little of this protein finds its way directly into foodstuffs, since most oil meal is fed to livestock or poultry, used for organic fertilizer or exported to earn foreign exchange. If the estimated 20 million tons of peanut, cottonseed, coconut and soybean meals available each year in the poor countries could be made into attractive, commercially successful protein foods, much of the world's protein hunger would be eliminated.

Some successful new high-protein products are beginning to appear. Prominent among these are popular beverages being developed by several private firms using oilseed meals. Vitasoy, a soy-based beverage manufactured and marketed in Hong Kong, has captured one fourth of the soft-drink market there. A caramel-flavored, soy-based beverage designed with the nutritional equivalent of milk is now being introduced on a pilot basis by the Coca-Cola Company in Brazil. Puma, a banana-flavored protein drink designed by the Monsanto Corporation, is now commercially manufactured and marketed in Guyana.

Eliminating Hunger

A global effort to eliminate hunger is a complex undertaking, extending far beyond agriculture and the capacity to produce food. To be sure, further advances are necessary, but we must ask two other questions: How can we devise a system which will distribute purchasing power more equitably both within and among societies, and how can we minimize the adverse ecological costs of attempting to produce the needed food?

It is unrealistic to consider eliminating hunger without a massive attack on global poverty, raising incomes to the level required to obtain the basic food nutrients for an adequate diet. As a nutrition map of the world shows, hunger is inextricably linked with abject poverty, concentrated in those regions where per capita incomes average less than $400 per year, essentially most of Africa, Asia and Latin America. There is no possible way of eliminating calorie-protein hunger with individual incomes in Bolivia, Ethiopia or India averaging only $90 per year.

A world seriously interested in eradicating hunger and malnutrition must be prepared to support a sharp acceleration in economic growth rates in the poor countries in the years immediately ahead. This in turn requires a much greater flow of resources from rich countries to poor than at present. A large share of the needed resources can be earned by the poor countries themselves if the rich ones will permit competitive access to their internal markets for such things as sugar, cereals and light industrial products. Beyond this, financial and technical assistance from the rich must also expand. The poor countries simply do not possess the internal resources to eliminate hunger in the forseeable future.

Beyond this, we must consider the distribution of wealth within societies, for, as Americans now know, producing an abundance of food within a country does not necessarily mean that everyone will be well fed. In countries where wealth is concentrated in a few hands, as in many Latin American societies, the incidence of hunger and malnutrition would be greatly reduced by a more equitable distribution of wealth. In agrarian societies, this may mean breaking up large land holdings through land reform, an effort few countries have been successful at. As population pressures build and rural poverty continues, or even worsens in some situations, the prospect of implementing effective land redistribution programs may be enhanced.

Another central component of a global strategy must be a crash effort to reduce birth rates everywhere, significantly slowing global population growth during this decade. Slowing population growth in the short term and stabilizing it over the longer term is essential not only to eliminate existing widespread hunger but to preserve the ecosystem and protect the future food supply for mankind as a whole.

Stresses on the earth's ecosystem are now such that even as we attempt to eliminate hunger and malnutrition, we must also begin to place some upper limits on the eventual over-all demand for food as dictated by the finite capacities of the earth's ecosystem. We do not yet have enough information to estimate these with precision, but we do know that at some point in the not too distant future the costs of continually expanding our food supply will become too great.

Eliminating hunger and malnutrition is a complex undertaking even in a wealthy society. At the global level the prospects for eliminating hunger are closely related to success in slowing population growth, in narrowing the North-South economic gap and achieving a more equitable distribution of wealth within societies.

II

Keys to Our Future

7

THE EDUCATIONAL CHALLENGE

Few problems facing mankind are as challenging as that of devising an educational system capable of responding to society's needs in the late twentieth century. If the quality of life for the majority of us is not to deteriorate, far-reaching changes in human behavior must occur in the years immediately ahead. Education becomes crucially important as a means of informing people of the need for change and for stimulating acceptance of new attitudes. For this reason education is selected, along with the need to stabilize population and to build East-West bridges, which is the key to reordering global priorities, as one of the three keys to dealing with the problems outlined in the preceding chapters.

The need to understand the accelerating pace of change, the consequences of the growing pressures of human activity on the ecosystem and the technological advances weaving all of mankind into a single community, each exerts new claims on the educational system. Yet for much of the world's population, the most fundamental education is still not available. For technetronic society, knowledge has become the central economic resource, while for the 700 million or so adults who are illiterate, the most basic tools for learning are still lacking.

Education's Changing Role

As the rate of change accelerates, the character of education changes, becoming a lifelong process. Informal education becomes more important relative to formal education. The day when a man was educated early in life, graduating from secondary school or college, prepared for a lifetime of work in his chosen vocation or profession, is largely past. Few of today's graduates can make it through even a decade of employment in a modern society without being vocationally refurbished in some way.

The accelerating rate of social and technological change puts added stress on the educational system. A paragraph in a recent UN report describes this well: "Those now in their active years were born in an economic, social, physical and cultural environment which differs enormously from the one they may still live to see. They were taught by teachers who had been reared in a world whose features are now fading rapidly, and they are called upon to instruct a new generation whose future living conditions are still shrouded in mystery. Basic human nature remains the same, but the necessary adaptations between man and his increasingly manmade environment are now changing with greater speed than ever before." As the pace of change quickens, the focus of education must be not so much how to live, but how to adapt.

It is becoming imperative that we alter our relationship with nature. In particular, this means altering attitudes toward childbearing and desired lifestyles. Our capacity to make these adjustments will directly affect the future well-being of all mankind. The educational system, broadly defined, must begin to provide the individual with much more information on the relationship between man and nature. A liberal education in the traditional sense continues to be important, but a basic understanding of man's place in the earth's complex and threatened ecosystem will be at least as essential in the decades immediately ahead.

Education is now recognized as the principal vehicle of social change. It is no longer simply a matter of mastering the three R's—reading, writing and arithmetic—nor is it merely a matter of skill acquisition, of preparing for a vocation or profession. For much of mankind it is the door into the twentieth century, it is the means to improving the quality of life, achieving social mobility and participating in the world's affairs. In traditional societies, education is available to those born to the wealthy, thereby ensuring the preservation of social strata. In modern society, the availability of education is related much more closely to the ability of the student. Admissions based on open examinations rather than family connections help ensure equality of opportunity, and have revolutionary consequences for both economic and social development. Indeed, a change as fundamental as the spread of literacy within a society can directly affect the distribution of power within that society.

We also need to develop a critical social awareness as individuals. Paulo Freire, Brazilian educator, defines the growing awareness by an individual of his relationship to society as a process of conscientization. Whereas Freire thinks largely in terms of the local and national community, I would expand his concept to encompass the global community, to encompass relationships among societies as well as among individuals within a society.

Educational systems everywhere are under great stress, in part because of the sheer lack of resources and in part because of the lack of relevance, a failure to change and adapt. In most poor countries, resources simply are not adequate to educate formally the enormous number of school-age children. In the rich countries the crisis in the universities, whether in Japan, France or the United States, is centered on the relevance of contemporary education to the circumstances in which today's young find themselves.

Literacy Trends

Five centuries have passed since the invention of the printing press, yet as of 1970 two fifths of the world's adults lack the capacity to take advantage of this invention. United Nations Educational, Scientific and Cultural Organization (UNESCO) estimates that the illiterate share of the world's adult population declined from 43 percent in 1960 to 39 percent in 1965. Although the share of the population affected is diminishing slowly, the number of illiterates is greater today than twenty years ago because of growth in population. The modern world is very much a world of words, and despite the new opportunities for learning made possible through radio and television, the illiterate person is severely handicapped.

Adult illiteracy is concentrated largely in Asia, Africa and Latin America. While illiteracy within the rich countries today is negligible, at least half and in some cases three fourths or more of the adults in many poor societies are illiterate. In 1963, UNESCO estimated that attaining literacy required from $5 to $8 per person, with costs generally lower for adults, since they acquire reading and writing skills more quickly than young children; in addition, the benefits are greater, for they are more immediately productive. Compulsory elementary education will eventually eliminate illiteracy, but several decades are required. Unfortunately, mankind cannot afford this delay.

Since World War II, governments have increasingly assumed responsibility for combating illiteracy, some developing novel and effective approaches to the massive teaching of literacy. Some are even taking legal action to spur the spread of literacy. Libya and Iraq are preparing legislation which would require illiterate adults to attend literacy classes. Cambodia and Ecuador recently passed laws requiring literate adults to help teach illiterate countrymen. Iran has established a National Literacy Corps in which all young people must do two years of national service.

According to Sir Charles Jeffries, a London educator, "Experience over the years shows that direct instruction can be and is probably best done by an army of volunteers who have undergone a very simple form of training designed purely to enable them to impart to others the elements of literacy. Only through the broad use of para-educational personnel is it possible to consider eliminating illiteracy on a global scale."

With the wide distribution of transistor radios throughout the poor countries, there has been a tendency to downgrade literacy. While it is true that information can move more freely in an illiterate society when transistors are present, it is also true that literacy constitutes a threshold of technical acculturation or assimilation. New farm practices can be effectively disseminated among illiterate farmers particularly when their beneficial effects are dramatic, as with the Green Revolution. But when the need is to introduce not new techniques but something more sophisticated, such as new forms of organization, then illiteracy becomes a serious constraint. Only those who can read, write and count, for example, can manage a cooperative, keeping its books, ordering supplies and paying dividends.

Constructive participation in the affairs of a society requires a high level of awareness, and such awareness develops through a process of information, enlightenment and training. The transmission of information orally is inefficient and unnecessarily limited in its means, but literacy makes it possible to expand these means and to maintain two-way communication between people and their leaders.

Education and Modernization

Education offers a means of improving human resources, of raising the productivity of people. In the words of Neal Jacoby: "Education holds the key to development. Development is not just change in terms of savings-income ratios, or export-GNP ratios; development is an enormously complex process involving changes in customs, habits, and ways of doing things. Development is a peasant plowing a furrow an inch deeper with the aid of a new steel mold board. It is a carpenter sawing five times as much lumber with a new power tool. It is a shoe manufacturer whose output has risen ten fold since changing from handwork in a cottage to machinery in a factory. It is a government clerk using double entry bookkeeping for the first time. To effect such rudimentary changes requires heroic effort. Multiply these instances a thousand times and one begins to understand the real meaning of development."

Maintaining even a moderate rate of economic growth entails widespread technological assimilation, extensive changes in the structure of employment, an elevation of employment qualifications in the modernizing sectors, and continuous gains in productivity per person. If the educational system is not geared to produce the needed manpower, development is slowed. If living levels are to rise, the economy must be improved. To do this, the tools of science and technology must be exploited. Such exploitation means adopting at least some of the values of a Western industrial society. The challenge lies in deciding which values to preserve, which ones to discard in seeking a balance to satisfy the need both for change and for continuity.

In the West, where industrialization and modernization were the natural outgrowth of internal social and economic development, education corresponded rather closely to economic needs, and educational services reflected the increasing technical requirements. In poor countries, however, the correlation of the two becomes exceedingly difficult when external factors determine the necessary technical level for labor and consequently impose high standards for education. Very often investment and economic development is inhibited by the dearth of trained or trainable labor, but simultaneously there is often a problem in utilizing educated personnel effectively in an undeveloped economy. The problems posed to educators in poor countries in making education relevant to economic development are totally without precedent in any earlier stage of development of Western nations.

The Pearson Commission Report dwells at length on the poor quality of educational systems in developing countries, drawing attention to the 70 percent dropout rate in primary schools and an overwhelming emphasis on academic curricula in secondary schools, despite the fact that only a small fraction of secondary-school students make it to the university. The report concludes that educational systems in poor countries are not designed to meet society's needs: "In too many instances children who finish primary school in rural areas seem rather less fit to become creative and constructive members of their own community than if they had never been to school. Education systems are not generally designed to produce such immediate skills or professions that correspond to the needs of industry, agriculture, or government in less developed countries. In these circumstances an educational system all too easily becomes an instigator of maladjustment and structural unemployment rather than an essential source of growth and development. An irrelevant education breeds discontent and frustration in countries of all levels. In the poorer countries this places an ominous burden on the entire social structure."

Phillip Coombs points out that professional myopia and parochialism has helped to litter the developing world with poorly functioning copies of educational models which are blindly borrowed from advanced nations and fit neither the needs and circumstances nor the pocketbooks of the importing countries. In addition, educational systems have tended to be unduly urban-oriented. This makes it not only irrelevant for the two thirds of the population which is rural, but adds further impetus to the swelling urban migration described in Chapter 5, despite the lack of opportunity in the cities. More emphasis must be placed on relevant rural education that will not only increase agricultural productivity but also provide the economic incentive to remain in the rural environment.

Among those countries attempting to design an educational system for local needs, Tanzania is perhaps furthest along. President Julius Nyerere feels strongly that since most rural people must remain in the countryside, there is a need for education for rural living, covering a much wider field of interest than the practice of agriculture. And now with widely distributed electric power, there is no longer the compulsion to aggregate the nonagricultural labor force. The ideas of Nyerere in Tanzania and the hopes of planners in India who are seeking development without overwhelming urbanization are therefore both relevant and feasible.

As we look to the future and at the capacity of various societies to improve the well-being of their people, we may well discover that the effectiveness with which countries confront their educational crises is a key determinant of this capacity. Not only must poor countries improve the quality of their education system, but they must simultaneously strive for much broader participation in the educational process. Phillip Coombs makes the case for this: "The industrialized countries of Europe achieved much of their economic growth with quite low educational participation rates above the primary level. It took them, however, 'a long time' to get where they are now economically and 'there is reason to believe' the higher participation rates of the United States, the Soviet Union and Japan at relatively earlier stages of their development paid substantial dividends in promoting their present high level of economic and technological advancement."

Evolving Educational Technologies

As the needs and demands of education in poor countries mushroom far in excess of the financial or human resources available to satisfy them, experimentation and innovation in educational methods becomes imperative. The electronics revolution is penetrating many remote areas where the population is largely illiterate. What is badly needed today is an assessment in each poor country of the entire range of available technologies, from the use of para-educational personnel for literacy training to the use of communications satellites for educational television, selecting from the panoply of available technologies the combination which best suits the needs of the individual country.

The prevailing educational model of a teacher surrounded by thirty students is an ancient one. The principal modification of this model occurred with the invention of printing, but this took place over an extended period of time. Prior to the printing breakthrough, knowledge was transmitted orally from teacher to students, placing a heavy burden on teachers. With printing, and eventually with the availability of textbooks, the teacher became much more efficient and knowledge much more diffused. The teacher supported by the textbook, however, is still a near-universal model of education throughout the world.

According to Lloyd Morrisett, one of the founders of *Sesame Street,* "After the invention of the printing press in 1456 it took hundreds of years for the tradition of print to be fully allied with that of verbal instruction. We cannot now afford so gradual a change in human habit." Morrisett's stress on the urgency of harnessing the electronics revolution for educational purposes is appropriate. There was, after all, a one-generation lag between the time television was commercially introduced in the United States and 1969, when its educational potential for children was realized with the introduction of the immediately successful program for preschoolers, *Sesame Street.*

In its first year, *Sesame Street* reached an estimated one half of all children between three and five years of age in the United States. Tests after six weeks indicated impressive gains in the abilities of viewing youngsters. Many of the five-year-olds entering kindergarten in the fall of 1971—the two-year alumni of *Sesame Street*—were semiliterate, at least partly as a result of watching it. This breakthrough is forcing many educators to take a second look at the educative potential of electronic communication. *Sesame Street* represents a fresh departure from children's programs, which often consist of commercials interspersed with cartoons. At a cost of $8 million in the first year (scarcely a penny per day per child reached), the returns on this investment in human capital appear extremely high. The *Sesame Street* approach permits the efficient use of that scarcest of commodities, the really creative teacher.

One indicator of *Sesame Street's* success is its adoption, almost overnight, by other countries. Within the first year of its going on the air in the United States, arrangements were made for its use in twenty other English-speaking countries, among them Canada, Australia, New Zealand

and including several Caribbean countries. *Sesame Street's* founders have resisted the use of the American-produced version in non-English-speaking countries, feeling the program should be produced and filmed in local cultural situations rather than merely dubbed in the local language. Foreign-language versions were filmed overseas in 1971, with Spanish and Portuguese versions for use in Latin America among the first. The possibility of producing a French version is under study.

This breakthrough in educational programing for television purposes, combined with the new possibilities for broadcasting from telecommunications satellites, opens some exciting new horizons in education. UNESCO's experts saw great potential in the satellite as the most economic means for quickly raising the educational level of the Indian population, which is 70 percent illiterate. The satellite system could achieve automatic television coverage, as quickly as each of the 570,000 villages in India could be provided with a television receiver. While many villages would be large enough to justify more than one community set, a single receiver is considered adequate as a first step. As for the urban and semiurban areas, most of them already have access to television. With 40 percent of the population under fifteen years of age, primary education in particular should receive a major boost. The UNESCO mission believed that widespread use of television would accelerate the enrollment rate and supplement the schools' limited curricula. Even those villages without schools would benefit, for if television sets and teaching assistants were made available to them, their children could obtain at least a fundamental education during the intervening period before schools were built and staffed.

The first concrete step toward implementing the UNESCO mission's report came in 1969 when the United States offered to loan an experimental distribution satellite to India for a one-year period, to conduct a pilot project which would experiment with the educational uses of television in 5,000 villages. The National Aeronautics and Space Administration of the United States has agreed to position the satellite within range of India in 1973. Initially, emphasis will be on broadcasting programs and instruction on practical subjects to the people at large, rather than on incorporating satellite television into the formal educational system. This will include such things as the planting and cultivating of crops and methods of family planning. If the one-year experiment proves successful, India hopes to introduce a nationwide educational television satellite system.

Such a system will not reduce the education budget. Indeed, it will probably require a much larger budget, for even with NASA supplying the satellite, the Indian government will still have to supply the receiving sets, a cost which eventually is likely to exceed that of the space segment by several times. The appeal of space television is not that it will absolutely lower ongoing education costs, but rather that it can potentially provide a much more satisfactory level of education to the *entire* population, children and adults alike, at a far lower cost than would otherwise be possible.

Other countries with widely dispersed populations, such as Brazil and Indonesia, have expressed strong interest in obtaining the use of a communications satellite. Regional groupings of smaller states, such as are already emerging in the Middle East and South America, may also seek satellite educational systems to give practical instruction, teach literacy to adults and strengthen the formal-education system.

There is a great need today to diversify educational institutions, moving beyond the near-total reliance on the existing formal systems of elementary and secondary schools, colleges and universities. Circumstances in the poor countries require a wide diversity of educational efforts, formal and informal, oral and literate, technical and political. Included in this could be such things as correspondence courses, combined literacy and awareness classes, apprentice training, educational television, business and vocational schools, radio classes and community-sponsored adult-education activities. Ivan Illich, an outspoken proponent of nonformal education, argues strongly for "deschooling" society entirely. He feels that existing educational systems in poor countries serve to maintain the social status quo and that the content of educational programs is not relevant to needs. Illich's argument are not without merit, but in my opinion he greatly overstates his case, losing credibility in the process.

In some poor countries it may be preferable to structure the educational system around the television set and educational auxiliaries, rather than around the village school. Expert television instruction might provide for less costly, higher-quality education than instruction from a teacher who was lacking even a secondary-school education. Although these techniques offer exciting prospects for improving both the quality and the quantity of education, the problems associated with their use in poor countries should not be underestimated. Using educational television, for example, requires classrooms with electricity, something not yet available in many rural areas. Maintenance skills must be available locally if "down time" is not to render the system ineffective. Missing several lessons in the middle of a progressive series is the end of it as far as students are concerned. Teachers must be trained in effective use of the new aids, achieving an understanding of the relationship of these aids to themselves and their role in the classroom.

As the urgency of reaching large numbers of children and adults in the rather immediate future becomes clearer, the possibilities of using satellite television for educational purposes is receiving more and more attention. Traditional educational systems are simply not up to doing the job in the time available, given the deficiencies in transportation and the limited number of skilled teachers.

Investment in Education

The growth of public education is one of the most significant social trends of the past century. Accompanying this has been a growing investment in education, particularly over the past two decades. Phillip Coombs puts it in perspective: "In developing and developed nations alike, the proportion of the gross national product devoted to formal education has risen in many instances from under two percent prior to 1955 to four percent or more at present, while in the same period the share of total public funds going to education has risen from under 10 percent to 20 percent or more . . ."

While the trend world-wide is upward, here too an enormous gap is developing between the rich countries and poor. The United States is in the vanguard of the global educational effort and seems destined to remain there with expenditures on education, public and private, of $50 billion a year, a sum exceeding the annual GNP of all but a dozen or so of the world's countries. Costs per pupil (in constant dollars) are projected to rise substantially from 1970 to 1975. One reason for the rising costs is steadily growing expenditures on electronic hardware in the form of programed instruction, computers and closed-circuit television. Expenditures on electronic hardware alone, totaling some $500 million yearly in the late sixties, are projected to reach at least $5 billion in 1975.

Contrasting with this are the poor countries which face difficult situations as they attempt to improve their educational systems. In a country with an average income of $90 a year, education may be a frill for many. Food and some semblance of shelter claim first priority. The gap between the United States and, for example, India in investment in education is enormous. These two countries, at opposite ends of the economic spectrum, have per capita annual incomes of $4,280 and $90, respectively, a ratio of nearly 50 to 1. Expenditures per student of elementary- and secondary-school age in the two countries are $839 and $5, respectively, a ratio of more than 200 to 1. Is it possible to prepare a person for life in the late twentieth or early twenty-first century with an annual educational expenditure of $5 per student, however low teachers' salaries might be?

Many poor countries, overwhelmed with the vast numbers of children of school age, are finding it impossible to keep up. Those countries with the least to spend on education are also those with the highest birth rates. Not only are funds in short supply, but the pyramidal distribution of age groups in a rapidly growing population means that in many cases the ratio of trained teachers to school-age children is decreasing. The school-age population is simply growing more rapidly than schools can be built and teachers trained and recruited within the educational budgets available. As a result, many governments which were once committed to universal education have quietly abandoned this objective for the foreseeable future.

These needs argue for a strong commitment of resources to education within the poor countries themselves. When the needs for education were determined largely by factors internal to a country, the size of the education budget was fixed by internal priorities. But in the late twentieth century, when it is in the interest of all mankind for people everywhere to achieve a high level of global awareness, the weighing of priorities must shift to the global level. What we must now do is examine the use of public resources at the global level, reordering priorities so as to provide at least an elementary education for all children everywhere.

Turning to the Media

One thing is now becoming evident: the traditional formal-education system is becoming less and less adequate to the needs of the late twentieth century. The pace of change is such that the inter-generational lag between the substantive education of a teacher and his use of that training makes much of his instruction irrelevant; hence the need to turn to the communications media for assistance.

The formal education system can no longer carry the load thrust upon it. Consider, for example, the environmental crisis. Awareness and understanding of this problem by adults has come almost entirely from the media, rather than from our formal-education system. So it must also be with many other urgent emerging problems such as global poverty, rising unemployment in the poor countries, and the extent to which malnutrition among infants can impair mental development. The first requisite to solving a problem is an understanding of it, and as far as many of the important global problems discussed in the preceding chapters are concerned, we lack even this.

The communications media include television, radio, newspapers, magazines and the book-publishing industry. Television, the first of these, is now heavily involved in education, mostly informal, though not entirely. The British are experimenting with an Open University, an effort to take higher education into homes via television. At present, 25,000 students are enrolled in this university without classrooms. Thousands more watch the lectures out of interest. The Japanese, offering a wide variety of courses via television, have exploited this medium for educational purposes very effectively.

With the advent of the transistor, radio has assumed an expanded role, penetrating every corner of the earth, including many places where TV is still many years into the future. Radio signals can be broadcast over long distances and can be picked up by low-priced receivers, bringing them within the financial reach of many low-income families otherwise isolated from the outside world. In rural economies, farmers make good use of broadcast information on weather conditions and forecasts, threats of crop disease or pest outbreaks, and market prices.

Newspapers and magazines, of course, play a major educational role today. If they recognize this central role they must play in a rapidly changing world, they might be even more important. Some periodicals now distributed globally include *The Economist* of London, *Time* magazine and *Reader's Digest*, the last with a phenomenal monthly circulation of 29 million in its various foreign-language editions around the world.

As the dimensions of human existence in the poor countries expand beyond the local village, the media, both electronic and printed, play an increasingly important role in shaping the individual's understanding of his relationship with the rest of human society. Values and attitudes affecting the way in which the individual relates to the remainder of mankind, both directly and through his relationship with nature, are partly if not largely shaped by the media.

The potential educational role of the communications media in poor countries is great. Not all new educational technologies are as exotic as communications satellite TV. One such example is the development of rural mimeographed newspapers in Liberia, which were initiated in 1963 with the publication of the *Gbarnga-Gbele News*. Within a year there were thirty or more brightly titled, four-page mimeographed newspapers covering the entire country, whereas none had existed before. National and foreign news for these local papers was gathered from a thirty-minute radio newscast originating each morning in Monrovia at dictation speed. Local news was obtained by the local editors; stories were short with brief headlines and short sentences using only simple words. The spread of these mimeographed newspapers, printed in English, throughout the Liberian countryside stimulated literacy programs, facilitated countrywide news coverage, and created a channel for communication between government, both national and local, and the rural population. The information flow was two-way, since excerpts of news taken from the rural newspapers and sent to the capital city news media were printed in the Monrovia papers under the heading "Around Liberia in Brief."

These local newspapers have made a remarkable contribution to the education of the rural population. As one Department of Education official states, "I have been engaged in rural school development in the Liberian interior for nine and one-half years and consider the community newspaper the most important educational device that has been introduced."

In addition to the new educational technologies per se, the communications revolution, which is at the heart of the evolving technetronic era, is going to have a far-reaching impact on educational processes. Increasingly, the distinction between formal and informal education will become blurred, with the relative importance of the former diminishing.

One of the most important effects of the expanded educational and communications networks will be to continue the trend toward increasing proximity of nations and cultures. In an interdependent world, civics must encompass not only the local community but the global community as well. Awareness of the interaction of problems on a worldwide basis must grow, and to do so the perspective of education and the communications media must change.

Among the more critical global problems is the vast gap between rich and poor countries. The existing gap in investment in education, already far wider than the economic gap, will probably act to preserve the existing economic imbalance. Indeed, the educational gap of this generation tends to become the technological gap of the next generation, and the economic gap of the following one. If this trend continues, it will not only perpetuate the growing rift between rich countries and poor but further aggravate it. Those who possess the major portion of the world's wealth must realize that it is in their interest to anticipate the global community for which the foundation is currently being laid. In this country we have recognized the importance of education and have reflected this in national priorities. But today we must look beyond the nation and recognize the importance of education for the world community as a whole by reordering global priorities to include a far greater transfer of resources from rich to poor for educational purposes.

The rich countries, which have effective, advanced systems of education, can assure their own national destinies up to a point, but no nation is secure unto itself in today's increasingly interdependent world. Security can come only within the framework of an informed and unified global society.

8

STABILIZING HUMAN POPULATION

Uncontrolled human fertility may pose a greater threat to our future well-being than any other single factor. Slowing population growth is a prerequisite to solving many of mankind's most pressing problems, including widespread hunger, rising levels of unemployment in the poor countries, the widening North-South gap, widespread illiteracy and a deteriorating physical environment for all mankind. We delude ourselves dangerously if we think there is a humane solution to these problems within this century without a pronounced reduction in birth rates.

As the explosive growth in human economic activity presses ever closer to the limits of our ecosystem, the need to control human fertility acquires new urgency, demanding a higher priority. The need is no longer merely to slow population growth but to stabilize our numbers. The longer this is postponed, the fewer goods and services there will be for each of us when economic activity also eventually levels off within the limits of our finite ecosystem. The urgency of stabilizing population becomes evident when we consider how low the average world-wide per capita production of goods and services now is, and how grossly inadequate it is for so much of mankind.

The global explosion in man's numbers since World War II is largely the result of efforts by the poor countries, assisted by the rich ones, to reduce their death rates without parallel efforts to reduce birth rates. In many ways the results have been disastrous. The point is not that death rates should not have been reduced, but that greater efforts should have been made to reduce birth rates at the same time.

Our present-day conception of the population problem traces to Thomas Malthus and his gloomy treatise published in 1798, in which he defined the population problem primarily in terms of food supplies and the threat of famine. Ever since, the threat of overpopulation has been perceived largely in his terms. This was still the case as recently as the mid-sixties, when the threat of massive famine on the Indian subcontinent loomed large and when national and international leaders were preoccupied with food scarcities in poor countries. But food shortages are but one consequence of uncontrolled population growth. As we enter the 1970s we are faced with a need to redefine the population threat, broadening its scope. The enormous growth in world population since the time of Malthus is now taxing many of the earth's finite capacities, not merely its capacity to produce food.

Population Trends

The current era, with a world population growth rate of 2 percent annually, doubling every thirty-five years, is unprecedented. It took two million years for man's number to reach one billion. The second billion came in one hundred years. Successive billions came even faster. At the present rate of increase, the sixth billion will require less than a decade. If the present growth rate were to be maintained until this time next century, it would then take a year to add one billion, three years to add the present world population.

	YEARS REQUIRED TO ADD ONE BILLION PEOPLE	YEAR REACHED
First billion	2,000,000	1830
Second "	100	1930
Third "	30	1960
Fourth "	15	1975
Fifth "	11	1986
Sixth "	9	1995

World population increased by 73 million in 1970, the difference between 124 million births and 51 million deaths. Globally, births exceeded deaths by a margin of 5 to 2. Stabilizing population growth requires that the number of births and deaths be brought into balance.

The annual addition to the world population of 73 million occurs primarily in Asia. Two countries, mainland China and India, contribute nearly 40 percent of the world increase. With Pakistan and Indonesia they account for half of the annual growth in man's numbers. Mainland China, though its population of 759 million is substantially larger than that of India, adds little more to world population than India, since its birth rate has begun to decline

Some of the relatively small poor countries add more to the world's annual population gain than some of the larger rich ones. Mexico, for example, now contributes more to world population growth than does the United States. The Philippines adds more people each year than does Japan. Brazil adds 2.6 million additional people in a year, while the Soviet Union adds only 2.4 million.

NATIONAL SOURCES OF WORLD POPULATION INCREASE, 1969

	Millions
Mainland China	14.43
India	13.83
Pakistan	4.38
Indonesia	3.39
Brazil	2.60
U.S.S.R.	2.43
Mexico	1.72
United States	1.64
Nigeria	1.38
Philippines	1.30
Japan	1.24
Thailand	1.19
Turkey	.96
U.A.R.	.93
Iran	.85
South Korea	.80
Colombia	.70
Burma	.64
Ethiopia	.53
Republic of South Africa	.48
All other countries	18.22
TOTAL	73.0

Source: Population Reference Bureau

Within individual countries the ratio between births and deaths varies widely from countries such as Ceylon and El Salvador where there are three times as many births as deaths, to East Germany, where they are essentially in balance. It is the latter which the world must emulate.

Economic and Social Costs

Rapid population growth in the poor countries is exacting heavy economic and social tolls, some of which may transcend several generations. The most obvious economic consequence of the runaway population growth in the poor countries since World War II is that they have largely, and in some cases entirely, offset increases in production. While production in some countries may have nearly doubled since 1950, so too has population, leaving little opportunity for improvement in living levels.

Rapid population growth results in a relatively youthful population and an excessively large number of dependent children to feed, support and educate. After fifteen or so years of rearing, training and educating, these children require employment, the provision of which also claims substantial economic resources. A decline in births would, therefore, not only reduce the dependency burden by reducing the number of children relative to adults, but it would also free capital for investment in employment-creating activity. Over the longer term (fifteen to twenty years), it would further alleviate pressure on the job market by reducing the numbers of new entrants.

Continuing rapid population growth in poor countries is steadily reducing the indigenous per capita supply of living space, fresh water, forest products, industrial raw materials, energy fuels and arable land. In many poor countries rapid population growth is interacting with a fixed arable land area, contributing to the massive rural-urban migration described earlier.

As man's activities place the earth's ecosystem under more and more stress, recognition of the relationship between world population size and the quality of life becomes inescapable. Population growth both reduces the per capita share of the earth's finite resources and accelerates consumption of nonrenewable resources.

But only recently have intellectuals begun systematically to address the question of what an optimum population would be. At a two-day symposium organized by the American Association for the Advancement of Science in December 1969, twenty-seven panelists focused on the question of an optimum population for the United States. The question was examined from several different vantage points, including food supply, health services, education and the psychic effects of crowding. Many panelists concluded that the United States, one of the world's more sparsely populated countries, has already passed the optimum population level. The prestigious National Academy of Sciences made the same point in a recent report: "Indeed it is our judgment that a human population less than the present one would offer the best hope for a comfortable living for our descendants, long duration for the species and the preservation of environmental quality."

As the relationship between the size of world population and the quality of human existence becomes better understood, political support for zero population growth (ZPG) will almost certainly be forthcoming. People are most reluctant to contribute consciously to a reduction in their standard of living. If more and more conclude, as the National Academy and others have, that we have already passed the optimum level of population, then the question becomes, In what way and how quickly can population growth be stabilized?

The economic costs of rapid population growth have been examined largely at the national level, but the adverse social and economic consequences at the family level may be even more serious. Despite difficulties in separating family size as a variable from other socioeconomic variables, a convincing case can be made from studies undertaken in the United States, Scotland, England and Wales, Colombia, Thailand and elsewhere that the well-being of both children and mothers is adversely affected by large families. Maternal death and illness are increased by high fertility, by early and frequent pregnancies and by the burden of caring for many children. The adverse effects on children show up in more frequent illness, more malnutrition, higher infant mortality rates and less satisfactory growth. Children from large families show on the average lower intelligence and verbal reasoning ability than those from small families. There is also growing evidence that bearing too many children in a short span of time will produce many of the same effects as excessively large numbers of children. Thus, the overall number of children per family as well as the interval between births appear to affect the well-being of both mothers and children.

After surveying a large number of studies examining the effects of family size on children, demographer Joseph Wray asks whether one might not consider the need to limit family size a "moral imperative." At the least, these studies suggest the need to broaden our concept of parental responsibility to encompass the obligation to limit family size on the behalf of children.

The Territorial Imperative

The concept of a territorial imperative, the need to defend one's territory from crowding by other creatures of the same or a different species, is frequently observed among animals in the wild. As man's number increase and as the competition for living space intensifies, both within and among societies, a modern version of the territorial imperative manifests itself. Local governments, particularly in the more attractive residential areas, are beginning to take action to consciously limit growth and immigration into these areas. City governments, faced with crowding and over burdened urban services, are attempting to limit growth in Djakarta, Bombay, Moscow, Oslo and Denver.

In the United States, numerous communities have begun to de-emphasize growth and the need to attract investment and people. In Oregon, for example, the Department of Economic Development had a publication called "Growing with Oregon," but recently the name was changed to "Oregon Quality." Oregon no longer strives to attract migrants to its principal residential areas. The president of the Florida State Legislature, Jerry Thomas, recently declared: "Florida no longer desires to be known as the fastest growing state of the Union." In California, the Los Angeles Planning Commission recently proposed a rollback in the zoning laws to provide for a future population of only 5 million as opposed to the current projection of 10 million. Voting on a recent election issue in Hawaii indicates that many natives not only want to arrest growth in migration but would like to limit tourism as well. The "growth is good" and "bigger is better" mode of thinking is rapidly being abandoned.

A similar change in attitude is beginning to occur at the national level in a number of countries. Australia, though rigorously limiting the immigration of non-Europeans, has invested heavily since World War I in programs designed to attract European migrants, particularly those with needed skills. But even Australia, one of the world's most sparsely populated countries, is beginning to have second thoughts on whether it should continue to encourage immigration. The British government recently introduced into Parliament a bill designed to curb immigration from Commonwealth countries. Though clearly racist in its thrust, it nonetheless reflects increasing sensitivity to crowding in the British Isles. India, largely as a retaliatory measure, and certainly a nominal one, is moving to prevent migration from Britain.

As governments adopt policies and find programs to slow their rates of population growth, they will become more sensitive to the contribution which immigration makes to population growth. For example, in the United States, where birth rates declined steadily for more than a decade, reducing the rate of natural increase to 0.8 percent per year, immigration now raises it to 1 percent, accounting for one fifth of the yearly population increase.

There are indications that as population pressure builds around the world, those governments of areas which are least densely populated will seek to restrict if not prohibit immigration. At the same time, the more densely populated countries will undoubtedly be seeking to alleviate population pressure through emigration, as indeed occurred in the nineteenth century in Europe, where population densities had increased far above those in many other areas. In a world in which man is becoming increasingly mobile, these pressures to emigrate could create an entirely new source of difficulties in international political relationships.

The Socioeconomic Threshold

Although much attention has been given to the need to reduce births, relatively little consideration has been given to the social and economic conditions required for a voluntary reduction in birth rates to occur. Historical experience indicates that fertility does not decline until a certain socioeconomic threshold is reached. This threshold varies among societies, being somewhat lower in East Asia than in Latin America. It also seems to be declining over time.

Poor countries such as South Korea and Taiwan, where birth rates are declining steadily, experienced exceptionally rapid socio-economic progress in the sixties. High economic growth, coupled with land and social reforms, had led to a more equitable distribution of income. As the general standard of living rises, large families are no longer needed for "old-age insurance." The accompanying rise in food supplies appears to stimulate interest in family planning. Some describe this relationship by arguing that "nutrition is an excellent contraceptive." Certainly there is no historical basis for expecting birth rates to drop voluntarily where there is widespread malnutrition and associated high infant and child mortality.

Other indicators of rising social and economic levels also bear a close relationship to declining birth rates. In Latin America this is particularly true for social indicators such as communications—as measured by telephones and newspapers—and education and urbanization. The adoption of contraceptive practices is clearly related to educational levels. Educated women have fewer children than those who are not educated, apparently because they perceive their interests differently. There is not yet any record of a largely illiterate society achieving a rapid reduction in its fertility levels.

No matter how extensive and available family planning services are, population control programs will be largely unsuccessful until the general standard of living is sufficiently raised to induce the necessary motivation to practice contraception. This is not to deny the urgent need to establish nationwide family planning services, for there is a sizable segment in every society which has already crossed the socioeconomic threshold—witness the high incidence of induced abortions in so many societies.

Preventing Births

Efforts to prevent births are not new, though some of the techniques now in use are. Techniques currently in use may be grouped into four types: abstinence, contraception, sterilization and abortion.

Abstinence from sexual relations is used in various forms. The rhythm method of birth control, approved by the Catholic Church, emphasizes periodic abstinence to avoid intercourse at the time of ovulation. One of the factors contributing to the reduction in Ireland's population by one half over the past 125 years was abstinence in the form of late marriages, and in the late nineteenth century, permanent spinsterhood for many Irish women. Mainland China discourages early marriage with a recommended minimum age of marriage of twenty-six years for women and twenty-eight for men.

Perhaps the most widely used method of limiting fertility is contraception in one form or another. The oldest form, coitus interruptus, is still widely practiced, particularly in traditional societies. Other techniques include the use of condoms, diaphragms and various spermicidal creams. The two new contraceptive practices which caught on rapidly during the sixties were the intrauterine device (IUD), or loop, and the pill. Condoms are relied on heavily by the Indian government in its family planning program. At present, free condoms are being disseminated at 20,000 health centers. Family planning programs in Taiwan and South Korea rely heavily on the IUD. The pill, somewhat more costly than other techniques, is now used by an estimated 20 million women throughout the world, mostly in the rich countries.

Sterilization of both men and women is becoming increasingly popular in such major countries as mainland China and India, and in the United States, where the shift in emphasis from sterilizing women to men, due to the simpler and less costly procedure of the latter, is proceeding rapidly, with vasectomy clinics now springing up in many communities. In 1970, male vasectomies, totaling 700,000, exceeded female sterilizations for the first time in history.

One technique widely employed to prevent births in virtually every society is abortion. While reliable data are not available for most countries, those authorities who are best informed estimate that there are now some 40 million induced abortions in the world each year. Had these pregnancies not been terminated by abortion, the increase in world population in 1970 would have been not 73 million but 113 million. The 40 million induced abortions, most of them illegal, attest to either an unfulfilled demand for contraceptives, the failure of existing contraceptive techniques, or a preference for abortion over contraception.

A commission appointed to study the abortion issue in India reports an estimated 3.8 million abortions induced annually, of which an estimated 180,000 result in maternal death. Survival odds for an American GI going to Vietnam in 1970 were much higher than for a pregnant Indian woman considering an induced abortion. Clearly, the willingness to take such grave risks is an index of desperation among women wishing to prevent unwanted births.

As the transition to modernization begins, the desire to limit births rises. Where this desire precedes the availability of contraceptive services, induced abortions may rise rapidly, reaching epidemic proportions as in some Latin American societies today. Widespread resort to induced abortions, where abortions are not legal and readily available, imposes heavy costs on health services for "medical salvage" procedures. In some large urban hospitals in Latin America an estimated one fourth of all maternity beds are required to treat post-abortion cases.

The need for abortion services is great, but abortions should not become a substitute for contraceptives which are far safer, cheaper and more humanitarian. In some societies where abortions were legalized and family planning services were not yet readily available, as was the case in Japan and parts of Eastern Europe, the number of abortions has often approached or even exceeded the number of live births.

National Strategies

A national effort to stabilize population must rest on an educational effort designed to familiarize people with the costs of continuing population growth. Pro-nationalist economic incentives, which most countries have in the form of baby bonuses or tax benefits, must be abandoned. While these may have served a useful purpose at a point in history when increases in population were desirable, they are now not only obsolete but diminishing our quality of life.

Beyond removing economic incentives it may be desirable, as in Singapore, mainland China and Tunisia, to adopt specific disincentives when the number of children per family exceeds a specified number, say two or three. In Tunisia, family allowances for industrial workers are limited to four children. Family allowances in mainland China are similarly influenced. Legislation passed in 1968 in Singapore restricts maternity benefits after the third child.

Governmental actions to reduce fertility are most effective when the entire range of policy instruments in taxation, education, health services, public law, food and nutrition, biological and social research, and social security are brought to bear simultaneously. This calls for both commitment at the top and coordinated planning and action by many different arms of government. The circumstances in which we find ourselves are such that governments must learn to use the various policy instruments at their control to influence the domestic demographic situation in the same way they do national economies.

Various economic incentives to reduce births are under consideration by governments elsewhere, including those of India and Malaysia. One proposal would reward a village with a low birth rate with government financed community improvements rather than payments to individuals. Under another plan couples with three children or fewer at the end of their childbearing period would be entitled to an old-age pension. Still another proposal would capitalize on the aspirations parents have for their children by providing an educational bond to cover the costs of advanced education in families with fewer than a designated number of children. The highly successful family planning program in Barbados has stressed the link between the costs of secondary-school education, which must be borne privately, and the effect of family size on prospects for advanced schooling.

Every effort must be made by governments to avoid any unwanted births. In some poor countries, achieving this objective will require the extensive use of paramedical personnel, as in mainland China, to extend the limited medical know-how and capital and technical assistance received from abroad. Beyond this, governments can raise the legal minimum age of marriage, thus reducing the likely number of children. The elimination of sexual discrimination in the job market creates opportunities for women and reduces the relative attraction of their traditional function of childbearing. This appears to be reducing birth rates in both Sweden and West Germany.

In many countries attempting to provide family planning services, success has been limited by the administrative capability in the agencies responsible. If family planning programs are to succeed, those in key management positions in these programs must receive the necessary training. This is an area in which an international family planning institute could train large numbers of civil servants in the management of family planning programs, much as the International Rice Research Institute provides training to agriculturalists in the latest techniques of rice production and the extension of new agricultural techniques.

It is important that all countries act to slow and stabilize their populations. For those countries which have already completed the demographic transition from high to low fertility, it will be much easier than for those only now beginning, but all countries need to establish the level at which they plan to stabilize their populations, then develop the policies, the programs and the timetables to bring this about.

The U.S. Responsibility

The United States has a unique opportunity to act responsibly on the world population problem, both because it possesses much more information on the magnitude and consequences of continuing rapid population growth and because it controls a third or more of the world's productive resources. Its vast information-gathering network collects data from all parts of the world. Its massive activity in government, universities and research institutes encompasses a great deal of research on the consequences of population growth. But in order for the United States to translate effectively its awareness of the population threat into a world-wide effort to stabilize man's numbers, it must first demonstrate its concern by moving toward the stabilization of its own population. This appears to be a reasonable prospect, despite the pronounced rise in the number of young people entering the reproductive age groups. Demographers are quick to point out that even if the U.S. population were to attain a net reproduction rate of unity, i.e., each couple exactly replacing itself, it would be several decades before the population would stabilize, since the couples now in the reproductive age groups constitute a disproportionately large percentage of the population. Our goal, then, must be not a net reproduction rate of unity, but a balancing of birth and death rates, giving us zero population growth.

In addition to the decline in birth rates over the past

decade, there are other encouraging developments. In late 1970, Congress passed and the President signed into law the Family Planning Services and Population Research Act. The objective of this legislation is to make available family planning counseling and contraceptives to any woman in the United States requesting them, free of charge if need be.

The other major development in 1970 was the signing by Governor Nelson Rockefeller of the law liberalizing abortion in New York State, making it solely a matter between a woman and her doctor. This law was the result of a nationwide effort by many groups, led by women's liberation, population, church and conservationist groups, to liberalize abortion throughout the country. Passage of the legislation in New York State was significant because with its nonresidency requirement for abortion it served to break the back of organized resistance to the liberalization of abortion throughout the United States. Its passage was a major factor accounting for the increase in legal abortions in the United States from 18,000 in 1968 to 200,000 in 1970, and an estimated 400,000 in 1971.

In the United States the number of unwanted births is estimated at 20 percent for society as a whole, though much higher in lower socioeconomic groups lacking family planning services. If the entire population had free access to family planning services backed by abortion on request, this would eliminate a large share of the current excess of births over deaths.

Another encouraging development on the U.S. demographic scene is the phenomenal growth of the newly established organization Zero Population Growth from 6,000 members in 40 chapters at the beginning of 1970 to 40,000 members in 400 chapters in 1972. During the summer of 1971, thirty-seven senators, ranging across the political spectrum from Senator George McGovern to Senator Barry Goldwater, co-sponsored a resolution urging adoption of

ZPG as a national objective. Exactly when zero population growth will be realized remains to be seen, but there are many favorable signs. Some social demographers believe the social forces now operating may bring the United States close to ZPG by 1980. They point to changing attitudes toward childbearing, modification of the family itself, and an upturn in age of marriage in the late sixties. To the extent that the women's liberation movement is successful in attaining equal opportunities, permitting women to seek fulfillment in activities other than childbearing, the number of births could be further reduced.

A Global Strategy

The dominant dimensions of the global population problem are its scale and urgency. The exponential character of population increase leaves little time with which to bring the explosion in man's numbers under control.

For several rich countries with low birth rates, more advanced medical services and education-communications facilities, zero population growth is both desirable and achievable within this decade. In addition to East Germany, which has already achieved ZPG, West Germany is on the verge of doing so. Indeed, the German-speaking population of Europe, including East and West Germany, West Berlin and Austria, totaling nearly 90 million, may stabilize by the end of 1973. Though a small segment of the global population, it represents a significant and highly encouraging beginning toward the ultimate objective of stabilizing global population. The remainder of Europe, the United States, Japan and the Soviet Union could be very close to ZPG by 1980, given the appropriate national educational programs and leadership. For the poor countries, additional time is required, but they too should be aiming for a low growth rate by the end of the next decade

Resources must be allocated on a massive scale in activities that will enable world population growth to be slowed quickly. This will require a heavy investment to provide family planning services to all couples throughout the world requesting these services, free of charge if need be. Two large countries, the United States and India, have already made a good beginning in this direction. This would make it possible to eliminate many millions of unwanted births occurring each year. The principal beneficiaries of these services will be that segment of world society already above the critical socioeconomic threshold.

Another key element of a global strategy must be educational, beginning with political leaders and then spreading until eventually it encompasses everyone, from the Indonesian rice grower to the American homemaker. An educational effort of enormous proportions, it must reach everyone, cosmopolitan and rural, male and female, leader and follower, literate and illiterate, rich and poor, transmitting an understanding of the finiteness of the ecosystem and drumming home the need to adjust procreative behavior to this pressing fact.

A successful global effort requires that countries with greater wealth and family planning medical resources share them with less fortunate societies. At present five of the richer countries—the United States, Sweden, Canada, Finland, and Japan—are providing family planning assistance through their bilateral aid programs. Others may soon follow. The United States has expanded its family planning assistance to other countries from $25 million to $125 million over the past five years.

United Nations leadership will be crucial in any effort to stabilize the world population. The year 1970 marked the establishment of a Population Trust Fund to be used to support family planning efforts among member nations. During its first year, member countries contributed $15 million. The target for 1971 was $25 million. The first grants under the program were a $300,000 grant to the United Arab Republic to import contraceptive pills and a $1.7 million grant to Pakistan to initiate support of its five-year national family planning program.

Other significant actions by the United Nations included the approval by the UNICEF executive board of the distribution of contraceptives through the organization's maternal and child health service, and the acceleration of the training of doctors and technicians for family planning by the World Health Organization. The World Youth Assembly, held in the summer of 1970, urged its sponsor, the United Nations, to provide free family planning information and services to any citizen requesting it.

A proposal was also moving ahead within the UN to establish a world population institute which would serve as a research center and information clearing house. The world sorely needs a family planning research center which would conduct research not only on contraception but also on motivation and delivery systems, serving as a global focal point for family planning activities, a place for governments to turn to for guidance in organizing family planning efforts. It should be independent of any nation-state or supranational institution, though maintaining liaison with the United Nations agencies and individual nation-states. Its staff would be international and interdisciplinary, its board of directors drawn from many countries.

This UN action represents a major breakthrough since the early years of family planning, when private organizations bore much of the responsibility for global family planning efforts. Among the private organizations active internationally are the International Planned Parenthood Federation, now in sixty-four countries, the Population Council, the Ford Foundation, the Rockefeller Foundation, the Commonwealth Fund and the Pathfinder Fund. In many instances these organizations, particularly the International Planned Parenthood Federation, have been instrumental in persuading the United Nations and national governments to take over and play an active role. Now governments are assuming more and more responsibility for reducing birth rates, as indeed they must if population is ever to be stabilized.

Resistance to Population Growth

Little by little, resistance to uncontrolled human fertility is mounting throughout the world; the costs of failing to slow population growth are simply becoming too high. Indeed, the 6.5 billion population projected for the year 2000 no longer appears to be a likely prospect. Pronounced declines in birth rates occurred in several countries, both rich and poor, during the past decade. Birth rates within the Soviet Union and the United States have been declining since about 1956. The U.S. birth rate of 25 per thousand in 1957 declined to 17.4 in 1968, dropping the rate of natural increase to roughly 0.8 percent per year. During the next two years the birth rate has turned modestly upward as the result of the sharply rising number of young women entering the reproductive age groups, reflecting the postwar baby boom. However, data for 1971 and 1972 indicate a resumption of the longer downward trend as public resistance to population growth deepens.

In the Soviet Union, birth rates closely parallel those in the United States, dropping to 17.9 per thousand in 1968 and yielding a rate of increase of less than 1 percent yearly. Together the Soviet Union and the United States contain one-eighth of the human race. Their progress in reducing birth rates is an encouraging factor on the world demographic scene. Outside Europe and North America, Japan was the first country to reduce its birth rate significantly, doing it in typically Japanese fashion within a short span of years during the fifties. For more than a decade now,

Japan's rate of natural increase has hovered around 1 percent yearly.

Following the Japanese example in East Asia are South Korea, Taiwan, Hong Kong and Singapore. Both Hong Kong and Singapore reduced their rate of population growth by one half between 1960 and 1970. Taiwan pulled its rate down from 3.3 percent in 1960 to 2.3 percent in 1970. South Korea plans to bring down its growth rate from 2.2 in 1970 to 1:5 by 1976. Together these countries contain 52 million people, but it is their success in reducing birth rates while still at a relative low level of development, rather than their size, that is noteworthy. Significantly, each has experienced a phenomenal economic growth, ranging from 7 to 11 percent yearly in recent years, and each has relatively high levels of literacy and nutrition for a poor country.

In Western Europe, birth rates have been declining in recent years. In addition to the German-speaking countries, Belgium and Sweden and the United Kingdom are also approaching zero population growth. Should these latter countries also succeed in stabilizing their populations within the next few years, it would be an enormously encouraging achievement. Their reduction in births to the point where they balance deaths would both contribute to a slowing of world population growth and set an example for other countries to follow.

Perhaps the most encouraging recent global demographic achievement is the progress made in reducing birth rates in mainland China over the past decade. Census data for Brazil indicate a growth rate during the sixties of 2.8 percent yearly, rather than the 3.3 percent projected earlier. Preliminary data from the 1970 census show that India has only 547 million people, instead of the 562 million estimated earlier, possibly indicating some unexpected progress in family planning. The most recent information indicates a very modest slowing of global population growth over the past few years. The global rate of 2 percent prevailing during most of the sixties may have declined to 1.8 percent as of 1972.

A possible breakthrough during the summer of 1971 provided a small ray of hope that new techniques might be found to rejuvenate India's lagging family planning program. A thirty-two-year-old district collector in Ernakulam, one of India's 363 administrative districts, organized a month-long family planning festival promoting vasectomies for men. Using a combination of economic incentives, political organization, education and superb management, this festival was astoundingly successful, resulting in the sterilization of 62,300 men during July. Twenty-four vasectomy tables, manned by a contingent of forty doctors, operated from early morning until midnight seven days a week. As each man left the operating table he was presented with a plastic bucket containing a new dhoti for himself, a new sari for his wife, a plastic raincoat or an umbrella, a ten-pound allotment of rice, and a lottery ticket to a 10,000-rupee drawing for participants to be held at the festival's end. Whether or not any other distict in India will ever put together the same highly successful combination of techniques and support remains to be seen, but if it does turn out to be a reproducible approach in other districts, it could represent a breakthrough in family planning for India comparable to the new seeds in agriculture.

In early August, only days after the Ernakulam family planning festival ended, the Indian Parliament passed legislation liberalizing abortion, making it in effect a matter between a woman and her physician. This was part of a wave of abortion liberalization in the past few years, following the earlier one which occurred in Eastern Europe and Japan during the postwar period. Among the larger countries which have recently liberalized abortion are Great Britain, East Germany and several states within the United States. Agitation for abortion reform is now under way in several European countries including France, West Germany and the Netherlands.

The emergence of the strong Zero Population Growth movement in the United States is enormously encouraging. With a burgeoning, politically active membership concentrated among youth, the organization was making its views felt in legislatures both in Washington and at the local level. Thanks to their efforts and to the growing concern over population growth, ZPG may soon become as much a part of the everyday vernacular as GNP is today.

Notwithstanding the various signs of resistance to population growth in many parts of the world, the battle to stabilize man's numbers has only begun. Mankind cannot hope to cope with the population threat without a frontal attack on global poverty so that hundreds of millions of people are raised above the socioeconomic threshold that facilitates fertility declines. This requires far more than investment in family planning services. A shift in global budgetary expenditures away from military purposes will hopefully follow the growing recognition by national political leaders that poverty and uncontrolled human fertility pose at least as great a threat to future well-being as does external aggression.

9

BUILDING EAST-WEST BRIDGES

Global poverty exists today not so much because of a lack of resources as because of a misuse of available resources. One of the principal factors preventing a massive attack on global poverty is the continued diversion of a large share of the world's public resources to military purposes because of the Cold War conflict between the United States and the Soviet Union. It has greatly distorted global priorities and polarized the rich countries into two camps, East and West, largely isolated from each other. Economic and social intercourse has been severely limited by restrictions or outright bans on trade, travel and investment across the "iron and bamboo curtains."

The incalculable economic, social and political costs of continuing the Cold War affect all mankind adversely. It has fostered an international ethos of competition and conflict among nations, hobbling the United Nations and contributing to its failure to thus far fulfill the hopes of its founders. Hamstrung by the political maneuvers and lack of wholehearted support by the great powers, it has not been able to address mankind's most pressing problems effectively.

The Cold War has generated a bizarre and costly arms race, draining the treasuries of both the Soviet Union and United States. Nearly 40 cents of every federal tax dollar is still used for military purposes. Global military expenditures in 1970 totaled $204 billion, much of it directly attributable to the East-West conflict. Not only is this a vast sum in itself, but it represents a large share of the world's public resources, the principal resources available for dealing with the world's growing social ills, such as uncontrolled human fertility, urban decay, the deterioration of our environment, and global poverty.

But the great cost of the Cold War conflict with its Koreas, Vietnams, and other lesser conflicts along the East-West political interface, is not limited to the impact on military spending and overall distortion in resource use. It also distracts political and scientific leaders from some of mankind's serious and worsening social ills. For several years an inordinate amount of the President's time, and that of the White House staff, has been devoted to the Vietnam war and the many related issues it has spawned. Fully half of the scientists in the United States are employed directly or indirectly by the military-industrial complex. It is one of the great paradoxes of the late twentieth century that the really serious threats to man's future existence are receiving so little attention while leading powers fritter away their financial resources, scientific talent and the time of their leaders on ideological conflicts. Historians looking back on this era in the distant future will surely be appalled at the short-sightedness of many aspects of international relations today.

At the height of the Cold War, development aid became a major instrument of foreign policy primarily for security reasons. It was used as a means of wooing and maintaining strategic friends in the so-called Third World. But as tension has lessened in recent years, this rationale for assisting the poor countries has weakened. The United States and the Soviet Union have stood virtually alone among the rich countries over the past several years in steadily reducing the resources devoted to helping the poor countries. Although a rapprochement is necessary to free resources on the scale needed to treat global social ills, it is not sufficient to ensure that these resources will be channeled to the most needful areas.

The superpowers must appreciate the stake they have in creating an international political structure based on a cooperative approach to those problems affecting the well-being of rich and poor alike. In the absence of an East-West rapprochement and a rapid reordering of global priorities, the gap between rich and poor may become politically explosive during this decade. In the words of Robert McNamara: "The outlook for the Seventies is that the fault line along which shocks to world stability travel will shift from an East-West axis to a North-South axis, and the shocks themselves will be significantly less military and substantially more political, social, and economic in character." It is against this backdrop that we must avail ourselves of every opportunity to build East-West bridges.

Postwar Conflict and Competition

The East-West relationship has so affected the pattern of research and development (R&D) expenditures, the structure of the global economy, and the ordering of global priorities that we cannot intelligently discuss the quality of life in the late twentieth century if we omit it. We will not, however, attempt to examine the complex political and strategic ramifications of the conflict, but simply take two points as given, namely, that the conflict exists and that its character is changing, and proceed from there.

Following World War II the most powerful victorious allies, the United States and the Soviet Union, began to perceive each other as mutual threats. Communism, avowedly an international movement, was bent on expanding its influence, while the United States was becoming more involved on every continent, creating an obvious conflict. The United States countered Soviet efforts to extend its influence into Western Europe with the Marshall Plan, NATO and support for West European unification in what eventually became the European Economic Community. The Soviets, in turn, formed the Council for Mutual Economic Assistance (COMECON) and the Warsaw Pact.

With both superpowers attaining nuclear weapons capability, the futility of nuclear war became clear, and the Soviet Union under Khrushchev attempted to alter the nature of competition by challenging the United States to peaceful competition on the economic front. This challenge was issued from a position of strength based on the remarkable postwar performance of the Soviet economy. The Soviets had converted the essentially feudalistic economy of 1917 into a leading global industrial power, challenging U.S. leadership in many areas.

Throughout much of the postwar period, Soviet planning was geared to overtaking the United States, both economically and technologically. During the late fifties Khrushchev, in his "We will bury you" statement, boldly challenged the United States in space exploration, in food production and in overall economic growth. He belittled the first belatedly launched U.S. satellite, quite small because of the limited thrust of available launch vehicles, calling it a "grapefruit." At about the same time he was opening the vast virgin-lands area for farming, promising the Soviet people that in seven years they would have more meat, milk, eggs and butter than their American counterparts.

Although the Soviets were well ahead in the space race

during the late fifties, the United States began to respond seriously to the multifaceted Soviet challenge during the sixties. As it turned out, it was American astronauts, not Russian cosmonauts, who first walked on the moon. Rather than exceeding the United States in production of livestock products by 1965 as Khrushchev had promised, the Soviets were importing millions of tons of wheat to fill internal deficits. Agricultural hopes had not materialized and industrial growth was slowing. By 1970 the concern was no longer when the Soviet Union would overtake the United States economically, but rather when they might be overtaken by Japan. With Japan's emergence as an economic superpower, the bipolar character of economic competition between the two superpowers began to change.

As the sixties progressed, internal situations in both countries were demanding attention. Issues of race, urban decay and poverty were creating unrest and conflict in the United States. Housing was in short supply in the Soviet Union; consumers were increasingly dissatisfied with the inability of the system to deliver quality goods. Environmental degradation and the alienation of youth were common to both systems.

In the U.S. economy, the distribution of wealth continues to be a problem. Despite great national wealth, millions of Americans are plagued by malnutrition. Medical services are far from adequate. Urban transport systems can only be described as primitive. Clearly there are many social needs to which the free enterprise system has not responded very capably.

The Soviet economy was experiencing great difficulty in shifting its economy, which was focused primarily on heavy industry, to a consumer-oriented economy providing services as well as goods. A centrally planned and directed economy may be very proficient in expanding steel production or constructing railroads, but it has difficulty keeping abreast of the latest women's fashions in the context of a five-year plan. Consumer-goods industries, to be satisfactory, must be sensitive to consumer desires and be service-minded as well as production-oriented. One of the principal obstacles confronting Soviet export agencies when attempting to market equipment, whether farm tractors or commercial jet aircraft, has been the traditional inability of the Soviets to supply parts and service their equipment. In centrally planned economies there is little incentive to worry about service; production becomes an end in itself.

The centrally planned economies lack experience in mass production and distribution of many lines of consumer goods. This is particularly true with automobiles, where the Soviet Union, Poland and Yugoslavia have turned to Western corporations for assistance. Fiat of Italy, one of the first Western firms to respond to Soviet overtures, now accounts for a large share of Soviet automobile production.

Research and development activities in the centrally planned economies are almost exclusively a public sector activity. This in turn means they are devoted largely to military, space and basic research. There is no counterpart to private-sector R&D of the sort characterizing Western corporations. As the centrally planned economies approach the more advanced stages of industrialization, they discover they lack the know-how and technology needed to create modern consumer-oriented economies. To develop this technology and know-how indigenously would take several years, and in some cases at least a decade or two. The only way to get the needed technology quickly is to turn to the West for it. In our shrinking world with its rising level of awareness, no government can expect to remain in power indefinitely without the most fearful repressive measures unless it can be responsive to the needs of its people.

Another crucial area in which the technological deficiencies of the centrally planned economies are proving costly is the computer industry. A modern postindustrial, or technetronic, society depends heavily on the efficiencies of the electronic computer in data handling and problem solving. In the early years of the computer era, the Moscow bureaucracy had great difficulty in deciding whether "computers were for real." When it finally did decide in 1955 that the computer had a place in a modern, centrally planned economy, IBM was already moving ahead with its third generation of computers.

The Soviets have not been able to overcome or even narrow the IBM lead. In the early industrial era, steel production was a useful indicator of progress, but as an economy moves into the technetronic era, the number of computers more accurately reflects the rate of progress and level of development. The lag of the centrally planned economies behind the rest of the world is striking. At the end of 1969 the Soviet Union had only 3,500 computers, while the United States had 70,000. In their efforts to compete in world markets the Soviets are severely handicapped by this gap in their technology. It comes as no surprise that Arthur Watson, as head of IBM International, was invited to Moscow to discuss the role his firm might play in the Soviet computer industry. In their efforts to overcome the lag in software technology, which appears to be even greater than that in hardware, the Soviets are now making their current generation of computers compatible with those of IBM so they can utilize IBM's software.

Other East European economies, suffering some of the same technological inadequacies and influenced by the earlier Soviet lack of regard for computers, are similarly handicapped in this key area. Six East European economies with 100 million people have only 750 computers, fewer than Switzerland and roughly the same as underdeveloped Africa.

Stalin's dream of a self-contained socialist community of nations is rapidly being abandoned as leaders in the centrally planned economies face the realities of modernization. Obtaining the technology needed, whether in the form of licenses, royalties, or imported equipment or consumer goods, requires hard currency, which can be earned only from the outside world. This helps explain several things, including the heavy emphasis on tourism in recent years (particularly in the Soviet Union and Yugoslavia), the exceedingly favorable rate of currency exchange given tourists from hard-currency countries, and the intense Soviet efforts to convert vast indigenous supplies of minerals, energy fuels and forest products into hard currency.

No political analyst can successfully analyze the future direction of East-West relationships without an understanding of the nature of the technological gaps now existing in the centrally planned economies and their economic and social consequences. These gaps will strongly influence attitudes in the capitals of the East toward relationships with the West for some years to come.

Arms Control and Military Détente

Several forces are converging to enhance the prospect for arms control. Dominant among these is the apparent military stand-off. Together the two military powers have accumulated a senseless level of destructive capacity capable of destroying every person on earth several times over. There is a growing realization on both sides that the distinction between first- and second-strike capacities in ecological terms is rather meaningless, since the resulting contamination of the environment would make the earth a radioactive wasteland unfit for human habitation. The desire by U.S. and Soviet leaders to see political systems in other countries fashioned in their respective images is ebbing. Both are also beginning to recognize that neither system has all the answers. As a result a much more pragmatic, less ideological way of thinking is emerging. Leaders on both sides are beginning to doubt whether war can realistically be considered an instrument of politics in the nuclear age.

Since the advent of the nuclear era, repeated attempts have been made to control the build-up of arms, particularly by the two superpowers. The efforts have been frustrated on both sides by military proponents fostering fear and distrust and equating deterrence with superiority. With intercontinental ballistic missiles (ICBMs) making a push-button nuclear war possible, the stakes appear too high for either the United States or the Soviet Union to even consider nuclear war as a feasible policy, since neither side is ever likely to achieve first-strike knockout (the capability to eliminate all effective retaliation in an offensive attack). A stalemate has thus been reached, yet the arms race is being perpetuated.

The history of disarmament since World War II shows only limited progress to date. Following the Antarctica Treaty, which banned all nuclear weapons from that continent, the Partial Test Ban Treaty of 1963 was the first major international agreement. Its full potential was diminished, however, with the authorization it gave to underground testing. The Soviet proposal to prohibit the use of the seabed for all military purposes was also diminished in import by the U.S. proposal and the closely allied final draft of the treaty, which prohibited only the emplacement of weapons of mass destruction on the seabed. Since such emplacements were not even under consideration, the Seabed Treaty in effect contributed little to disarmament. The Non-Proliferation Treaty, aimed at controlling the spread of nuclear armaments, has not yet been signed by several countries with advanced nuclear technology—Israel, South Africa, India, Pakistan, Brazil and Argentina— although the last two have pledged themselves to the use of nuclear power solely for peaceful purposes in the Latin American-Free Zone Treaty.

The urgency of the present Strategic Arms Limitations

Talks under way since late 1969 stems from the imminent danger of a change in the approximate nuclear parity which exists between the two countries. This precarious balance was nearly upset several times during the two and one-half years of the SALT negotiations as both sides were active in the development and deployment of new weapons systems. However, in an unprecedented agreement signed between President Nixon and Soviet party leader Brezhnev in late May of 1972, both nuclear powers agreed to put limits on the growth of their strategic nuclear arsenals.

A commitment was made to establish a ceiling of 200 launchers for each side's defensive missile systems. An agreement concluded on offensive systems, due to run five years, freezes land-based and submarine-based intercontinental missiles at the level now in operation or under construction. However, the SALT treaty in itself promises no more than a slowdown in the arms race. Further accords are essential in order to fix limits on, and later to pave the way for the reduction of, the numbers of warheads that can be carried by offensive missiles and the number of strategic bombers permitted each side. Unless these agreements are forthcoming, the lid placed on the arms race may be only a temporary one.

Convergence of the Two Systems

Although satisfactory arms limitations have not yet been achieved, military détente between East and West is clearly in evidence. The ideological relaxation permitting this also underlies the gradual convergence of the two systems. Trends in several areas indicate that the U.S. and Soviet economic systems are converging, with the stark differences of a generation ago gradually diminishing.

Within the Soviet Union, decentralization of economic activity is under way, reducing control from Moscow and delegating more authority to the local level. The Soviet economy is now being transformed from a vast collection of individual factories, managed through a massive central planning and administrative mechanism, into multiplant groupings, designated "firms," whose chief executives' fortunes depend on how efficiently they manage their factories. These multiplant groupings are in many ways patterned after those of the Western corporations. As of 1969, 563 such firms existed in the Soviet Union. According to *Pravda*, they performed much better than the remainder of the economy in raising both total output and labor productivity. Although the short-term tides ebb and flow, the longer-term trend is clearly toward modification of the system.

Economic reforms in some of the East European countries have been even more dramatic. Hungary initiated a reform beginning in January 1968 which also emphasized decentralization. Under this reform, central government planning is largely reduced to the provision of guidelines. Factory managers have a great deal of freedom in contracting with customers and suppliers, negotiating their own prices and other terms of contract. They sometimes even procure raw materials or other needed products directly in foreign countries. Managerial success is measured by profits earned. Bonuses are very large for successful managers compared to those for workers, providing strong incentives for management. At one time, prices of an estimated million products were fixed by central planners in Budapest, but this has now been reduced to less than a thousand products; even here many of these prices are only ceiling prices, leaving room for competitive cost cutting. Unlike Yugoslavia, Hungary does not have workers' councils to participate in the management of its economic enterprises. In this sense the Budapest reform is even more far-reaching. It is even anticipated that the management of various firms in Hungary will be allowed to invest their profits in other enterprises.

This reform movement has not been without its ideological dilemmas. The Hungarians are, for example, working hard at the task of balancing the special privileges guaranteed workers in a socialist society with more incentives for the managerial class and for those whose positions have a direct influence on profits.

In the West meanwhile, the trend points toward greater government involvement in a wide spectrum of activities. The U.S. government is playing an increasingly dominant role in managing the economy through fiscal and monetary policy and through the financing of research and education. Social security benefits, health services, and the purchase of goods and services by federal, state and local governments are expanding more rapidly than is the economy, with the result that the public sector accounts for a larger share of the GNP each year. Significantly, there is no indication that this trend will be arrested or reversed.

Recently, when other, more indirect measures to curb the inflation and rising unemployment failed, President Nixon put direct government controls on the economy with his wage-price freeze. Although this is less structured and hopefully temporary by comparison to the Eastern economies, it clearly implies the responsibility and authority of the government to control the economy and ensure its proper functioning.

Direct ownership of the means of production and the control that went with it, once the hallmark of capitalist societies, are becoming less and less common as large corporations, sometimes owned by millions of stockholders, control more and more of the means of production. Separation of ownership and control is also the dominant mode in the Soviet Union where ownership is public and control is in reality largely in the hands of technocrats very much as in many U.S. corporations.

This convergence is evident from within the Soviet Union. Harrison Salisbury comments on Andrei Sakharov's thinking: "He believes in the 'convergent' theory which has been propounded by Western theorists, both socialists and non-socialists, under which the societies of both Russia and the United States seem to be borrowing valuable features from each other, thus leading in the long run to the creation of systems which are more and more compatible and which do not carry inevitable seeds of military collision and fatal war." This is not to imply that the two systems will become quite similar within the next decade or so. Far from it. But it does indicate that there is now some gray in a situation that once seemed quite black and white.

Both economies are making increasing use of, and being shaped by, technology, a factor which is ideologically neutral. Computers have the same characteristics wherever they are produced or used. Both economies have large, often ponderous bureaucracies, though the U.S. economy seems much more flexible and has a stronger incentive structure. As advancing technology increasingly determines the organization of society and way of life, differences between the two systems will begin to diminish.

East-West Economic Interface

Throughout most of the postwar period, contacts along the economic interface between East and West have been limited. Initially the limitations were due to the Stalinist dream of an economically self-contained socialist community of nations, and to restrictions by Western countries on trading with the East, particularly in strategic goods. In recent years economic intercourse between East and West has begun to expand on several fronts, including finance, trade and the internationalization of industrial production. The ideological relaxation following the death of Stalin, the need for Western technology, and the desire of Western firms and governments to expand exports have contributed. West European leaders De Gaulle of France and Brandt of West Germany helped strengthen both economic and political ties with the Soviet Union.

The need for hard currency in COMECON countries explains the concerted effort to expand trade with the West. In recent years COMECON trade with the West has increased much more rapidly than internal trade. Trade between some centrally planned economies, particularly Soviet-China trade, has actually declined, though almost entirely for political reasons. A decade ago this trade flow totaled $1 billion each way, but by 1969 it had dropped to $56 million. By 1969, the U.S.-Soviet trade flow was triple that between the Soviet Union and China, and growing rapidly. In many instances it is more advantageous for the centrally planned economies to trade with Western economies to get the capital goods and technology they need.

One of the most promising direct trade links between the U.S. and Soviet economies is the import of U.S. feed grains. Agronomically handicapped by a short grazing season and the lack of a corn belt, Soviet agricultural planners have continually been frustrated in their efforts to develop a modern livestock economy capable of supplying the meat, milk and eggs demanded by Soviet consumers. Late in 1971 when American maritime unions waived a longstanding demand that at least 50 percent of U.S. shipments to the Soviet Union be carried in American ships, effectively lowering the cost of U.S. feed grains to the Soviets by several dollars per ton, the Soviet Union was quick to respond. The initial purchase was for 129 million bushels of corn, barley and oats valued at $136 million. Given the vast supplies of low-cost exportable feed grains in the United States and the growing demand for livestock products in the Soviet Union, the above agreement could represent but the beginning of a continuous flow of U.S. feed grain to the Soviet Union.

Central to the effort to expand trade with the West is the export of energy fuels, particularly petroleum and natural gas. Pipelines originating in the natural-gas fields in the Soviet Union now extend not only to COMECON countries but are also being extended into West Germany, Italy and Austria.

The Soviets have deeply penetrated the West European energy market by providing large quantities of petroleum and signing contracts for massive long-term deliveries of natural gas. Negotiations are now under way with Japan for an underwater pipeline to link Soviet gas fields in Sakhalin to the northernmost Japanese island of Hokkaido. The expanded network of natural-gas pipelines originating in the Soviet Union, but extending well into Europe and Asia, is a dramatic example of growing East-West economic integration and interdependence. At the same time that Soviet energy export agencies are penetrating Western markets, other East European countries are diversifying their sources of energy, reducing dependence on the Soviet Union. Yugoslavia today obtains only one half of its petroleum from the Soviet Union. Rumania, whose indigenous reserves are gradually being depleted, is turning to Iran for the petroleum needed to keep its refineries going.

The Soviets are also negotiating with the Japanese for construction by the latter of a port at Nakhodka on the Japanese Sea costing $80 million. This would facilitate the flow of raw materials from the Soviet Union to countries on the Pacific periphery.

Soviet economic strategy departs from those of other members of COMECON in that it has vast stores of natural resources which it can export to obtain badly needed foreign exchange. Other members, lacking such natural resources, must compete in the world market for consumer goods and industrial products. The pressure to reform their economies thus tends to exceed that of the Soviet Union.

Writing in *Foreign Affairs,* Marshall Goldman indicates that "Although it would have been unthinkable a decade ago, Communist countries are encouraging mutual producing and merchandising arrangements between Communist and capitalist firms. As of early 1968 there were 120 such agreements between firms in Eastern Europe and firms in the West, involving varying degrees of participation and sophistication."

Coca-Cola is being produced in Hungry, Yugoslavia and Bulgaria. West German textiles are made into clothing in a Polish sewing factory and then marketed in the West under a West German label. An Italian firm collaborates with a Czech firm to produce motorcycles, with the Italians producing the frames and the Czechs the motors. A French manufacturer supplies diesel engines for locomotives manufactured in East Germany. A recently signed agreement links Hertz auto rental service with Intourist.

Besides forming multinational firms in both banking and sales modeled after those in the West, the Soviets are also creating Western-style distribution organizations in the West, often in joint ventures with local partners. They are adapting goods to suit consumer tastes, advertising and otherwise acting like good capitalists. In France, for example, Russians own two thirds of ACTIF-AVCO, a company that imports Soviet tractors and farm equipment, re-equipping them on an assembly line with French tires and seats, repainting them a brighter red, and selling them to French farmers. Russians sit on the board of directors of this firm; two vice-presidents and half a dozen engineers are also Russians. Tractor sales in 1969 totaled 1,200, up from 150 in 1967.

Watches have been the big success story in the exporting

of consumer goods. The Soviets have nosed out the Japanese to become the second largest world producer and exporter, producing yearly some 17 million watches and exporting 9 million. Sales abroad are handled by such firms as Global Watches, which is entirely British-owned. This firm suggested that Soviet watches be redesigned to suit Western tastes by the use of cases and dials from Switzerland. In 1968, sales of Soviet watches by Global Watches totaled 300,000 in the U.K. market, second after Timex.

If the Soviets are to become an integral part of the modern international economy, they must adapt their economic system accordingly. Brian Quinn, professor of business at Dartmouth, describes some dimensions of the adjustments they must make: "Interestingly, it is quite doubtful that even the huge national enterprises of Russia can compete internationally in the future—unless the U.S.S.R. changes its existing policies to conform to the multinational mode. To succeed, Russian enterprises will have to make investments in plants, research, distribution, and service facilities at optimum locations relative to their world markets. Many of these will of necessity be in non-communist countries. Unless Russia permits such investments and allows decentralized decisions to be made in its overseas units, Russian industry may not be able to produce in sufficiently low-cost locations, provide adequately flexible service, or understand world markets well enough to participate in trade for high-technology items. Russia may be forced to follow capitalist practices or remain content to sell primarily undifferentiated bulk items on world markets."

COMECON has recently set up an International Investment Bank in Moscow, patterned in some ways after the World Bank. It has $1.1 billion in capital, one third of which is convertible currencies so it can be used to buy some types of equipment and licenses in Western markets. It will also, hopefully, serve as a vehicle for attracting investment capital from Western countries.

Third-Country Bridges

While attention focuses for the most part on direct ties between the United States and the Soviet Union, some important indirect ties are developing. One of the most interesting is the investment by Japan, now the world's third-ranking economic power, in both economies. Japanese firms are investing heavily in the development of forest and mineral resources in both Siberia and Alaska. In Asia the same thing is occurring with the two Chinas. Some Japanese firms do business with Peking and others with Taiwan.

With the relaxation on restrictions governing trade of U.S. subsidiaries with the centrally planned economies, a multitude of opportunities for new trade ties are appearing. Subsidiaries of U.S. firms in Canada, long chafing under restrictions imposed by the United States, are beginning to trade with the centrally planned economies, including mainland China, as are U.S. subsidiaries in Western Europe. In 1970, mainland China asked an Italian truck manufacturer, the Robert Perlini Company, to use American engines and spare parts in eighty dump trucks to be purchased under a $4.2 million contract. The U.S. Department of Commerce subsequently approved the proposed GM sale of engines to the Italian company for inclusion in the trucks destined for China.

An even more impressive example of a Third Country economic bridge between the U.S. and Soviet economies occurred recently in Finland. The Westinghouse Corporation signed a contract in 1970 to provide an ice-condenser containment system for a nuclear power station being built in Finland by the Soviet Union. The Atomic Energy Commission granted U.S. approval. An Italian firm has a contract with the Soviets to establish a chain of fourteen U.S. style supermarkets in several of the larger cities in the Soviet Union. Equipment for the supermarkets was made in Italy under license from U.S. firms, leading the Moscow representative of Sirce Materprim, the Italian contractor, to quip, "America comes to Moscow via Italy."

Each new economic link, either direct or indirect, can enhance the prospect of closer political cooperation and eventual disarmament. Thus far, the links are tenuous and relatively few. Despite the gains of the past few years, economic integration across the East-West barrier remains trivial compared with that between West European economies, say France and Germany, or between the United States and Canada. But a beginning has been made and the pace of East-West economic integration is quickening. While encouraging new economic ties have been formed between the West and Eastern Europe, including the Soviet Union, mainland China still remains very much outside the economic fold.

Bringing China into the Fold

Almost any conventional economic, social or political indicator shows that mainland China is largely isolated from the world community, even following its admission to the United Nations in October of 1971. Its economic ties with the rest of the world are fragile, its international trade less than that of Norway, a country of 4 million people. Taiwan, once a tiny offshore province of China, has a volume of international trade which is now larger than that of the mainland. Since China relies heavily on barter, its ties with the world monetary system are almost nonexistent. There is no foreign investment in China or Chinese investment abroad. It has a modest foreign aid program concentrated heavily in a few African countries in projects such as the Tanzanian-Zambian Railway now under construction. Despite its great size, it ranks near the bottom of the list of countries in international tourism. Formal diplomatic ties in the West are still limited. As of early 1971, for example, the only formal diplomatic ties with Western Hemisphere countries were with Canada, Chile and Cuba.

Mainland China is unique among the world's countries today in that it is isolated from both East and West. Although it is a member of the socialist community, 80 percent of its trade is with Western countries. Japan is, in fact, its principal trading partner. Japan, Hong Kong and Western Europe are its leading suppliers. Hong Kong, the principal market, provides a crucial link with the outside world and a valuable source of hard currency for the Chinese economy.

Considering the circumstances in which the world finds itself today, the continuing exclusion of China from the world community is clearly not in the global interest. Global cooperation in preserving the environment, in disarming and reducing military expenditures, and in creating an integrated global economic system is not possible without China, which contains one fifth of mankind.

Over the past year or two there have been some encouraging signs that China may be recovering from its internal "cultural revolution" and preparing for a somewhat more active role in world economic and political affairs. Many countries throughout the world now seem more favorably disposed toward China and China toward them. Following China's admission to the United Nations, several countries have recently established formal diplomatic ties. The new era of "ping-pong diplomacy," which was initiated by an invitation to a U.S. ping-pong team to visit China, was followed by invitations to U.S. newsmen and scientists and to presidential adviser Henry Kissinger. The latter laid the groundwork for the highly publicized eight-day visit by President Nixon himself in February of 1972.

U.S. economic policy toward China is also becoming more flexible. The trade embargo imposed on China at the time of U.S. intervention in the Korean War was relaxed somewhat in December 1969, when the U.S. government terminated its efforts to prevent foreign subsidiaries of American firms from engaging in commerce with China in nonstrategic goods. Curbs were further eased in June 1971, permitting imports from China without restriction and subjecting exports to China to fewer restrictions than before. Prior to the February 1972 summit talks in Peking, a presidential directive ended restrictions applying solely to China. These moves appear to be spurring interest in direct trade with China within the U.S. business community, particularly since some of mainland China's principal imports —wheat, fertilizer and commercial jet aircraft—are items in which the United States is the leading world supplier.

The demand for hard currency to import the technology needed to industrialize one of the world's most rural economies may also be a factor underlying China's growing interest in becoming an active member of the international community. There are indications, for example, of efforts to expand tourist facilities. The government-operated airline, Chinese Aviation, is seeking landing rights in Western countries to obtain a larger share of hard-currency expenditures on international travel.

All in all, there are hopeful signs that China may eventually become, for the first time in its history, an integral part of the world community. Certainly full membership and participation for China in the world community of nations must be high on the international agenda in the years immediately ahead.

A Bridge-Building Strategy

A successful strategy for building bridges between East and West must be based on the identification and pursuit of common interests. A combination of forces is coalescing to provide just such a solid foundation from which a U.S -

Soviet rapprochement can be worked out. Spheres of influence in the traditional East–West-power-politics sense are becoming less meaningful than they once were, in part because the cost of maintaining these spheres is very high, as the United States is learning in Vietnam, and the Soviet Union, to a lesser degree, in Cuba. To some extent, these traditional spheres of influence are being replaced by a series of North-South trading blocs between the United States and Latin America, Western Europe and Africa—largely through associate memberships with the European Economic Community—and between Japan and East Asia. Still another North-South economic relationship may be forming between the Soviet–East European group in the North and India, Bangla Desh and Ceylon in the South, though the trade ties are still tenuous and investment ties are negligible.

Both the United States and the Soviet Union are acquiring a vested interest in peace and stability, since it is only then that the two governments can turn their attention to pressing internal matters. Perhaps the most urgent issue facing the Soviet leadership today is how to achieve the higher living standards the Russian people are demanding. A fundamental question is whether Russia's economy can satisfy popular expectations, maintaining her position as a superpower during the seventies and eighties. Closely related to this is the question, Can the Soviet economy, with its reliance on barter and, as yet, lack of an effective counterpart to the multinational corporation, become an integral part of the world economy?

The Eastern countries are attempting to create consumer economies, and it is in the U.S. interest to help them do so. Samuel Pisar, in his definitive work on the future potential and prospects for East-West trade, proposes several specific actions to facilitate the expansion of this trade. In addition to liberalizing restrictions on the list of Western goods which could be shipped to the Eastern economies, he recommends that Western governments and business leaders actively oppose any boycotts imposed on goods imported from Eastern Europe. He further proposes that penalizing tariffs on Eastern goods should be abolished. On the part of the Eastern governments, he suggests that they should attempt to accommodate their economic system to the outside world. This would be accomplished in a substantial degree by following the lead of Hungary in reforming its economy as discussed earlier. He also suggests that the Eastern governments should trade on the basis of strictly commercial considerations, not political or ideological motives, and that they should strive for currency convertibility, eventually eliminating the dependence on barter, a rather primitive technique for exchanging goods.

A giant step toward East-West rapprochement was taken with ratification of the West German–Soviet treaty to "renounce the use of force in their future relations." West German Chancellor Brandt described the occasion as an opportunity "to turn over a new page in the story." For Moscow the treaty was particularly important, since it related to the possibility of greater commercial, financial and technological exchange between Eastern and Western Europe. Soviet Premier Kosygin expressed the hope that it would become a "model for relations between all countries with different economic systems," and he raised his glass of champagne to "better relations in the interests of the peoples of both countries and peace in Europe and all the world."

Without the Moscow-Bonn agreement, and the general relaxation of international tensions which accompanied it, the U.S.-Soviet summit in May of 1972 would likely have been more a ceremonial than a substantive affair. To be sure, détente has not caused the more troublesome aspects of U.S.-Soviet relations to disappear; Indochina and the Middle East are still thorny issues. However, what the two superpowers chose to do at the Moscow summit was to put aside these problems and to emphasize the areas in which they both agree greater cooperation is desirable. It is in this context of wanting to gain greater acceptance at home for the principle of expanding cooperation between Washington and Moscow that the summit produced agreements in a number of important fields.

In preparation for a docking of orbiting U.S. and Soviet spacecraft in 1975, American astronauts are to be trained in the Soviet Union and Russians in the United States. The two governments also set up a permanent commission on scientific and technical cooperation, an arrangement which reflects the growing Soviet appetite for Western technology of all kinds. Finally, attention was given to the potential benefits to be derived from the exchange of research results in both cancer and heart disease, and in cooperation in a wide range of matters relating to protection of the environment.

Although the two governments were unable to reconcile all the differences required to conclude a trade agreement during the President's Moscow visit, they did establish a joint commission to devise a comprehensive trade agreement. The assignments of the joint commission include negotiations to extend "most favored nation" status to the Soviet Union, and to devise arrangements under which credits will be provided to finance sales by each nation to the other. In light of these developments, and the continuing liberalization of U.S. licensing of exports to Russia, substantial increases in trade between the two nations appear imminent.

Some bridges being built between East and West are large ones, such as the agreements just mentioned; others are small by comparison. A meeting of U.S. and Soviet scientists to discuss the pollution-control technologies is in itself rather minor. Soviet efforts to expand tourism and augment their foreign exchange earning capacity have led them to accept Diners' Club credit cards for payment of bills in the Soviet Union. Pan American Airways now has landing rights in Moscow, and Aeroflot, the Soviet national airline, has landing rights in New York. Daily flights now link the two cities.

These are but a few of the micro-détentes occurring almost daily. Individually, these events are not of historic importance, but collectively and cumulatively they can bring about a gradual bridging of the gulf between the two superpowers. As fragile economic ties are strengthened, including trade, tourism and investment, improvements in political relations will hopefully follow.

The United States and the Soviet Union are both grossly guilty of neglecting the world's social ills while pursuing their own selfish interests. Over the past few years the commitment to international development from both superpowers has declined steadily. U.S. aid levels have dropped disastrously over the past five years, amounting to a virtual abandonment of the world's poor. Soviet commitments, much smaller to begin with, are far below levels of the mid-sixties.

This decline in aid, coming just as U.S.-Soviet relations are improving, forces us to re-examine our foreign policy motives and national priorities. It is clear that the East-West conflict absorbs an inordinate amount of public resources, but it is becoming equally clear that a cessation of Cold War animosities will not of itself suffice to raise our concern with global poverty as measured by economic assistance provided. Large reductions in military expenditures in both East and West are necessary for a rational reordering of global priorities, but they are not sufficient. In an increasingly interdependent world, we must also realize that problems of the poor countries quickly become those of the rich as well, and continuing neglect of them may inevitably lead to a universal deterioration in human well-being.

There now exists a historic and unprecedented chance

for the United States to take the lead in putting U.S.-Soviet relationships on a new and constructive footing, permitting the two countries to work together to address effectively some of mankind's pressing problems. China appears anxious to take its place in the community of nations, to play an active role in world affairs. Whether its role will be primarily a constructive or disruptive one remains to be seen; nonetheless, the prospects for East-West rapprochement are better than at any time since the Cold War began.

It is not likely that U.S.-Soviet rapprochement and the complete normalization of relations will occur abruptly as a result of a single dramatic event. It is more likely to occur over an extended period of time, as a result of patient, protracted exploration and negotiation. Often it will be a matter of two steps forward and one backward. There will be ample opportunity for both sides to be frustrated and disappointed.

All of mankind, but especially the poor, have a stake in U.S.-Soviet rapprochement. At question is whether the rationale of Cold War competition used by both countries to justify large-scale economic and technical assistance to the poor countries can be replaced by one based on a desire to create a workable world order and to improve living levels in the poor countries. If this can be done, then it should be possible to achieve a much more rational use of resources, making many of the world's problems much more manageable. Beyond this, the international climate for cooperative address of the world's most pressing problems could improve dramatically.

Creating a Global
Economy

10

THE GROWING ECONOMIC
INTERDEPENDENCE OF NATIONS

A subsistence economy is, by definition, independent of the rest of the world. It has little need to export or import. But as an economy modernizes, it customarily imports an increasing variety of products, both raw materials and manufactures. Other things being equal, a modernizing economy becomes successively more integrated into the global system as measured in economic, social and political terms. This is not to say that a modern economy cannot reduce its dependence on certain imports by using its technological capabilities to develop substitutes, but usually it can do so only at a cost.

At the same time that the modern nation-state is becoming progressively more integrated into the world economy, it is also assuming increasing social responsibilities toward its people. Its importance as an administrative unit is clearly on the rise. As Theodore Geiger points out, there is among the rich countries "a long-term trend toward increasingly comprehensive and active management of their

economic systems. The purposes are to assure that resources will grow at an adequate rate, that they will be
allocated to meet the expanding diversity of high-priority
national objectives and that there will be neither significant
unemployment, on the one hand, nor excessive inflation on
the other. . . . In addition to their previous activities, governments now seek to provide minimum incomes and equal
opportunities to all, assure rising standards of education
and health, protect and improve the physical environment,
rebuild the cities, foster and finance the advancement of
knowledge, support the arts, expand recreational facilities
to meet greater leisure and earlier retirement, and in a
growing variety of other ways, better the quality of life for
an increasing population." This assumption of new functions and responsibilities by governments reflects an evolving set of values and an expanding social consciousness
within modern societies.

The freedom of action of an individual government to
discharge these responsibilities to its citizenry is sometimes
hindered by increasing interdependence, but it is important
to recognize that the capacity of a national government to
improve the well-being of its people is now directly dependent on its access to technology, energy supplies and raw
materials from abroad and to foreign markets for the products it produces most efficiently. If it cannot draw widely
upon the world's resources, it will be severely handicapped
in efforts to raise the quality of life of its people.

Indeed, international economic integration has two important advantages, one essentially economic and the other
essentially political. In economic terms it promotes more
rational, more efficient use of the earth's resources. The
political plus is that it enhances the prospects for reducing
international conflict. Both of these have far-reaching social
consequences, linking improvements in the quality of life
to the creation of a unified global economy.

Although global trends indicate a steady growth in

interdependence among nations over the past two decades in international trade, international production, international monetary matters or international technology exchange, it would be a mistake to assume that nationalism is everywhere on the wane. It is still a very potent force. Economic nationalism takes many forms. In the United States it takes the form of resentment by labor groups toward imports of low-cost textiles manufactured in poor countries such as Hong Kong, Taiwan or India. The U.S. steel industry pushes for government action to limit imports of steel from Europe and Japan. France drags its feet as the European Economic Community moves toward political as well as economic integration. Rumania initially declined membership in the recently established COMECON investment bank in Moscow for fear that the financial pool to which it contributes would be used for purposes which it does not approve. Peru and Tanzania restrict investment from abroad because it signifies foreign control of their embryonic industrial economies.

Although the desire for economic independence is strong, global trends indicate that the benefits of economic integration are, on balance, a much more powerful force. Countries are sacrificing independence in many areas, becoming economically integrated and interdependent, because they believe they will be better off if they do so. Traditional economic relationships consisted of international trade, conceived and analyzed with international trade theory, but this conceptualization is no longer adequate to explain the movement toward a unified global economy. It does not, for example, explain international financial flows, the Eurodollar market, the overall workings of the international monetary system, or the emerging global market for technology. Nor does it explain the internationalization of production, an entirely new way of organizing global economic activity, which is of enormous importance today with its volume far exceeding that of international trade.

Energy interdependence is a relatively new form of interdependence, materially different from other forms. Interruptions in international flows of petroleum may affect not merely whether certain products are produced but indeed, in the case of a modern economy, whether that economy can function at all. Measuring international trade does not include the sale of services across international borders which account for an increasing share of global economic activity. Tourism is the largest single source of foreign exchange for a number of countries. In Greece, foreign exchange earnings from services such as shipping and tourism even exceed those from exports of goods. The largest single item in Turkey's foreign exchange earnings is remittances from several hundred thousand members of its labor force working in Europe.

The development of many natural resources for power or transport purposes often requires binational or multinational collaboration. Development of the Indus River system shared by India and Pakistan has involved close cooperation between the two countries, a cooperation which continued even when they were at war. The St. Lawrence Seaway, a joint U.S.-Canadian project, is now a major North American transport artery contributing to the economic advancement of both countries.

Rapidly unfolding technological and economic developments are affecting the global political structure. Increasingly, the political power of the nation-state is being shared with supranational institutions and multinational corporations. Neither traditional economic nor political theory is capable of analyzing and explaining this process.

Sacrificing Sovereignty for Affluence

National sovereignty frequently interferes with the efficient organization of economic activity, the global dissemination of technology and the attainment of a higher standard of living for much of mankind. Cherished though it is, national sovereignty is being gradually but steadily sacrificed for affluence. This is most evident in Europe, the region where the nation-state originated. The economic sovereignty of European community members is being steadily exchanged for the more rapid economic progress which economic integration makes possible.

National economic sovereignty is sacrificed in many ways. Membership in the General Agreement on Tariffs and Trade brings with it certain obligations regarding national behavior in international trade relationships. Membership in the International Monetary Fund places certain constraints on the formulation of economic policy. William McChesney Martin described it well in a September 1970 lecture in Basel: "The progress I have been describing [international monetary cooperation] originated between and has been accepted and welcomed by sovereign states. One often hears it said that the existence of a world central bank is inconsistent with the maintenance of national sovereignty. So it is, if by sovereignty one means what has traditionally been implied by that phrase—the unfettered right of national governments to act in whatever way they may choose in economic, financial, or defense matters. . . . What we have been witnessing has been a willingness of nations, by the exercise of their sovereign rights, to recognize that the national interest can no longer be pursued in isolation but is dependent on cooperative action with other nations. This necessarily involves some limitation on national freedom of action in deference to the common good. . . . It could even be said that what were once the principal objectives of sovereign powers—the maintenance of economic prosperity and of effective defense—can now only be achieved by the acceptance of cooperative international arrangements which by their very nature impose limitations on the sovereignty of all the nations concerned."

Exploiting modern technology requires a high degree of training and specialization, heavy capital investments and large-scale production, all facilitated by economic integration. Excessive economic nationalism could impede modernization in poor countries, by deterring the inflow of foreign capital and know-how.

In the late twentieth century the nation-state must consider various trade-offs between sovereignty and independence on the one hand and cooperation and economic integration on the other. Nations behave very much like people in this respect; they want to be independent but also want to be able to enjoy the fruits of integration and interdependence. The conflict between the desire for independence and the need for integration continually plagues the movement toward a unified global community.

Among the more newly independent ex-colonies, national sovereignty is still a cherished attribute of independence, and the sacrifice of sovereignty for economic progress is painful indeed. But if West Germany and Belgium recognize that *they* are anachronisms as independent economic entities, then the Philippines, Ghana, Colombia and the scores of other developing countries whose economies are far smaller must eventually take note as they strive to modernize. With time, rising aspirations throughout much of the world will accelerate and broaden this exchange of sovereignty for affluence, affecting not only virtually every country, but eventually the organization of global society itself.

Economies of Scale

One of the most compelling reasons for economic integration, either within groups of countries or world-wide, is the prospect of exploiting the large-scale economies associated with modern manufacturing technologies and research and development efforts. The development and exploitation of many modern technologies require vast markets, some exceeding even the largest national economy in size.

A recently discovered technique for producing nitrogen fertilizer, which reduces production costs by about one third, requires a plant with a production capacity of at least 200,000 tons of nitrogen per year. Countries with less than 20 million people may not be able to justify a modern nitrogen fertilizer plant in terms of their own requirements. Only when prospects for exports into the world market are good or when several smaller countries are combined into one economic grouping can a modern plant be seriously considered.

Electric power grids tying West European countries together reduce the total generating capacity needed to meet the sum of individual country needs. Electrical power generating facilities now nearly completed in Paraguay will be used to provide electric power for neighboring Brazil and Argentina as well. If efficiencies of power transmission were to make the transmission of power over long distances feasible, continental power grids, permitting the system to distribute daily peak power requirements which vary with time zones, would permit vast savings in generating facilities.

Research and development costs in many high-technology fields are prohibitive unless results can be exploited in large markets. This is certainly the case with the computer industry where International Business Machines, currently holding 70 percent of the world market, has in many ways outgrown the U.S. economy. It could not fund its vast research and development (R&D) program if it did not have access to the world market for computers.

One of the most widely publicized new technologies with an enormous R&D cost is the supersonic transport, with a price tag of $1.4 billion. For the American version (SST), now abandoned, the cost was nearly $20 per taxpayer—

just to build a single prototype. The retail price of such a plane would have been an estimated $40 million. Among the world's 160 nation-states, only two, the United States and the Soviet Union, possessed the economic and technical resources to launch such a venture unilaterally. Even after combining their resources and expertise, Britain and France have had continuing doubts of their ability to see the project through.

The same holds true for space exploration. Thus far only the United States and the Soviet Union have been willing to spend the enormous sums involved in the serious exploration of outer space. The formidable costs explain why there are a number of cooperative efforts under way to launch research satellites, principally instrumented satellites assembled by other countries, using U.S. launchers and boosters to put them into orbit. With time we may see much more cooperation in this area, including extensive cooperation between the United States and Soviet Union.

Technological Interdependence

As modernization proceeds, countries become increasingly dependent on technology imported from abroad. Every dimension of our lives is affected. The space programs in both the United States and the Soviet Union rest on the foundations of early German rocketry. New dwarf wheats revolutionizing cereal production in Asia were bred in Mexico. The most commonly used abortion technique in New York City, the vacuum aspiration method, was developed and perfected in mainland China. Creation of INTELSAT has enabled the entire world to benefit from the solar-powered telecommunications satellite technology financed by U.S. taxpayers.

Countries can obtain technology from abroad through imported products, private investment or through the purchase of patents and licenses. When the Soviets wanted to take advantage of Western advances in computer technology, they imported computers from the West. India, desiring the same technology, attracted investment by IBM in computer manufacturing facilities within India. The Democratic Republic of the Congo, needing tires for replacement purposes on imported vehicles, acquired this technology through investment by Firestone. Japan has chosen to satisfy many of its technology needs through thousands of licensing agreements with foreign firms.

Buying and selling technology internationally is big business today. It has, in fact, given rise to a new concept, the "technological" balance of payments, i.e., the foreign exchange spent versus that earned in importing and exporting technology. An analysis of 1964 data on international technology transactions indicates five countries—the United States, the United Kingdom, West Germany, France and Japan—each account for just over one tenth of world imports of technology as such. Together they account for 61 percent of all imports of technology, leaving only 39 percent for all other countries. Interestingly, the most technologically advanced countries are the biggest importers of technology.

Japan has the largest technological balance of payments deficit of any country. But the foreign exchange earned by Japanese firms selling licensing rights abroad is on the rise and will one day undoubtedly exceed the import of technology if the national R&D budget continues to expand at the recent rate.

The United States has the largest technological balance of payments surplus. Receipts from the sales of technology abroad increased from $362 million in 1956 to an estimated $2.2 billion in 1970. Expenditures on imported technology totaled $229 million in the latter years. U.S. exports of technology now exceed the total exports of countries such as Colombia, Nigeria or the United Arab Republic. This rapid growth of international technological transactions is closely associated with the phenomenal growth in the size and number of multinational corporations since 1950.

More and more, the new technology used in any given country originates outside that country. No country is self-sufficient today. As technology continues to advance, R&D programs of any given country are becoming more concentrated and specialized. Although no comprehensive worldwide data on international technological transactions are available for an extended period of time to give us a precise picture of trends, we do know that U.S. exports of technology, now accounting for about one half of the world total, grew at 11 percent yearly from 1956 to 1969, doubling every seven years. In the late twentieth century, technology is a global commodity, and one with a rapidly expanding market.

Our focus thus far has been on commercial transfers of technology, but important advances are occurring in the noncommercial field as well. Some 83 nations and 40 international organizations meeting in Paris during the fall of 1971 approved plans for a world-wide system of science information storage and exchange to be known as the World Scientific Information System, or Unisist. If approved by a UNESCO conference scheduled for late 1972, it would be in operation in 1973. Among other things, Unisist would provide abstracts of the 2 million articles appearing in 35,000 scientific journals published throughout the world in 50 languages. Abstracts would be stored in such a form as to be suitable for computer searching, giving scientists in any country or organization participating in the system ready access to all published material on any given topic.

Mineral Interdependence

Four aspects of mineral interdependence stand out: the consumption of virtually all critical minerals, both metallic and nonmetallic, is rising rapidly; known reserves are often concentrated in a few locations around the world; the global distribution of minerals bears little relationship to areas of consumption; and rich countries are becoming increasingly dependent on poor ones for mineral supplies.

No country or continent is endowed with all the raw materials needed by a modern industrial society. Geologist Preston Cloud points out that "no part of the earth, not even on a continent wide basis, is self-sufficient in all critical metals. North America is relatively rich in molybdenum and poor in tin, tungsten and manganese, for instance, whereas Asia is comparatively rich in tin, tungsten and manganese, and apparently less well supplied with molybdenum. Cuba and New Caledonia have well over half of the world's total known reserves of nickel. The main known reserves of cobalt are in the Republic of the Congo, Cuba, New Caledonia and parts of Asia."

Interdependence among nations is commonly viewed in terms of dependence of poor countries on rich ones. And so it is with capital and technology. But with minerals, dependence of rich countries on poor ones is far greater and increasing year by year. Those countries industrializing earliest are depleting their indigenous supplies of many of the basic raw materials required by modern industrial economies. Thus the rich countries, particularly the United States, Japan and those of Western Europe, with their rapidly rising consumption of minerals required to support their affluence, are becoming increasingly dependent on the poor countries with their largely unexploited mineral reserves. In Western Europe, consumption of eleven basic industrial raw materials—bauxite, copper, lead, phosphate, zinc, chrome ore, manganese ore, magnesium, nickel, tungsten and tin—exceeds production. In the case of copper, phosphates, tin, nickel, manganese ore and chrome ore, nearly all needs must now be met from imports.

The growing dependence of the United States on imported raw materials to fuel its expanding industrial economy and rising levels of affluence is becoming a matter of national concern. Of the thirteen basic industrial raw materials required by a modern economy, the United States was dependent on imports for more than one half of its supplies of four of these in 1950: aluminum, manganese, nickel and tin. By 1970 the list had increased to six, as zinc and chromium were added. Projections indicate that by 1985 the United States will depend on imports for more than one half of its supplies of nine basic raw materials, as iron, lead and tungsten are added. By the end of the century it will be dependent primarily on foreign sources for its supply of each of the thirteen raw materials except phosphate.

U.S. imports of energy fuels and minerals in 1970 cost $8 billion, but this is projected to increase to $31 billion by

U.S. DEPENDENCE ON IMPORTS OF PRINCIPAL INDUSTRIAL
RAW MATERIALS WITH PROJECTIONS TO 2000

RAW MATERIAL	1950	1970	1985	2000
		percent imported		
Aluminum	64	85	96	98
Chromium	n.a.	100	100	100
Copper	31	0	34	56
Iron	8	30	55	67
Lead	39	31	62	67
Manganese	88	95	100	100
Nickel	94	90	88	89
Phosphorus	8	0	0	2
Potassium	14	42	47	61
Sulfur	2	0	28	52
Tin	77	n.a.	100	100
Tungsten	n.a.	50	87	97
Zinc	38	59	72	84

Source: Data are derived from U.S. Department of the Interior publications.

1985, and to $64 billion by 2000. This dramatic projected growth in dependence on imports implies that the United States must support a very liberal international trading system if it is to earn the foreign exchange needed to finance future import requirements of industrial raw materials. As competition for dwindling reserves of high-grade mineral deposits intensifies, the U.S. economy will become much more vulnerable to external forces beyond its control, such as collective bargaining by supplier countries, or to strikes either in foreign mines or in the shipping industry. This situation forcefully underlines the U.S. interest in a cooperative world order in which resources are freely shared.

Known remaining resources of many minerals are concentrated in a few poor countries. Four of them, Chile, Peru, Zambia and Zaire (the Congo), supply most of the world's exportable surplus of copper. Three others, Malaysia, Bolivia and Thailand, account for 70 percent of all tin entering international trade channels. Australia, Mexico and Peru account for 60 percent of the lead entering international trade.

Mineral reserves are important to agriculture as well as to industry. Of the three principal nutrients in chemical fertilizer—nitrogen, phosphate and potash—the first is available in virtually endless amounts from the atmosphere, but supplies of the latter two depend on mining underground reserves. Unfortunately, the world's supply of these two minerals is concentrated in a few spots. Canada has most of the world's known reserves of potash within its borders. The United States, Morocco and Tunisia account for most of the phosphate entering international trade. The overwhelming majority of countries are dependent on imports for most if not all of their supplies of supplemental plant nutrients, making their internally produced food supply rather dependent on external mineral supplies.

World mineral consumption is dominated by the United

States which consumes from one fourth to one half of most minerals. In per capita terms Americans consume perhaps twenty times as much metallic ores as the average person living in the poorest countries. If consumption in these countries should ever begin to approach levels now prevailing in the rich ones, pressures on mineral supplies, particularly the scarcer ones, would quickly become a matter of global concern.

As consumption rises and reserves are depleted, concern over the future supply of certain minerals is rising. The Stanford Research Institute reports that "the world consumption of mineral ores has been increasing throughout this century, interrupted only by the two world wars and in some instances by the Depression. Otherwise the trends of increase are remarkably regular. If the periods required for consumption to double are used as a measure, these are found to be short: 9 years for aluminum and petroleum, 10 to 15 for iron, 12 to 15 years for copper, 17 years for zinc, and 20 years for lead. The inevitable result is that the more accessible ore supplies in older industrial countries are worked out to the point where further mining becomes too expensive. The search, therefore, shifts to new sources of supply." This implies, of course, that as the sharply climbing global consumption curve presses against the remaining reserves, those in control of them stand to benefit. This helps explain the much tougher bargaining position recently taken by poor country governments in dealing with multinational corporations where the mining and export of mineral resources are involved.

Energy Interdependence

Among the most striking forms of interdependence evolving as the world economy modernizes is energy interdependence. In 1925, only 14 percent of the world's energy fuels crossed national borders; by 1967 it had risen to 31 percent. In the early seventies it is even higher and beginning to climb very rapidly.

Only a small fraction of the world's 160 nation-states are self-sufficient in energy fuels; the vast majority look to imports for some, if not most, of their energy needs. Only a handful—Saudi Arabia, Venezuela, Algeria, Indonesia, Libya, Kuwait, Iran, Iraq, Nigeria and a few others—are significant net energy exporters. Japan depends on imports for 99 percent of its petroleum needs. Western Europe is only slightly less dependent, importing 96 percent of its petroleum.

Prior to 1970, the United States was only marginally dependent on petroleum imports, but this is changing rapidly. As its petroleum consumption climbs at 3 to 4 percent per year and domestic production declines, even with Alaska's North Slope coming into production in the mid-seventies, the gap between production and consumption is projected to widen rapidly. Projections show the United States will be dependent on imports for more than half of its petroleum supply by 1985, with the bulk of imports coming from the Middle East.

The energy required for day-to-day living climbs sharply as incomes rise. Early man's daily energy consumption approximated 100 thermal watts per person. It consisted entirely of food intake and approximated his minimum biological requirement. This curve rose slowly over time as man learned to harness other forms of energy. The discovery of fire and the use of firewood for cooking and heating raised energy intake to about 500 thermal watts. As man learned to harness the winds to sail ships or turn windmills for drawing water and developed the water wheel to power mills of various kinds, his energy consumption increased further. Then with the industrial revolution and the use of coal it began to increase more rapidly. Finally, with the use of petroleum, hydroelectric power and the energy locked in the atom, the energy consumption curve began to climb sharply, reaching an average of almost 10,000 thermal watts per person in present-day United States, a hundredfold increase over that of our preagricultural ancestors.

Modern, or technetronic, man is an enormous consumer of energy, dependent on it for mobility (automobiles, elevators, airplanes), for manufacturing material goods of all kinds, for producing food (plowing, milking cows), for light, for heat (homes or food preparation), for cooling (refrigerators or air conditioning) and even for thinking (calculators and computers). The technology which permits high-income man to consume so much energy also makes him highly vulnerable to any disruption in the international system which would interfere with the movement of energy fuels. Depriving high-income man of his energy supply might affect not merely his well-being but his prospects for survival as well. Consider food production: without fuel for tractors, high-income man without draft animals would be reduced to hand cultivation, a precarious prospect. By contrast, low-income man relies largely on draft animals and so would not be greatly affected in any event.

As the exponential energy consumption curve presses against finite reserves of energy, particularly petroleum, the international energy market is changing from a buyer's to a seller's market. It was not uncommon in the early days of the petroleum industry for oil companies investing abroad to retain 90 percent of the income from oil, with the government of the country in which the oil reserves were located retaining the remainder. Since the 1950s, "50–50" has been the common slogan of the oil companies. But this is rapidly being abandoned as the host countries press for an ever larger share of the returns. On balance, division of returns between governments and companies is probably now close to 70–30, almost a reversal of the situation prevailing thirty years ago.

In a five-year oil accord between the six Persian Gulf states and twenty-three oil companies concluded in February 1971, the companies agreed to additional payments of $10 billion over the next five years. This translates into higher prices for gasoline and fuel oil, particularly in Western Europe and Japan, which are so heavily dependent on the Middle East for their oil imports. How long this trend will continue is unknown. With the increased economic competitiveness of nuclear power, oil producers are anticipating a massive shift away from oil in the coming decades—a shift spurred by the higher prices. Over time this should place eventual limits on the bargaining power of the oil exporting countries.

But for the present and foreseeable future, the oil-exporting countries are in the driver's seat. Half a dozen Middle Eastern countries with a combined population of 50 million (scarcely 1 percent of the world population) controls over half of the world's known reserves of petroleum, and because of their limited internal consumption, a far greater share of total exportable reserves. During 1971 and 1972, the bargaining focus has shifted from that of obtaining a larger share of oil revenue to obtaining an equity position (ownership) in the international oil company subsidiaries operating in the exporting countries. Some countries, notably Algeria, had already negotiated a strong equity position in 1971. But more generally, members of the Organization of Petroleum Exporting Countries (OPEC) issued a statement in the fall of 1971 indicating that they plan to negotiate as a group for 20 percent equity in the subsidiaries operating within their countries. In essence, the oil-exporting countries are attempting to convert their strong bargaining position into some control of the international energy economy. They are seeking economic power as well as a greater share of the income. Saudi Arabia's aggressive bidding for drilling concessions in the North Sea in competition with international oil companies was further evidence of this effort.

At present the confrontation on the terms over which oil is exported from the principal exporting countries is taking place between the eleven principal exporters, all members of OPEC, and the twenty-three international oil companies. At some point, a confrontation might become a more direct one between governments in the rich countries and those in the oil-rich countries, particularly if prices continue to rise, creating serious political problems within the principal consuming countries.

The quest for oil and the desire by the industrial countries to reduce their overwhelming dependence on imports from a few exporters is driving them to seek oil in various offshore areas. This is particularly evident in northern Europe, where Britain, Norway and the Netherlands have divided up the North Sea between them and are parceling out concessions. Many of these concessions are 110, 150 or even 185 miles offshore, far exceeding the widely accepted territorial limit of 12 miles.

Monetary Interdependence

In the intermeshed global economy of the late twentieth century, changes in trade, fiscal and monetary policy in a major industrial country can affect the rate of economic growth, employment levels, the rate of inflation, and currency values throughout the entire global economy. There is a widespread awareness among national leaders that countries cannot go it alone in formulating economic policy, in part because the consequences of doing so are so costly. To again cite William McChesney Martin: "The 1930's demonstrated all too well the dangers of economic nationalism and taught the lesson of economic interdependence—that each nation's prosperity depends upon the prosperity of its neighbors."

The economic disasters of the 1930s led to the creation of a supranational institution, the International Monetary Fund, to bring order into the international monetary system. The IMF does this by establishing the rules within which member countries formulate economic policy, by attaching conditions to loans required by member countries when their monetary reserves are low, and by continuously analyzing and assessing the economic policies of member governments in terms of their impact on the international economy.

Over the twenty-five years since its creation, the International Monetary Fund has gradually strengthened its position as a supranational institution. A recent major step in this direction was taken in 1968 when it was granted the authority by its member countries to create additional international monetary reserves, in the form of Special Drawing Rights. This assumption of a central banking function at the global level must be considered the forerunner of eventual additional steps in this direction.

Another major step which threatened the Fund initially but which may eventually strengthen its position came indirectly on August 15, 1971, when the United States, faced with a severe balance-of-payments crisis, announced that the dollar would no longer be redeemed in gold. Freeing the dollar from the price of gold and the movement toward more flexible exchange rates is a major step forward because the world is now forced to consider replacing the dollar with a truly international currency, namely the Special Drawing Rights.

The effect that a change in national economic policy can have on other economies was very much in evidence following adoption of the new economic policy by the United States as described above. Export earnings and economic growth rates were quickly affected in a number of countries, ranging from economic giants such as Japan to poor countries, closely tied to the U.S. economy. It used to be said that if the United States sneezed, Europe would catch pneumonia. This is less true than it once was, but what the long-term effects of the U.S. action will be remains to be seen. Needless to say, the international monetary system is very fragile. It exists and functions only because of the cooperation and mutual confidence of national governments

Trade and Economic Integration

Recent trends in world trade and production indicate how rapidly a global economic system is emerging. During the sixties, world trade increased 8 percent yearly, doubling in nine years, while world production of goods and services increased only 5 percent yearly. The share of global production entering international trade channels increased steadily throughout the decade, reaching an estimated $280 billion worth of goods in 1970. Barring adoption of regressive trade policies, it is expected to nearly double again by 1980, reaching $500 billion. Not only will the quantity of goods crossing national borders be much greater in absolute terms but it will represent a far greater share of global production than at present, resulting in a far more integrated, tightly knit global economy than exists today.

As a group, the Western industrial countries and Japan have expanded exports much more rapidly than either the centrally planned or poor countries. In 1969 the former accounted for 71 percent of world exports in contrast to 18 percent for the poor countries, and somewhat surprisingly, only 11 percent for the centrally planned economies, including mainland China. Economic systems of the latter group, containing some 1.25 billion people, appear to lack the flexibility needed to capitalize on comparative advantage in the world economy.

Among the world's 160 countries, a handful—the United States, West Germany, the United Kingdom, Japan and France—stand out in international trade. The principal bilateral relationships are those between the United States and Canada, the United States and Japan, and Germany and France (the latter pair despite a history of rivalry and wartime enmity). If recent trends continue, the U.S.-Japanese trade flow will eventually become the leading bilateral trading relationship.

Most of the quarter century since World War II has been spent undoing the damage done to the world trade system by the rising tide of protectionism during the 1930s. The several rounds of tough, intense international negotiations required to regain the liberal trade conditions prevailing before World War I were conducted under the auspices of the General Agreement on Tariffs and Trade (GATT), an organization created expressly for this purpose in 1947.

The latest round of GATT negotiations to reduce international trade barriers, the Kennedy Round, lasted from 1964 to 1967. The most ambitious and comprehensive effort to reduce tariffs in history, its full impact will be realized over a period of several years. The industrial countries reduced tariffs on an estimated 70 percent of their dutiable imports, two thirds of these by 50 percent or more. In total, tariffs were reduced on about $50 billion worth of traded goods. Once the tariff reductions negotiated in the Kennedy Round are implemented, world trade will again be as liberal as it was in the halcyon pre-1914 period.

The Kennedy Round of negotiations did not, however, erase all trade barriers. Tariff reductions were concentrated on industrial products leaving agriculture highly protected, preserving the existing irrational and inefficient global production patterns for many important farm commodities. And even as tariff barriers fell, new nontariff obstacles to trade were contrived to prevent full realization of the negotiated reductions. On balance, however, tariff declines will act to expand trade flows, integrating national economies more fully into a single world economy.

Regional Economic Groupings

Perhaps the most convincing evidence of the declining economic viability of the independent nation-state in the modern world is the formation of multinational economic groupings, such as the European Economic Community. Of the world's ten largest economies all but two, the United States and Japan, are integrating their economies within a regional framework. Although a major share of the world economy outside of the United States is included in regional common markets, the path to completely integrated common markets is not a smooth one. Many efforts to form common markets abort; progress in others is painfully slow. Experience to date indicates that advanced industrial economies are more successful than preindustrial ones. But the overall trend is clear: national economies are integrating at a record pace, losing their distinctive national identities.

In many respects, regional economic groupings are an intermediate step between the nation-state and a single integrated world economic system. As economic integration progresses, political independence invariably declines or, stated more positively, when economic integration occurs political cooperation inevitably follows. For example, during the Kennedy Round of trade negotiations lasting from 1964 to 1967, the six member nations of the European Economic Community did not participate individually, but rather as a group, speaking and negotiating as a single political entity. As integration proceeds in various economic groupings, this should become more and more common, with the pursuit of common economic interests being invariably followed by the identification of common political interests. Over time we can also expect stronger ties, and in some cases, integration among various economic groupings. There are instances where this is already in progress, as between the European Free Trade Association (EFTA) and the European Economic Community (EEC).

The EEC—West Germany, France, Italy, Belgium, the Netherlands and Luxembourg—is in many ways the father of the common markets. An outgrowth of the European Coal and Steel Community, it was officially launched in 1955 with the signing of the Treaty of Rome which called, among other things, for the complete elimination of tariffs on trade within the group by July 1, 1968. Despite numerous crises along the way, this target was reached on schedule. This is not to say that all goods move freely among member countries, since numerous nontariff restrictions remain.

Benefits of economic integration within the EEC have taken many forms. The larger market has permitted larger scale, more efficient production. National corporations, through mergers and acquisitions across national boundaries, are becoming continental in scope. This enlarged market has attracted foreign investment, largely by U.S.-based multinational corporations, on a scale without precedent in this or any other region. The overall result has been more rapid economic growth and lower-priced products than would otherwise have prevailed. Not only are production and marketing being regionalized but so also is publicly sponsored research in such advanced technology areas as nuclear power, communications and space exploration, thereby avoiding needless duplication.

As of 1972, the economies of the six Common Market members have been closely woven together. Not only do goods and capital flow freely and in steadily increasing volumes, but so do tourists, students, workers and businessmen. At present the market for goods and services within the EEC is in excess of $400 billion yearly, one seventh of the world market. Already the largest single market outside the United States, it will become even larger as Britain, Ireland, Norway and Denmark, which are applying for membership, are added.

The prospects for political integration within the EEC may also be improving slowly. Headquartered in Brussels, the principal administrative body, the Common Market Commission, has 8,000 employees, often referred to as "Eurocrats." In addition there is a European Parliament in Strasbourg and a European Court of Justice in Luxembourg. Among the Common Market's numerous accomplishments are the negotiation of associate memberships with eighteen other countries (mostly former French colonies), the decision to move toward a common currency, and an agreement reached in late 1970 by the six foreign ministers to move toward a common foreign policy.

COMECON, the East European counterpart of the EEC, encompasses the Soviet Union, Bulgaria, Czechoslovakia, Hungary, Poland, Rumania, East Germany, and since 1962, Mongolia. Formed in 1949 as a response to the unification of Western Europe provided by the Marshall Plan, it has a gross regional product of $370 billion a year, slightly smaller than the EEC. Handicapped by a lack of enthusiasm among its members and its cumbersome attempts at multinational central planning, its success to date has been limited. Scientific research, concentrated within the Soviet Union, has been rather uneven among sectors, being quite advanced in weapons and space exploration but quite deficient in housing, household appliances and other consumer goods.

Among the developing regions, planning for economic integration is most rapid in Latin America. Like Europe, it has two common markets, but one, the Latin American Free Trade Association (LAFTA), is quite large and the other, the Central American Common Market (CACM), is very small. The LAFTA is continental in scope, including virtually all of the South American continent plus Mexico. The CACM comprises the five Central American republics of Guatemala, Honduras, El Salvador, Costa Rica and Nicaragua.

Of the two regional markets, the smaller is the senior one; it began in 1958 with a multilateral treaty providing for free trade in 20 percent of the goods produced. Although it is still fragile, integration of the member economies has proceeded rapidly, attracting a substantial volume of investment from abroad that otherwise would not have been forthcoming. Growth in intraregional trade (which, along with the ability to attract investment, is a principal indicator of success) has risen rapidly, multiplying sevenfold between 1958 and 1965. Production, particularly that from new investments, is becoming regionally oriented; the individual economies are being bolstered by it. Eventually, however, the CACM must seek wider affiliation with the LAFTA if its people are to benefit fully from available modern technology.

The LAFTA, which came into existence in 1960 with the Treaty of Montevideo, has moved slowly during its first decade. Bogged down in recent years in disagreements and trade arrangements for petroleum and wheat, which account for 25 percent of intraregional trade, it has not progressed very far. Intraregional trade as a proportion of total trade did double during the 1960s, though starting from a narrow base.

Within the LAFTA, the smaller members fear domination of the community by the larger ones, prompting Bolivia, Chile, Peru, Ecuador, Colombia and Venezuela to form a subregional grouping, the Andean Common Market. While remaining members of the LAFTA are participating in its generally slow liberalization of trade, these countries want to emulate the CACM and proceed to integrate their economies rather rapidly.

Among the major geographic areas, regional economic groupings have been slowest to form in Asia. Although intraregional trade looms large in the total trade of countries in the region—about one third in 1965—there is not a regional or even subregional economic grouping in the process of being formed. One reason obviating the need for this might be the complementary nature of Japan's highly industrialized economy with the rural economies of East Asia.

In Africa, the East African community—Tanzania, Uganda and Kenya—is the only grouping to achieve any significant progress in integration. A holdover from British administrative days, the unit of three countries is now forming a common market, but it remains a tenuous arrangement. The community faces two serious problems: first, it contains only 30 million people and is therefore scarcely large enough to form an industrial base; second, since Kenya is more advanced economically, it tends to attract most of the outside investment and to otherwise dominate the group. Three other economic groupings were formed during the sixties in West and Central Africa, but none of these seems to have progressed far in liberalizing and expanding intragroup trade.

In North America, the United States and Canada, the world's first and ninth largest economies, though not officially a common market, are closely integrated in terms of both trade and investment. Trade between the two is by far the largest of any two countries. The same is true for investment. Although these two economies do not have common external tariffs or free internal movement of goods, they are nonetheless highly integrated.

11

THE MULTINATIONAL CORPORATION

Technological advances in communications, transportation and management over the past few decades have greatly increased the optimum size of business firms, creating multinational or global corporations, some of which are larger in economic terms than the countries in which they operate. Once these technological advances permitted a few firms to begin to operate multinationally, others were forced to do so also in order to remain competitive. What began as a few special cases is becoming an epidemic, reshaping the global economy.

While multinational corporations (MNC's) are growing in number and size, their popularity is not. Corporations suffer from a split image. Some believe the MNC to be the key to modernization of the global economy, a major force in reducing international conflict and eliminating global poverty. To these, it is the most effective global disseminator of technology and a creator of wealth. To its critics it is a mercenary institution designed to exploit labor and the poor countries, profit-oriented and entirely devoid of a social conscience. In reality, the multinational corporation is neither the epitome of righteousness as its supporters claim nor the unmitigated evil its detractors make it out to be. On one point most would agree: it is emerging as one of the dominant institutions of the late twentieth century.

Internationalizing Production

The internationalization of production may be the most significant economic phenomenon of the late twentieth century, one which will eventually affect not only the structure of the world economy but the global mode of political organization as well. International production results when inputs come from more than one country. Most often this means combining capital, technology and management from one country with labor and raw materials from another, but there are innumerable variations on this general theme. Management and technology, for example, may come from one country, capital and labor from another, and raw materials from a third. Each of these inputs may come from a different country. Increasingly, components of a single product may originate in several different countries.

Traditionally, economic relations among nations have been dominated by international trade. Each country tended to specialize in those goods which it produced most efficiently, at least in relative terms. Economists explained and analyzed international trade with the law of comparative advantage. But today economic relations between countries are increasingly dominated by international production. The theory of international trade assumes national specialization in products and immobility of the various production inputs, an assumption no longer valid. What is needed to explain the workings of the international economy today is a new theory, a theory of international production.

According to calculations by Judd Polk, U.S.-based firms alone had direct investment abroad of $70 billion in 1969. Assuming $2 of annual output for each $1 invested in plant and equipment, these investments now yield $140 billion in output yearly. This volume of goods produced abroad, with at least some inputs—usually capital, management and technology—from the United States is four times that of U.S. exports. Production resulting from indirect U.S. investment abroad is estimated at $70 billion, assuming conservatively $1 of output for each $1 invested. Both direct and indirect investment thus give a total of $210 billion of production abroad, which is partly U.S. in origin. On the domestic side, Polk estimates that one tenth of the U.S. gross national product of $1 trillion is associated, directly or indirectly, with investment from abroad. International production world-wide now totals an estimated $450 billion of a gross global product of nearly $3 trillion. Growing at 8 to 10 percent yearly, this sector is expanding far more rapidly than the GGP, heralding the eventual emergence of a global economy which is organized much more along economic than political lines.

There is a tendency in many countries to equate foreign investment with U.S. investment. In part, this is not only because overseas investments by U.S.-based firms are far larger than those of any other country, but also because there is more information available on activities of the U.S. firms, much of it gathered by the U.S. Department of Commerce. It is well known, for example, that U.S. firms control more than half of all the manufacturing in Canada. What is not so well known is that Canadian per capita investment in the United States, led by such corporate giants as International Nickel and Massey Ferguson, is far greater than U.S. per capita investment in Canada. On balance, foreign investment by U.S.-based firms and those based in other industrial countries is roughly proportionate to the size of the GNP of each country.

In response to the earlier wave of investment by American firms in other countries, particularly Canada and Europe, foreign firms are now beginning to invest much more heavily in the United States. This phenomenon was recently brought home to me quite forcefully on a personal level when I received a gasoline credit card from British Petroleum with a letter explaining that it replaced the Sinclair credit card I was then carrying in my wallet, since British Petroleum had taken over part of Sinclair's U.S. chain of service stations. It was not until several months later that I discovered from a news article that not only is British Petroleum a foreign firm but it is 49 percent owned by the British government. In early 1971 Imperial Chemical Industries of Great Britain acquired Atlas Chemical, a Delaware-based firm, making the former the world's leading producer of chemicals.

Investment by foreign firms in the United States is not limited to British enterprises. A Japanese firm is building an aluminum smelter in the United States, and a West German firm a steel plant. Mitsubishi has attached a "Made in USA" label to one of its turboprop executive jets, the MU-2, manufactured in Texas. It is the first airplane made by a foreign company in the United States. Piedmont Airlines is now using the Nihon airplane YS-11, a 60-seat twin turbojet, for many of its short-haul flights. This plane is built in Japan but uses Alcoa aluminum, Goodyear landing gear and Rolls Royce engines.

As the internationalization of production expands, it is causing many corporations to alter their organization and outlook. Initially the internationalization occurred as national corporations organized international divisions to coordinate overseas activities. As long as these activities were marginal to the parent firm this was a sensible way to organize, but as the overseas operation expanded, this was no longer adequate. The MNC is now moving toward a global corporate structure, organizing along functional lines—production, R&D and marketing—rather than along geographic lines. Corporate strategies are being formulated increasingly on a global scale in terms of utilizing R&D results, selection of production sites, procurement of raw materials, and marketing of products.

The Size of Modern Corporations

The emergence of the MNC and its rapid growth put the larger ones on a par economically with all but a small number of the largest nation-states. One way to compare the size of nation-states and MNC's is to rank them together according to gross national product and gross annual sales, respectively. While this overstates somewhat the relative size of the MNC, it does afford a rough comparison. Such a listing provides some interesting and striking comparisons. The first 22 entries are the 22 largest nation-states ranging from the United States to Argentina. Each of these is larger than any of the existing MNC's. The 23rd entry on the list is General Motors, with gross annual sales of $24.3 billion in 1969. Its sales are larger than the gross national products of Switzerland or Pakistan, which follow it on the list. Standard Oil and Ford, ranking 27th and 29th, are bracketed between the Republic of South Africa and Austria.

Of the top 50 entries in the merged list, 41 are nation-states and 9 are MNC's. Of the second 50 entries, 18 are nation-states and 32 are MNC's. In the first 100, countries outnumber corporations, but only by 59 to 41 (See table.)

Table 1. Ranking of Countries and Corporations According to Size of Annual Product* for 1970 (in $ billion)

Rank	Economic Entity	$	Rank	Economic Entity	$
1	United States	974.10	34	Norway	11.39
2	U.S.S.R	504.70	35	Hungary	11.33
3	Japan	197.18	36	ROYAL DUTCH/	
4	Germany, West	186.35		SHELL GROUP	10.80
5	France	147.53	37	Philippines	10.23
6	United Kingdom	121.02	38	Finland	10.20
7	Italy	93.19	39	Iran	10.18
8	China, Mainland	82.50	40	Venezuela	9.58
9	Canada	80.38			
10	India	52.92	41	Greece	9.54
			42	Turkey	9.04
			43	GENERAL	
11	Poland	42.32		ELECTRIC	8.73
12	Germany, East	37.61	44	Korea, South	8.21
13	Australia	36.10	45	IBM	7.50
14	Brazil	34.60	46	Chile	7.39
15	Mexico	33.18	47	MOBIL OIL	7.26
16	Sweden	32 58	48	CHRYSLER	7.00
17	Spain	32.26	49	UNILEVER	6.88
18	Netherlands	31.25	50	Colombia	6.61
19	Czechoslovakia	28.84			
20	Rumania	28.01	51	UAR	6.58
			52	Thailand	6.51
			53	INTERNATIONAL	
21	Belgium	25.70		TEL. & TEL.	6.36
22	Argentina	25.42	54	TEXACO	6.35
23	GENERAL		55	Portugal	6.22
	MOTORS	24.30	56	New Zealand	6.08
24	Switzerland	20.48	57	Peru	5.92
25	Pakistan	17.50	58	WESTERN	
26	South Africa	16.69		ELECTRIC	5.86
27	STANDARD OIL		59	Nigeria	5.80
	(N.J.)	16.55	60	Taiwan	5.46
28	Denmark	15.57			
29	FORD MOTOR	14.98	61	GULF OIL	5.40
30	Austria	14.31	62	U.S. STEEL	4.81
			63	Cuba	4.80
31	Yugoslavia	14.02	64	Israel	4.39
32	Indonesia	12.60	65	VOLKSWAGEN-	
33	Bulgaria	11.82		WERK	4.31

Rank	Economic Entity	$	Rank	Economic Entity	$
66	WESTINGHOUSE ELECTRIC	4.31	82	GEN. TEL. & ELECTRONICS	3.44
67	STANDARD OIL (Calif.)	4.19	83	NIPPON STEEL	3.40
68	Algeria	4.18	84	Morocco	3.34
69	PHILIPS GLOEI-LAMPEN-FABRIEKEN	4.16	85	HITACHI	3.33
			86	RADIO CORP. OF AMERICA	3.30
70	Ireland	4.10	87	GOODYEAR TIRE & RUBBER	3.20
71	BRITISH PETROLEUM	4.06	88	SIEMENS	3.20
			89	Vietnam, South	3.20
72	Malaysia	3.84	90	Libya	3.14
73	LING-TEMCO-VOUGHT	3.77	91	Saudi Arabia	3.14
74	STANDARD OIL (Ind.)	3.73	92	SWIFT	3.08
75	BOEING	3.68	93	FARBWERKE HOECHST	3.03
76	DUPONT (E.I.) de NEMOURS	3.62	94	UNION CARBIDE	3.03
			95	DAIMLER-BENZ	3.02
77	Hong Kong	3.62	96	PROCTER & GAMBLE	2.98
78	SHELL OIL	3.59	97	AUGUST THYSSEN-HUTTE	2.96
79	IMPERIAL CHEM. INDUSTRIES	3.51	98	BETHLEHEM STEEL	2.94
80	BRITISH STEEL	3.50	99	BASF	2.87
81	Korea, North	3.50	100	MONTECATINI EDISON	2.84

* The indicators used are gross national product for countries and gross annual sales for corporations. Though not strictly comparable (a value-added figure would have been more appropriate for industry), they are sufficiently close for illustrative purposes. Data for the centrally planned economies (excluding mainland China) and for the General Motors Corporation are for 1969.

The emergence of the MNC as a dominant global institution, in many ways challenging the nation-state, is a novel characteristic of the last half of the twentieth century. Indeed some MNC's have assumed the trappings of the nation-state. It was once said that the sun never set on the British Empire. Today the sun does set on the British Empire, but not on the scores of global corporate empires including those of IBM, Unilever, Volkswagen and Hitachi. Standard Oil of New Jersey has three times as many employees stationed overseas as the State Department. Its six-million-ton tanker fleet is half again as large as that of the Soviet Union. General Motors is owned by more than a million stockholders, a group comparable in size to the population of Liberia.

The average rate of growth of MNC's substantially exceeds that of national economies. Growth generated within the firm as well as mergers and acquisitions contribute to this rapid corporate expansion. In West Germany, for example, the twelve largest industrial firms increased their sales by a whopping 22 percent in 1969, the greater part of the increase due to acquistion of smaller firms. The two largest steel firms in Japan, Yawati and Fuji, merged in 1970 to form the Nippon Steel Corporation. Nippon offiicals are confident that within a year or two, Nippon output will exceed that of U.S. Steel, long the world's largest steel producer by a wide margin. Japan's ten auto firms are joining forces with the prospect of reducing their ranks to three or four during the early seventies.

With bankers concerned because loans were outstanding and governments did not want small national corporations to fall too far behind the multinational giants, the pressure for merger intensified throughout the sixties in Western Europe and Japan. In 1960 Great Britain had eleven independent auto makers, among them Austin Motor Company, Morris Motors Ltd., Guy Motors Ltd. and Jaguar Cars Ltd. A series of mergers between early 1960 and 1970 resulted in the formation of one giant firm, British Leyland Motor Corporation, second only to Volkswagen among Europe's auto producers. France's State Planning Agency has arranged mergers in several industries. Two French firms now produce two thirds of the country's steel. Renault and Peugeot, two of the three remaining French-controlled automobile firms, are loosely affiliated, cooperating in a wide range of matters. And so it is with industry after industry in the industrial economies of Europe and Japan.

In the next stage, transnational mergers will probably become more common as large national firms attempt to expand still further. Some analysts, among them Richard Barber, estimate that by 1980 some 300 large corporations will control 75 percent of all the world's manufacturing assets. He further adds: "The transition from a world economy in which thousands of companies competed with each other to one in which 300 giant industrial firms dominate the scene is of nearly immeasurable public consequence." Others feel this is not likely to happen, pointing out that new firms are continually springing up and that the distribution of production between large and small firms has not changed much in recent years. Although this seems generally true for the past, new technologies in communications, transportation and management at least suggest the prospect of concentrating a steadily expanding share of the gross global product in a few hundred global corporations.

Industrial Complementation Agreements

Industrial complementation agreements reflect decisions made by a group of countries to permit free trade in the products of a certain industry, such as automobiles, computers or petrochemicals. Consider, for instance, four countries interested in developing a petrochemical industry. One country may supply petroleum from indigenous reserves, one may do the refining, one may have a lubricants enterprise, and the fourth may have a plastics industry or some other petrochemical enterprise. Products would then move freely among these countries, enlarging the market for all and justifying investments which otherwise might not be practical.

Industrial complementation agreements may involve either the manufacturing of several related products in different countries or the manufacturing of components which are eventually assembled into a final product. The hypothetical petroleum-petrochemical complementation agreement described above is an example of the former type. The industrial complementation agreement worked out by International Business Machines with Argentina, Brazil, Chile and Uruguay in the computer industry is an example of the latter. Components are manufactured in Brazil and assembled in Argentina. A Chilean firm is licensed to produce punch cards and the entire operation is headquartered in Uruguay. In exchange for these arrangements the four countries now constitute a duty-free zone for all IBM computers, components and punch cards.

By far the most ambitious complementation effort conceived to date is one by the Ford Motor Company to build an Asian Ford. In many ways an Asian version of the Model T, it is to be small and rugged in design, cheap to operate and a combination car-pickup for transporting passengers and goods. Components will be produced in individual countries and then transported from country to country by what amounts to a conveyer belt of ships; except for Singapore, every country involved will assemble the vehicles for local sale. Ford expects to establish an electric- and plastic-parts factory in Singapore, engine foundries in Thailand and Taiwan, axle and transmission factories in Indonesia, and a diesel-engine plant in South Korea. A plant is also scheduled for Malaysia, possibly one for India, and even one for mainland China if it should open up. By 1980, Ford plans to invest $1 billion in the regional complementation agreement.

An agreement negotiated between the United States and Canada in 1965 abolished tariffs on automobiles and parts, permitting free movement of both across the border. Before the agreement, Canadian plants of U.S. firms had been established in order to overcome the high Canadian tariff on imported cars. These plants were too small to operate economically, resulting in a high production cost. Today all this is changed. Ford supplies its entire North American market for its Maverick model from its Canadian plants. Chrysler, which used to produce six models in Canada, now produces only two models there, but these supply much of the U.S. market as well as Canada. Direct effects on trade are reflected in the climb of U.S. imports of cars, trucks and parts from Canada from practically nil in 1964 to around $3.1 billion in 1970. Imports into Canada from the United States also increased, though on a considerably smaller scale.

The basic principle underlying industrial complementation agreements is the enlargement of a market beyond the national market for a product or related group of products in exchange for the sharing of production among the countries involved. Industrial complementation agreements are much less difficult to negotiate than are regional economic groupings, which are far broader and more complex, and whose consequences are much less certain. Another advantage of these agreements is that their impact may be almost entirely positive in terms of employment, balance of payments and economic growth, especially if the group of countries involved is entirely dependent on imports for the product or products in question. These agreements can often serve as a useful intermediate step as economies move toward regional integration. The initiative for the formation of regional economic groupings comes from national governments, whereas that for industrial complementation agreements more often comes from MNC's. Individual firms, with their more detailed information and understanding of the market for their products, can see an opportunity for creating a market for a product or group of products large enough to justify an investment much more readily than governments.

Transferring Technology Across Borders

MNC's are composed of a complex of widely varied modern technologies ranging from production and marketing to management and financing. Because it operates in many countries, the MNC serves as a vehicle for transferring a wide range of technologies across national borders. Indeed, it is by far the most effective agent yet devised for disseminating technology across national borders, dwarfing in its effectiveness other types of institutions such as the UN Special Agencies, international professional societies, private consulting firms or bilateral assistance agencies. Unfortunately, the great bulk of this transnational flow of technology occurs among the rich countries. Relatively little moves in a North-South direction. This poses a problem for the poor countries because there is no alternative institution capable of transferring technology on the scale required. Even the centrally planned economies of Eastern Europe, including the Soviet Union, recognize the need to involve MNC's in their development, particularly in advanced-technology areas such as computers and certain consumer-goods industries like automobiles.

Several billion dollars' worth of technology are exported and imported each year in the form of licensing rights and patents. The United States, the leading exporter of technology, exported $2.2 billion worth in 1970. Perhaps 90 percent of this total moves within corporate channels, most of it within the same corporation. The sale of technology between governments is very small by comparison.

Within the field of production, technology transferred may range from the concept of mass production as pioneered by Henry Ford to a process for synthesizing Dacron

fibers. Marketing know-how is sometimes even more difficult to come by than production expertise. The financing
of modern corporate activity is an intricate matter in which
experienced corporate financiers have a great deal to offer.

Technology is transferred by the MNC in many ways
across national boundaries. An advance in technology
made in one country in which a firm is operating may be
made available almost simultaneously in all other countries
in which it operates. Technology is also transferred through
licensing arrangements between firms. For example, since
1950 Japanese firms have entered into some 9,800 licensing
agreements with foreign firms for the purchase of technology.

Nonproprietary technologies, such as management practices used by firms investing in a given country, are often
emulated by local firms. The same is true for marketing,
particularly product promotion. European firms, for example, have absorbed a great deal of know-how from
American firms operating in Europe.

The National-Corporate Interface

The nation-state and the MNC are the two dominant
institutions in the world of the late twentieth century. In
some ways these two institutions are quite similar, in others
quite different. The nation-state is primarily a political
institution, the MNC an economic one. Behavior of the
first is decided in large measure by the ballot box, and of
the second by the marketplace. Neither of these two institutions acts solely in the public interest. Response to the
electorate in the democratic nation-state is often strongly
modified by the influence of the special-interest groups.
This is particularly true where restrictions on campaign
funding are lax, as in the United States. The MNC not only
responds to the marketplace, but through its Madison

Avenue style of advertising, it attempts to create and shape consumer tastes and wants.

The nation-state and the MNC are similar in that both engage in long-term economic planning and both allocate resources—financial, human and natural resources. Planning in the nation-state is geographical in character, relating to its territorial confines. The MNC is often global in scope but confined to a particular industry or sector, such as pharmaceuticals, automobiles or food processing.

The nation-state uses the budget mechanism along with a wide array of economic policies both to directly allocate and to indirectly influence the use of resources. MNC's formulate a global strategy and in the process make decisions on where to procure raw materials and components, in which capital markets to seek financing, where to locate plants, offices and research laboratories, and in which parts of the world to concentrate marketing efforts. To paraphrase Judd Polk, technological progress, particularly in communications and computers, has created a situation in which for the first time men are in a position to treat the world itself as the basic economic unit in pursuing that core economic problem: seeking the most efficient combination of production inputs.

For the past few centuries the world has been neatly divided into a set of independent, sovereign nation-states, including in some cases their colonial extensions. With the emergence of literally hundreds of multinational or global corporations, this organization of the world into mutually exclusive political entities is now being overlaid by a network of economic institutions, creating a complex political-economic matrix. Within this matrix there is often overlap between countries and corporations in functions, responsibility and authority. In this sense there is no clear line of demarcation between countries and corporations.

Fortunately, the broad interests and objectives of the nation-state and MNC usually coincide, but occasionally they conflict. This is becoming more of a problem, given the enormous size and range of activity of many modern MNC's relative to that of smaller nation-states.

Many decisions once considered the province of the nation-state are now being made by externally based MNC's, particularly in such matters as the nature, timing and location of investment. These decisions may affect the employment level, the rate of economic growth, the balance of payments, or whether a given natural resource is developed. A planning commission sitting in Kampala, the capital of Uganda, may make certain decisions concerning, say, the creation of additional employment, but critical decisions influencing the number of new jobs to be created in Uganda may be made in the executive offices of MNC's headquartered in Saint Louis, Amsterdam or Osaka.

In addition to the overlapping responsibility, the rules which govern the relationship between the nation-state and the MNC are determined on a country-by-country basis, and they vary widely between countries, even those with adjacent borders. Rules are often changed at the whim of national leaders or when governments change. There is no universal set of rules governing the interface between these two dominant sets of institutions. Rules are outdated, often going back to the days when corporations were national rather than multinational. National governments cannot always deal satisfactorily with MNC's relying solely on their national laws and national policies. The net result of this situation is a great deal of confusion, suspicion and distrust.

Another sticking point in relations between nation-states and MNC's has been efforts by some nation-states, notoriously the United States, to use foreign subsidiaries of U.S. corporations as instruments of foreign policy. This issue of extraterritoriality was a particularly trying one for Canada whenever subsidiaries of U.S.-based corporations wanted to trade with mainland China or some other centrally planned economy. *The Economist* of London reports a specific instance involving U.S. subsidiaries in France: "Two French companies illustrate the extent to which the United States attempts to influence its subsidiaries abroad. An attempt to export some Caravelle airliners to Communist China was blocked at the instigation of the U.S. State Department on the grounds that since a significant part of the aircraft's electronics equipment was supplied by U.S. firms the aircraft was within the reach of the trading-with-the-enemy provisions." Fortunately, late in 1969 the United States rescinded its policy of trying to force foreign subsidiaries to hew to its foreign policy. Subsidiaries of U.S. firms may now trade with whatever country they choose, at least in nonstrategic goods. This progressive step should to some extent lessen concern over the use by nation-states of MNC's domiciled within their boundaries to further their own interests.

One of the important sources of friction between the nation-state and the MNC is that agreements between the two are often broken, most frequently by governments. This is a common occurrence in countries where governments change hands frequently, as is the case in many poor countries, either through elections or coups d'état. Scarcely a week passes in which a government somewhere in the world is not either overthrown or threatened with overthrow. Bolivia, with 186 coups d'état in its 145 years of existence, is a dramatic case in point.

At present there is not an effective legal means of resolving disputes between corporations and national governments. The International Court of Justice in The Hague, seemingly a logical institution to resolve national-corporate conflicts, refused to rule on these disputes, claiming they are beyond its purview. As things now stand, the relationship between governments and foreign investors is a troubled one in many countries. The contour of the interface between the two sets of powerful institutions is to a substantial degree shaped by the relative negotiating strengths of the two parties in a given situation. National governments must offer certain terms in order to attract investors. Expropriation by a government or even a threat of expropriation can quickly dry up the inflow of external capital and technology. Large multinational corporations which have ruthlessly exploited the smaller, weaker poor countries in the past are finding they are no longer welcome in many parts of the world. At the same time, political leaders in these countries who wish to use the multinational corporation as a convenient whipping boy must rise above temporary political expediency lest the economic costs of their actions far exceed personal or partisan gains. A favorable view by the international business community of a particular country is a valuable asset and should not be sacrificed lightly.

Social Responsibility

The past two decades have witnessed an enormous growth of corporate power at the global level without a corresponding growth of public accountability in the conduct of business affairs. Although the behavior of MNC's, governed largely by the profit motive, frequently coincides with the public interest, it sometimes conflicts.

In its efforts to achieve the most efficient possible combination of productive resources, the MNC contributes to the creation of a more equitable world order. It raises investment capital in countries where it is abundant and interest rates are low, investing in poor countries where interest rates are high. Likewise, it attempts to locate its more labor-intensive operations where wages are lowest, thereby helping to raise incomes in poor countries. The MNC uses the most efficient technology available irrespective of the country of origin. The net effect world-wide is to provide a higher level of living for a given use of resources and effort than would be possible without MNC's. In this sense the MNC is, almost by definition, socially constructive on the international scene.

Unfortunately, not all actions are constructive. MNC's have been grossly negligent in environmental matters, often resisting efforts by governments to legislate and enforce pollution controls. The role of U.S.-based MNC's in joining forces with the armed services to lobby for greater defense expenditures is despicable. Lobbying by influential U.S. firms is responsible for the U.S. violation beginning in 1972 of the United Nations boycott of Rhodesian chrome ore (voted by the Security Council). Scores of MNC's with investments in South Africa are virtually ignoring apartheid there. Beyond these specific actions which illustrate the seamier side of corporate behavior, actions to alleviate some of the world's leading social ills, such as poverty, overpopulation and rising unemployment do not occupy a very prominent place in corporate strategies.

The issue facing the community of nations is how to harness the capacities and resources of MNC's to more effectively meet man's social needs. Can the MNC's collectively evolve a socially responsible code of conduct or must this be imposed through regulation at the international level? There are some within the business community, such as Business International President Orville L. Freeman, who urge the former, but progress to date does not provide much basis for hope. Barring an unexpected breakthrough it may be necessary to take action at the international level.

Within the United States various proposals have been made to have at least one representative of the public interest on the board of directors of each large corporation. Including such an individual in a board directorate would at least ensure that the public interest was voiced within the corporations' inner councils even though it might not be heeded. Along with its need to acquire a greater sense of social responsibility, the MNC also needs to be denationalized.

Denationalizing the Multinational Corporation

One of the greatest problems facing the MNC is its ancestry, its beginnings as a national corporation. The close association of the MNC with its government and with the interests of the country in which it is domiciled make actions of the MNC suspect in the eyes of other governments. For example, until quite recently the U.S. government required overseas subsidiaries of U.S.-based firms to adhere to its national policies in such areas as antitrust and trade with the centrally planned economies.

Pressures brought to bear on foreign governments by the U.S. government on behalf of U.S.-based multinational corporations are particularly troublesome. This is perhaps epitomized by the Hickenlooper Amendment to the U.S. foreign aid legislation which directs the U.S. government to discontinue aid to countries which expropriate holdings of U.S.-based firms without adequate compensation.

If the MNC is to realize its full potential for raising living standards around the world, it must be willing to divest itself of its national ties, particularly where the ties are to the more influential nation-states such as the United States and, increasingly, Japan. Only as it becomes truly multinational and global can it function at full effectiveness. The day when the MNC can expect the government of its country of origin to represent its interests in other countries is fading. Achieving a genuinely multinational character requires that employment, ownership and R&D activities acquire a multinational character. Some firms are moving rapidly in this direction. For example, less than half of all ITT employees are Americans. IBM has fewer than one hundred Americans in management positions in its vast overseas operations. For several years, the chief executive heading IBM activities outside the United States was a Frenchman.

Encouraging progress has been made during the past few years in broadening the base of corporate ownership. Shares of a long list of multinational corporations are now listed on securities markets in more than one country.

When Japan's Sony Corporation was added to the 1,317 listings on the New York Stock Exchange in September 1970, it became the thirty-third foreign based firm to join the list. It was the sixth such firm to be added to the Big Board list in 1970, following British Petroleum and Plessey Corporation of Britain, Northgate Exploration, Northern and Central Gas of Canada, and Norlin Corporation of Panama. Sony's reason for requesting a U.S. listing was that 35 percent of the firm's output is sold in the U.S market. British Petroleum is deeply involved in the development of Alaskan oil reserves, and in addition owns 25 percent of Standard of Ohio. Shares of a large number of U.S.-based firms are traded on stock exchanges abroad, most of them in Europe.

As computer communications technology continues to advance it seems quite likely that a single world market for shares of corporations will emerge. Ultronics, a subsidiary of General Telephone and Electric, recently teamed up with Reuters to organize a world-wide system providing price quotes on corporate shares and commodities. At present the system is operational in Europe and covers some 10,000 stocks and commodities. Stock exchanges included are Düsseldorf, Frankfurt, Hamburg, Munich, London, Amsterdam, Milan and Zürich. Outside Europe, there are *Stockmaster* subscribers in Hong Kong, Beirut and Latin America. Japan and Australia are also subscribers.

Even the Soviet government has toyed with the idea of subscribing to *Stockmaster* in Moscow.

The result of this information becoming available globally is the gradual emergence of a single world market for securities, with continuous trading in one market worldwide, twenty-four hours a day. The opening price on the New York Stock Exchange will in the future be influenced not so much by the closing price of the preceding day in New York as by trading progressing through the night around the world, time zone by time zone, from New York to Los Angeles to Sydney, Tokyo, Singapore, Beirut, Frankfurt and London.

Trends of the past two decades indicate that the multinational or global corporation is profoundly affecting the economic relationships among nations. These mammoth economic entities are responsible for the internationalization of production, finance and ownership, and for the increasing integration of national economies into a single global economy.

12

RESTRUCTURING THE GLOBAL ECONOMY

Several forces are acting to restructure the global economy in the late twentieth century. While economic forces loom large, there are important and potentially powerful social, ecological, technological and political forces at work as well. Some are longstanding, while others are just beginning to emerge. Among the potentially most influential forces is the spreading concern over the increasingly inequitable distribution of wealth among societies. As the world becomes smaller, awareness of the inhuman nature of the widening gap between superaffluent and poor societies is rising. Many among the rich are troubled by the widening gap. The poor are finding it less tolerable.

Meaningful progress in eliminating the poverty which blights human society will not occur with anything less than a restructuring of the global economy. Both international investment and trade need to be further liberalized, creating conditions where capital and technology can flow more readily across national borders. Over the longer run this should distribute global economic power more evenly, reducing the traditional concentration of wealth within the North Atlantic community. Hopefully, this will be done in such a way as to avoid an uncontrollable backlash from adversely affected labor and industry in the North and a psychology of exploitation in the South.

Accompanying this concern over the inequitable distribution of wealth is the growing leverage which the poor countries can and are beginning to exercise in world markets and in political relationships with the rich countries, given their control of a disproportionately large share of the world's remaining exportable reserves of petroleum and industrial raw materials. Closely associated with this is the growing dependence of rich countries on cooperation of the poor to help reduce atmospheric and oceanic pollution, to control international narcotics flows and to exploit oceanic resources peacefully.

Wide variations in wage levels among societies are also acting to redistribute economic activity as multinational corporations (MNC's) locate more of their labor-intensive activities in low-income countries. Unfortunately this trend toward a more equitable global distribution of economic activity is strongly opposed by segments of organized labor in the United States because they feel it reduces employment in the United States. The Burke-Hartke Act, introduced in Congress in late 1971 and designed to restrict investment by U.S. firms abroad, is strongly supported by some labor unions. However, available evidence indicates that direct foreign investment by U.S. firms is, on balance, very much in the interest of U.S. workers. Foreign affiliates of some 330 U.S.-based MNC's purchased 5.1 billion dollars worth of goods from the United States in 1965, the latest year for which data are available. Perhaps even more importantly, the opportunity of importing lower priced components from foreign affiliates in some industries, notably electronics, enables the U.S. firms to remain competitive where they would otherwise lose out. At best, restrictions on international investment and trade would reduce employment in the United States, and, at worst, set off a round of rising protectionism comparable to that of the thirties.

In many ways paralleling the impact of widely varying wage levels among societies on the global economic structure are the widely varying levels of industrial pollution. As pollution levels in advanced industrial economies begin to approach or exceed safety tolerance levels established by health authorities, additional production costs attributable to pollution control will rise, causing corporations to invest in countries with less pollution and less stringent or even nonexistent pollution controls. Japanese industrialists, faced with one of the world's most polluted areas, are talking of locating pollution-intensive industrial activities in poor countries in much the same way they take advantage of low-cost labor in the same countries. U.S.-based international oil companies are avoiding pollution control regulations by locating refineries in the petroleum-exporting countries. The head of one U.S.-based oil company estimates that seven new refineries will be needed in the northeastern United States by 1975, but is convinced that all will be built overseas, supplying the U.S. market from there, because of the costly pollution controls existing within the region. U.S. environmental regulations affecting construction of new oil refineries can easily raise production costs 10 to 15 percent. As long as pollution levels remain relatively low in the poor countries and as the ecological stresses in the heavily industrialized countries increase, the need to rationalize global production in ecological terms will also increase.

Still another factor which may affect the global distribution of economic activity is the change in life styles occurring within the more affluent societies. Most evident among the young, it reflects both a decision to abandon the pursuit of materialism and a desire to accommodate consumption habits to a finite ecosystem. If enough young people within the more affluent societies adopt these attitudes, it could eventually slow economic growth rates. If at the same time economic growth in the poor countries continued at a rapid rate, their relative economic position would improve over time.

There are also indications that consumers in the rich countries, particularly the United States and Japan, are beginning to organize as they become less tolerant of the high prices for consumer goods associated with protection of inefficient industries and firms. Just how effective consumer groups will be when their interests run counter to organized labor and affected industries remains to be seen. As yet it is too early to determine how much changing life styles and the organization of consumer interests will affect the global distribution of economic activity.

Most forces acting to alter the global economic structure affect primarily North-South economic relationships, but there are some forces altering East-West economic relationships. After nearly a quarter century of limited economic intercourse between the centrally planned economies and other countries, important economic ties are beginning to form across this barrier. For the Western industrial societies and Japan, economic rapprochement provides access to vast supplies of petroleum, natural gas and industrial raw materials, particularly those of the Soviet Union. For the Eastern economies, economic intercourse can provide access to sorely needed technology from the West. In addition the Soviet Union may not be able to develop the efficient modern livestock industry required to satisfy consumer demands without importing low-cost feed grains from abroad, and notably from the United States, which supplies half of all feed grains entering the world market. Barring the unlikely prospect of a lasting setback in improving the political interface between East and West, new

East-West economic ties could be an important force in shaping the global economy during the seventies.

Rationalizing Global Production

At present, the global economy is not very rationally organized since national boundaries are being used to protect highly inefficient production of many products, particularly agricultural and light industrial products in the rich countries. This inefficient production contributes both to unnecessarily high prices for selected consumer products in the rich countries and to rising unemployment in the poor ones.

The cost to consumers of tariff and quota restrictions on imports is reflected in higher prices of imported products, a restricted variety of available goods, and higher prices on some domestically produced goods. In addition, because of inefficiencies which frequently develop in industries not exposed to external competition, consumers also often pay higher prices for some domestically produced goods. The range of models of consumer goods, such as automobiles and TV sets, has been greatly broadened within the U.S. market through imports. According to Fred Bergsten of the Brookings Institution, tariffs and import quotas on such things as petroleum, steel, sugar, fresh and frozen meat, and dairy products such as milk, cheese and butter, cost U.S. consumers an estimated $12 billion per year in higher prices. Andrew Brimmer, a member of the Federal Reserve Board, estimates that passage of a bill introduced into Congress in 1970, providing for quotas on textile and shoe imports, could alone cost consumers an additional $3.7 billion per year by 1975, amounting to $54 per family. European consumers pay dearly for the protection of inefficient production of cereals, sugar and livestock products within the European Economic Community. Millions are jobless in the poor countries because of protectionist trade policies in the rich ones.

These circumstances prevail at a time when labor is relatively scarce in several European countries and in Japan, but when unemployment is rising in the poor ones. There are various ways of achieving a better global balance between these two factors of production. One is to import labor into the rich countries, as is done in northern Europe where a few million workers, largely from lower income countries bordering the Mediterranean, are in residence with labor visas. Another way of achieving a better worldwide balance between labor and capital is to export jobs by investing abroad in labor-intensive activities. Both the United States and Japan have invested widely in labor-intensive industries in East Asia, Mexico and elsewhere. Still another way is for the higher-wage countries to import labor-intensive products such as textiles or fruits and vegetables.

As unemployment levels continue to rise in the poor countries and the full social and political dimensions of the employment problem unfold during the seventies, the world will be forced to take inventory of ways of dealing with it. The poor countries need to consider liberalizing restrictions on foreign investment to attract capital, while the rich countries need to open their markets to labor-intensive exports from the poor countries.

The existing international economic system, with its protection of inefficient production in the rich countries, seems designed more to preserve global poverty and unemployment than to eliminate it. The recently completed Kennedy Round of trade negotiations under the auspices of the General Agreement on Tariffs (GATT) was largely of, by and for the rich countries. It was a major step toward creating a vast northern industrial market but it did not significantly liberalize trade for agricultural commodities or labor-intensive, industrial products such as textiles.

In agriculture, the sixties witnessed rising agricultural protectionism and increasingly distorted production patterns. A steadily increasing share of the world's supply of cereals, livestock products and sugar was contributed by high-cost, inefficient producers, invariably at the expense of the more efficient producers.

Cereal prices within the European Economic Community, protected by the trade barriers erected around the Common Market, are nearly double those of the world market. As a result of these barriers, a German livestock producer pays almost twice as much for feed grains as his American counterpart. Consumers bear the burden of increased prices for livestock products.

In Japan the government support price for rice is nearly triple the world market level, making Japan the most flagrant violator of free trade of any cereal producing country. Not only is Japan no longer an importer, but its internal prices are overstimulating production, forcing the export of rice with heavy subsidies. This severely depresses prices in the world market for countries that must make their living from exports of rice.

A similar situation exists in the world wheat market, where the subsidy required to export high-cost French wheat is equal to the world market value of the wheat itself. France's exportable surpluses of barley are marketed outside the Common Market with an enormous subsidy, as are its exports of wheat. If Pakistan's effort to export soft wheats materializes and becomes a matter of competing subsidies between the French and Pakistani treasuries, there can be little doubt of the outcome despite Pakistan's competitive advantage.

The situation with sugar is even worse. If there is any commodity in which the poor man living in the rural tropics has an advantage over temperate-zone producers,

it is in the production of sugar. If economics alone prevailed, there would be little if any beet sugar produced
in the world. Sugar would come from cane, virtually all of
it from the tropical and subtropical countries. Beet sugar
costs between 7 and 10 cents per pound to produce, while
cane sugar costs 2 to 4 cents. The United States adopted a
more protectionist sugar policy following the Castro take-
over in Cuba, by reducing its imports of sugar in favor
of more costly domestic production, much of it from beets.
At present, approximately 60 percent of U.S. sugar needs
are met by domestic production. The situation is far worse
in several European countries where inefficient sugar-beet
production is subsidized to the point where some now export sugar.

The sugar situation is closely paralleled in the world
textile industry. This industry is one of the most labor-intensive and least sophisticated in which developing countries can invest. Because of high labor content of textiles,
the poor countries, with their low wages, can produce
clothing much more cheaply than can the rich countries.
Nonetheless, the rich countries are discriminating against
textile imports from both Japan and the poor countries.

Changing prices of labor, capital and technology both
within and among countries can lead to changes in competitive position. Advancing technologies and diminishing
natural resources may do the same. Global production
patterns which seem rational today may not be so tomorrow. Japan, which paid its tuition into the modern era
with exports of raw silk, is now itself a net importer of this
labor-intensive commodity. Japanese textile exports have
been viewed as a dire threat to textile industries in Europe
and the United States, but Japan itself, faced with competition from Taiwan, Hong Kong and other low income
countries, is already importing cotton yarn and may be
a net importer of textiles within a few years. Therefore, the
impact of legislation introduced into the U.S. Congress

during 1970 to limit textile imports would be borne largely by the poor countries.

In the Western Hemisphere, the production of fruits and vegetables is shifting southward from the United States into Mexico and the Caribbean countries with their lower-cost labor. As transport technologies advance, seasonal variations among countries can be more fully exploited to create additional rural employment in the Southern economies. Rising exports of fresh winter fruits and vegetables from Mexico and the Caribbean area to the United States and Canada illustrate this, as do exports from some of the Mediterranean countries to northwestern Europe. The newly paved road that passes through Afghanistan and the Khyber Pass could make the Soviet Union an important market for Pakistan's winter fruits and vegetables, much as the United States now is for Mexico.

Present restrictions on imports not only lock the U.S. economy into low productivity, low-wage industries but also limit the dynamic character of the U.S. and world economy. At a time when inflation is a serious threat, restrictions on imports fuel inflationary pressures. Indeed some European countries, including the Netherlands, West Germany and Switzerland, have in the past unilaterally reduced trade barriers in order to combat inflation.

But this is only part of the problem. Because the protection against exports from poor countries reduces export earnings and incomes of these countries, the U.S. government, like those of other industrial countries, has a foreign aid program which has the effect of at least partly offsetting the losses due to its protectionist policies. The net effect is that the average person pays more for the products he buys because of protectionism, and then has his taxes increased to support foreign aid so he can pay to offset the damage. In other words, the consumer-taxpayer must pay both coming and going. If protectionist measures were eliminated, the consumer in the rich countries would be better off, as would the worker producing sugar or working in the textile mill in the poor countries. And for the poor country, increasing foreign exchange earnings through expanded trade has a great advantage over aid in that it does not need to be repaid.

The key issues in achieving a more rational and equitable global economic structure are: who bears the cost of making adjustments and how can these costs be minimized? Should the costs be borne by the affected industries and workers alone or should they be borne by society at large? The answer obviously is the latter. As things stand, U.S. consumers are now paying 12 billion dollars for existing protectionist measures. Presumably then, the public at large could spend any amount up to 12 billion dollars per year in adjustment assistance to finance retraining and upgrading of labor skills, and conversion of plant and equipment into other lines of production. Effective adjustment assistance expenditures would likely cost consumer-taxpayers only a fraction of trade protectionism. In addition, it would make the economy more flexible and capable of adjusting to new opportunities and challenges in an increasingly dynamic, integrated global economy. Labor, business and consumers would all be better off than in a highly protected, inflexible national economy.

Modest efforts to redress the imbalance in economic power between rich countries and poor are now under way, taking the form of generalized preferences to poor countries for industrial products. Imports of most industrial and a few agricultural products into the European Economic Community from poor countries were exempted from all duties on July 1, 1971. Japan and the United Kingdom followed with similar moves. The U.S. intent to liberalize imports from the poor countries has been delayed by its balance-of-payments crisis.

Although granting generalized preferences by the rich

countries is not an insignificant gesture, it is perhaps less consequential than it initially appears, because the number of industrial products in which the poor countries are competitive is limited and because quotas are imposed on products where growth becomes too rapid. From those products in which they are competitive, such as shoes and textiles, the rich countries are removing tariffs but substituting the authority to impose quotas which could be even more restrictive. What would help the poor countries greatly would be the opening of rich-country markets to farm imports, particularly sugar, and increasingly, cereals. But this is not yet in prospect.

The net effect of rationalizing economic activity on a world-wide basis is more jobs, lower prices, higher living levels, and a more equitable distribution of wealth and income among countries. Indeed, such rationalization is in the interest of all countries. Only the political influence of the special interests must be overcome to achieve it. An exemplary act reflecting the spirit of global economic integration was taken by Britain in the fall of 1971 when the British government ordered that labels on goods indicating the country of origin be removed. After November 30, 1971, British consumers were no longer able to tell where goods were made, not even whether they were British.

Disseminating Technology

A central question before governments in the poor countries is how to acquire the technology needed to improve the quality of life of their people. As indicated in the preceding chapter, there are two ways of obtaining needed technologies—to develop indigenously or to import. Some countries have relied heavily on the exploitation of imported technologies, developing little of their own. Others, principally the earlier countries to modernize, meet more of their needs indigenously.

The manner in which today's poor countries acquire technology is largely influenced by the circumstances in which they find themselves. Rapid population growth, common to virtually every poor country, requires continuous technological innovation merely to maintain the status quo in living standards. Stated differently, countries now trying to modernize are faced with pressures which the earlier ones were spared.

Professor James Brian Quinn of Dartmouth points out the strategic role that technological innovation plays in economic growth today: "The growth impact of technology multipliers [such as the introduction of time sharing with computers] can vastly outweigh the Keynesian demand stimulation effects of the investments that initiated them. Quite often large increases in productivity or value added can actually be accomplished through introduction of a series of management technologies or minor process improvements which involve almost no capital investment. In fact, throughout many societies the primary force needed to stimulate growth is not so much capital investment as technological advance. This viewpoint changes the entire growth formulation issue. Knowledge flows become as important to growth strategies as monetary flows. And national policy makers must learn to attack the new problems this approach poses."

A strategy to import technology must consider both basic forms, proprietary and nonproprietary. The former consists of those technologies developed by corporations or other commercial firms and held under patent. Examples would be a process for making synthetic fibers or the design of a particular machine tool. Nonproprietary technologies are those developed in the public domain by institutions such as the U.S. Department of Agriculture, the National Institutes of Health or international research institutes, or those technologies such as improved accounting practices, which are of such a general nature that they are part of the educational offering.

Whether technology is in the private or the public domain, governments must create the conditions under which it can be successfully imported and adopted. For example, successful importation requires a human resource base of knowledge and skills capable of using the technology.

If the technology is privately held by a multinational corporation, then it may be available only through licensing. This requires capital, and more specifically, foreign exchange. Privately held technology can be imported in the form of equipment embodying a certain technology, such as earth-moving equipment, or equipment for a new factory, in which case the cost of the new technology is included in the equipment itself. Foreign know-how can also be obtained through direct investment, either wholly owned or in collaboration with local firms. If the desired technology is available only through direct investment, then the potential market must be large enough to make the investment worthwhile, providing one of the most compelling arguments for regional integration. Certainly the member countries of the Central American Common Market were much more successful in acquiring new technology from external investment as an integrated economic unit than they were individually.

Brian Quinn points out that "when a high degree of know-how and capital intensiveness characterize the manufacturing process, direct investment may be by far the best way for a country to obtain technology, and perhaps the only feasible way for a company to provide it. Such investments can allow the country to eliminate the decades of time required to educate people, develop processes, and generate investment sources internally."

Among those countries which have been very successful in exploiting the technological resources of the multinational corporation to achieve domestic economic and social objectives are Taiwan, South Korea and the Ivory Coast. These countries have evaluated investment proposals from abroad partly in terms of the technology contribution these investments would make. The challenge to the national leadership is to identify and attract the technologies desired.

Nonproprietary technology can be acquired in a variety of forms. Foreign technicians, either in residence or on short-term consultancies from rich countries or international agencies, are one of the most important sources. At present an estimated 200,000 technicians from North America, Europe and Japan are in residence in poor countries. This is essentially the manner in which both the United States and the Soviet Union acquired basic space technologies from the Germans following World War II, when both eagerly sought German space scientists.

Another widely used technique to obtain technology from the more advanced countries is by sending students for training. A predominant share of the estimated 135,000 foreign students attending U.S. colleges and universities are from poor countries. Many are also studying in other advanced countries. One drawback of this approach is that students often elect to remain in the country in which they are studying, contributing to the brain drain. Another is the inapplicability of much of the education acquired to conditions in the poor countries.

Still another way of disseminating technology is in the form of products such as vaccines or new seeds. The introduction of vaccines in the poor countries has greatly reduced the incidence of infectious diseases. International agencies such as the Agency for International Development (AID), bilateral aid programs of other donor countries, and the UN specialized agencies often serve as a vehicle for these technologies.

High-yielding Mexican wheats were introduced into Turkey on a large scale by the U.S. AID mission in Ankara under the direction of James Grant, now president of the Overseas Development Council. AID technicians not only introduced the new seeds and verified their adaptability to growing conditions in Turkey, but AID also financed the importation of 22,000 tons of the new seeds.

A similar, even more dramatic example occurred in West Pakistan. Once it was determined that the high-yielding Mexican dwarf wheats were adapted to growing conditions there, these seeds were imported en masse. In 1967 Pakistan imported 42,000 tons of Mexican wheat at prices only slightly above world market prices. This shipment of seed, planted on more than a million acres, yielded enough seed when harvested to plant the country's entire acreage of wheat. Virtually without cost to Pakistan since the research investment had already been made in Mexico by the Rockefeller Foundation, this new technology enabled Pakistan to increase its wheat crop 60 percent in four years. A similar approach in India permitted a doubling of its wheat crop in six years.

The period since the end of World War II has witnessed the emergence of a variety of new institutions which have in effect institutionalized the transfer of technology across national borders. In the field of agriculture, for example, this includes multinational agribusiness corporations, bilateral and multilateral assistance agencies, and institutions such as the International Rice Research Institute based in the Philippines and the International Corn and Wheat Improvement Center located in Mexico. Technology generated in supranational institutions is usually more accessible to the international community than is that developed within a particular nation-state.

Transferring technology from rich countries to poor poses problems in that many technologies being used in the former are often not appropriate for use in the latter. Most often they are capital-intensive, designed to minimize labor use. Conditions in the poor countries are quite the opposite. Capital is scarce and labor is exceedingly abundant. Multinational corporations are thus handicapped because their technology evolves almost entirely in an environment where capital is abundant and labor scarce. One notable exception is Japan, where many industrial technologies appear much better suited to use in the densely populated, poor countries than are those from, say, the United States. On this note we turn to what is clearly one of the most promising developments in the restructuring of the world economy and the global diffusion of technology—the emergence of the Pacific Basin as an identifiable economic grouping.

Emergence of the Pacific Basin

The process of modernization, originating in England with the industrial revolution, spread slowly to other countries in the Atlantic community through what is sometimes described as the spin-off effect. Development outside Europe and the Atlantic community has, with few exceptions, been slow. Over the past few decades, however, a new community of nations situated on the periphery of the Pacific Basin has emerged as an important economic group.

The recent emergence of the Pacific Basin as a focus of economic activity has occurred so rapidly and so abruptly that its consequences have not yet been fully taken into account by world political leaders. Since the industrial revolution, the most rapidly growing economic region has always been part of the Atlantic community, either Western Europe or North America, but during the sixties this era came to an end as East Asia greatly outdistanced both.

At the heart of this remarkable economic performance was the 12 percent rate of economic growth attained by

Japan during the sixties. A rate of economic growth unmatched by any other country, it propelled Japan to the front ranks of the world's economic powers, surpassing traditional leaders—France, the United Kingdom and West Germany—and placing Japan third after the United States and the Soviet Union. With Japan's emergence as a global economic power, all three of the world's ranking economic powers—the United States, the Soviet Union and Japan—fronted on the Pacific, only one on the Atlantic.

The economic transformation of Japan into an economic superpower over the past two decades deserves examination. In 1950 Japan, still suffering from the devastation of World War II, was barely among the top ten economies of the world in terms of gross national product. Measured in terms of international trade, it compared less favorably, trailing even India. Several factors have contributed to its unprecedented rate of economic expansion since then. Perhaps the most important has been the high proportion of income saved and invested. Investing more than $1 of every $3 earned in new production capacity each year, Japan's rate of capital formation has been by far the highest in the world. Contributing to this high rate of investment have been exceedingly low military expenditures made possible in part by the U.S.-Japan defense treaty, and also the low birth rate of the past fifteen years, which has reduced investment needs in social services and created a very low dependency ratio.

Within the United States, the emergence of the Pacific Basin grouping was accompanied by a western shift in the economic center of gravity which both contributed to and was stimulated by the emergence of Japan and the statehood granted Hawaii and Alaska. Paralleling this was a westward shift in the political center of gravity as population moved westward and as California, now the most populous state, displaced New York, previously the leading state in national political representation.

The year 1968 was a turning point of sorts when Asia displaced Europe as the leading overseas market for U.S. farm products, a position Europe had held since the first exports from Jamestown. The United Kingdom, which historically had dominated Australia's trade with the rest of the world, was replaced by the United States as the principal supplier and by Japan as its principal market, thus weaving Australia into the Pacific community and weaning it from its traditional commonwealth status. These events should not be viewed as temporary phenomena, but rather as part of long-term sweeping trends which are reshaping the global economy.

Although there is no formal regional common market within either East Asia or the Pacific community, there are, nonetheless, extensive ties developing in both trade and investment. The largest bilateral trading relationship in the world today is that between the United States and Canada; that between the United States and Japan also ranks high and could eventually become the world's largest. In effect, an informal Pacific economic community is emerging based on the natural economic complementarities of the region. Also playing a major role are advances in ocean transport. Engineering advances permitting construction of much larger, more efficient vessels are shrinking the once formidable expanses of the Pacific. These engineering advances, many achieved by the Japanese, are reducing shipping costs by as much as two thirds through use of mammoth ocean-going freighters capable of carrying 100,000 tons of cargo and with a crew little larger than that required for the earlier generation of ships with scarcely a tenth of their capacity.

Japanese firms today are investing heavily in raw-material sources, especially in the sparsely populated areas of the Pacific periphery such as Siberia, Alaska, Western Canada, Australia and the outer islands of Indonesia. Both U.S. and Japanese capital and technology are combining with low-cost labor in manufacturing activities in South Korea, Taiwan and Hong Kong.

Transpacific economic ties are developing at a rapid pace in the internationalization of production, international trade, tourism and technology transfer. The bilateral flow of technology between the United States and Japan is the second largest in the world. Impressive though the rate of economic integration among the countries bordering the Pacific has been over the past decade, there are many indications that the rate at which new economic ties are forming among members of the Pacific community will continue at an equally rapid pace during the 1970s.

Emergence of the Pacific community signifies a major dispersal of global economic power. For the first time in modern history, a non-European country has become a leading economic power. Japan is today serving as a center of growth for those countries in East Asia which are geographically and culturally close in much the same manner that England did for neighboring West European countries in an earlier period. Indeed, the spin-off effects of the phenomenal Japanese economic growth are now evident in South Korea, Taiwan, Hong Kong, Indonesia, Thailand and Malaysia.

Beyond this, Japan is beginning to serve as a broker of technology between the advanced industrial countries of the West and poor countries throughout the world. Although Japan still has the largest technological balance-of-payments deficit of any country, it is now beginning to export technology in significant quantities. Technology imported from the West is often modified to accommodate smaller-scale firms and the lower, indigenous cost of labor, making it much more suitable for eventual export to the labor-surplus, poor countries. Japanese exports of technology climbed from $2 million in 1960 to $34 million in 1968, with more than half going to poor countries. In this respect Japan is unique among the industrial countries, since other industrial countries export technology primarily to one another. In 1964, for example, only 8 percent of all international technology transfers occurred between rich and poor countries. Japan's unique role is further illustrated by the respective relationships of the United States and Japan with Taiwan. Although American investments in Taiwan far exceed Japanese investments, Japan has entered into almost five times as many technology agreements as has the United States. Similar situations exist for several other Southeast Asian countries.

The Japanese government, concerned over the large deficit in its technological balance of payments, is encouraging an internal expansion of R&D activities with the hope of both reducing dependence on imported technology and expanding exports. To facilitate the latter, all income from exports of technology is exempted from income tax.

Swords to Plowshares

The emergence of the Pacific community during the sixties represents a geographical redistribution of global economic activity and power. As the seventies begin, a movement is under way to redistribute resources along functional lines, specifically from military to social purposes. In the United States, numerous groups are pressing hard in this direction, putting the military-industrial complex on the defensive.

As of 1970, global military expenditures totaled $204 billion, *exceeding the total income of the poorest half of mankind*. Of this total, the United States and the Soviet Union account for two thirds, and rich countries as a whole account for over 90 percent. While poor countries contribute an insignificant amount to the total, their expenditures are rising more rapidly. In many Middle Eastern and

Far Eastern countries, military expenditures constitute a larger percentage of GNP than in any rich country. For example, while the average expenditure in rich countries is about 4 percent of GNP, none spends over 10 percent of GNP for military purposes. However, while most of the poor countries spend between 1 and 2 percent, fourteen nations spend over 10 percent of GNP for military purposes, some as much as 25 percent.

These figures become even more lamentable when one compares them to the total national expenditures. In 1971 the United States defense budget consumed 37 percent of federal expenditures, but even more shocking is the case of Pakistan, where the military accounted for 49 percent of national spending in 1969. The present rate is undoubtedly even higher. Other examples of developing nations which spend a disproportionate percentage on the military include India (34), Brazil (31), Argentina (22) and Ghana (12), countries which are nominally at peace.

The arms race in many poor countries is often a matter of prestige as well as defense in regional conflicts. Brazil, for example, ordered two guided-missile destroyers in retaliation for an Argentinian purchase of an aircraft carrier, despite the fact that the prohibitive cost of operation has kept the first destroyer in port since delivery.

Much American aid is allocated specifically to the military. Although it may be argued that those nations which receive military aid would divert development funds and obtain arms from other sources if the United States were to discontinue its aid, there are several arguments against American funding. For one, the United States supplies nearly half of all major weapons going to Third World countries. By being the major supplier, it has often helped to escalate conflicts and arms build-ups through extended commitments. In several cases the U.S. supplies aid to both parties in a conflict, as is the case with Israel and Jordan or Pakistan and India. Furthermore, much of the equipment sent overseas is suitable for counterinsurgency, the morality of which becomes questionable when the recipient country is ruled by an oppressive regime.

Redistributing Resources

Thus far we have discussed various means of distributing income and wealth more equitably among countries, including the liberalization of international trade and investment, steps to facilitate the movement of technology across national boundaries, and the dispersal of economic activities associated with the emergence of the Pacific Basin—but this is not enough. The widening gap between rich countries and poor calls for a much greater effort. As a starter, the Pearson Commission Report recommended that all rich countries adopt a goal of transferring 1 percent of their GNP to the poor countries in the form of economic aid. Several countries, including the United Kingdom, Sweden, the Netherlands, West Germany, Canada and Japan, have agreed to this. Among the leading industrial countries, only the United States and the Soviet Union have failed to commit themselves firmly to this goal.

The World Bank, which commissioned the Pearson Commission Report, plans to double its lending in the poor countries over a five-year span. This, combined with the rising levels of economic assistance from the countries cited above, represents movement in the right direction, but again, it is not enough. For the time being at least, the United States appears to have abdicated its leadership which has loomed so large in the world since the Marshall Plan launching. Though the world's wealthiest country by far, it ranks twelfth in the share of GNP given as aid, allotting less than one half of 1 percent of its GNP to foreign assistance, including military assistance.

Other countries too could do much more. Japan, for

example, has a GNP which is now roughly the same size as that of the United States when it launched the massive Marshall Plan in 1947 to reconstruct Europe. The size of the Japanese economy, combined with its low level of military expenditures as a result of dependence on U.S. military protection, means it has a capability for doing much more. Indeed, given its close cultural and geographic ties to Asia, most of which is pathetically poor, it may face rising pressures to share its wealth with its less fortunate neighbors.

At present economic assistance to the poor countries depends heavily on annually appropriated funds by national legislatures, not always the most predictable of groups. One way of supplementing bilateral national contributions to economic assistance would be to tap new sources of funds now becoming available. One proposed scheme for doing this would channel some or all of the newly authorized Special Drawing Rights directly into poor countries where they could put them into circulation with purchases of goods and services in the world market. At present this windfall in resources is allocated among International Monetary Fund (IMF) member countries according to their voting rights, giving a handful of wealthy countries the lion's share and further reinforcing the existing concentration of wealth.

A second potential source of development funds could be part of the income accruing to an international oceanic regime which would license or perhaps even tax countries and firms wishing to exploit fish, mineral and energy resources in international waters. Again, this could be organized as an automatic transfer of funds to poor countries, isolating it from the sometimes tempestuous political crosswinds which affect bilateral political relationships.

Economic and Political Integration

These last three chapters have demonstrated that economic integration among nations is proceeding steadily on several fronts. It is no longer merely a matter of expanding international trade but of internationalizing production, and of increasing technological, monetary and energy interdependence. The internationalization of production introduces a massive and intimate form of integration which far overshadows the more traditional international trade. Resulting from the evolution of the multinational corporation, it is greatly increasing the economic interdependence among countries, particularly the more technologically advanced ones. National economies are being woven together by the increasingly complex web of corporate activities, much of it resulting from the concentration in various specialized phases of production within individual nation-states. The procurement of raw materials, manufacture of components, and intermediate and final assemblies for a given product can easily involve a score of countries.

Every major form of international economic integration is expanding far more rapidly than the global economy, growing at 4 percent per year in the early seventies. International trade is expanding at 8 percent yearly, while the internationalization of production and tourism are growing at 10 percent yearly. The share of global energy consumption crossing national borders is also rising. Monetary interdependence and cooperation today involve not only the maintenance of stability but the creation of new monetary reserves as well. What national leaders must recognize is that this growing economic interdependence and integration has far-reaching political implications.

As living levels rise, consumer needs become more diverse, exceeding the capacity of any national economy to supply. Gains in prosperity in much of the world over the past generation can be attributed in large measure to the emergence of an international economic system. Economic activities in countries which lack internal reserves of minerals and petroleum would, if isolated from their sources of supply, come to a virtual halt.

As economic integration among nations proceeds, it eventually begins to make war both more costly and less probable. Where integration has proceeded furthest, the prospects of war have diminished most. The United States and Canada do not guard their common borders. No one any longer gives serious thought to France and Germany going to war again, though they did so repeatedly for generations.

Continually advancing technology has also seriously undermined the traditional rationale for war. Throughout most of history when technology changed little, if any, from one generation to another, and levels of productivity were low and essentially fixed, the only way for a group to raise its living standard measurably was by suppressing another, as through slavery in ancient Greece or through colonialism as practiced by the European colonial powers. With steady technological advance, it becomes much easier to improve living standards by investing in research and development activities and in new production capacity than in military conquest. The net effect of this change, though not always fully appreciated, is also to reduce the prospect of international conflict among the more advanced nation-states. Although much of the form of the earlier period of international power politics is being retained, its substance is diminishing rapidly.

If the multinational corporations continue to expand their activities as projected, they will contribute importantly to continuing economic integration and indirectly to a reduced prospect of conflict between the more thoroughly integrated countries. Like nation-states, they have a strong vested interest in a smoothly functioning international system. To the extent that economic integration continues to make war a less practical instrument of foreign policy, the prospects will improve for creating a socially and politically unified global community and for restructuring the global economy to eliminate poverty.

IV

Creating a Global Infrastructure

13

A GLOBAL COMMUNICATIONS SYSTEM

Communications are the essence of community. Without a global communications system there is no global community. Arthur Clark points out that the United States was truly united only with the advent of the railroad and the telegraph. So, too, a unified world is now a real possibility with the jet plane and the communications satellite. Today man is being challenged to use new technologies to create the global communications system required by an increasingly interwoven, interdependent world.

Man's capacity to communicate with other members of his species, evolving over hundreds of thousands of years, is marked by four distinct and revolutionary developments. The first was the evolution of spoken language, the origins of which are lost. The second was the emergence of written language several thousand years ago. The invention of printing late in the fifteenth century marked the beginning of the third communications revolution. The fourth, the electronics revolution, is now under way. Like each of those before it, it promises to influence profoundly man's political, economic and cultural evolution.

Forming a Global Communications System

The first step in the establishment of a global communications system was taken on April 6, 1965, with the successful launching over the Atlantic of "Early Bird," the world's first commercial communications satellite. With a capacity equivalent to 240 telephone circuits, Early Bird immediately increased transatlantic communications capacity by nearly 50 percent and made live transoceanic television possible for the first time. This increase was achieved with a communications satellite weighing 85 pounds, only slightly heavier than the baggage allowance on a first-class international air fare.

With the positioning of an INTELSAT III satellite over the Indian Ocean in mid-1969, the final link in a global communications system was in place. For the first time in history, given the necessary transmitting and receiving equipment, it was possible to communicate between any two points on earth via a single electronic system.

Prior to the launching of telecommunications satellites, intercontinental telecommunications services were provided by high-frequency radio and underwater cable. Arrangements for communicating across national boundaries were bilateral, between government agencies or commercial carriers. There were no multilateral or global agencies.

The institutional framework for establishing a global system began with the Communications Satellite Corporation (COMSAT), a unique, privately owned U.S. communications carrier company operating under a mandate from Congress. It was incorporated in early 1963 under provisions of the Communications Satellite Act of 1962, which enunciated a national policy "to establish in cooperation with other countries a commercial communications satellite system as part of an improved global communications network which will be responsive to public needs and national objectives, which will serve the communications needs of the United States and other countries, and which will contribute to world peace and understanding."

International Telecommunications Satellite Corporation (INTELSAT) was created by the international agreements which were opened for signature in Washington, D.C., in August 1964. At a conference held in Washington in May 1971, agreement was reached under which COMSAT would be gradually relieved of its managing responsibilities, transferring these to an internationally appointed director general of INTELSAT. The U.S. majority representation on the board of governors would end, constituting at most 40 percent of the board in the future. In addition, an assembly was to be established in which each of the seventy-nine members would have an equal voice. This group would then make recommendations to the board of governors but would have no decision-making power.

In the short period since INTELSAT was established, significant progress has already been achieved. The economic flexibility and versatility of the global communications satellite system is radically improving communications among a large number of the world's countries. At present INTELSAT's membership of seventy-nine countries collectively accounts for 95 percent of the world's international telecommunications traffic.

Hardware in the INTELSAT system consists of the space segment and the ground segment. The space segment consists of the five satellites now in synchronous orbit, two of them over the Atlantic, one over the Indian Ocean, and two over the Pacific. The ground segment consists of ground stations and related transmission and receiving equipment. As of 1970, some twenty-five of the member countries were a functioning part of the system. Another ten, including Kenya, India, Korea, Nigeria, Senegal, Cameroon and Ethiopia, are expected to have their earth stations ready in 1971.

The communications capability of telecommunications satellites is enormous, and will increase with each generation. Early Bird, the INTELSAT I satellite, which increased transatlantic cable communications capacity by 50 percent, had 240 telephone circuits and could carry only one TV signal. INTELSAT IV has expanded the capacity to approximately 9,000 voice circuits and 12 TV signals, while INTELSAT V, if and when it is launched, is expected to carry some 20,000 voice circuits.

Telecommunications satellites greatly reduce the cost of long-distance communication. One reason for this is the great reduction in the material resources required. A communications satellite weighing less than 500 pounds can replace 150,000 tons of transoceanic cables. Moreover they are powered by solar energy. Solar cells in the shell of the satellite convert solar energy into electrical power, enabling the satellite to both receive and transmit signals. Since telecommunications satellites have been in service, the cost of a three-minute station-to-station, off-hours telephone call from London to New York has been reduced from $9 to $5.40. The cost of transmitting color TV programs across the Atlantic has fallen by 81 percent in two years. The prospect is for further reductions in cost as even more efficient equipment goes into operation. In addition to conveying large volumes of information more cheaply, communications satellites are also more reliable.

The development of computers, with their vast capacity for storing information and their linkage to telephone networks, often via telecommunications satellites, is opening up a vast new front in the communications revolution. Richard Barber describes this as follows: "By 1975 over

half and perhaps 75 percent of all computers in the United
States will be linked by a communications facility. Thousands of these computers will be internationally connected
either through underseas cables or communications satellites. As an intensely practical matter this means that just
about all of the information stored in computers will be
retrievable almost anywhere by almost anyone with access
to a computer terminal. This will necessitate the creation
of computer information utilities that will serve either as
large data banks or as 'brokers' between information
sources." John Diebold elaborates further: "The areas of
computer-based and communications-based capabilities
will be brought into existence by, and will create the demand for, major new industries. The first major entre-
preneurial opportunity is the industry which supplies the
system and the equipment. This is already a several billion
dollar industry. The second industry is the about-to-bloom
data utility industry, analogous to the electric utility industry. A large central processor handles information at a
very low unit cost, just as a large generator produces electricity for many customers at a low unit cost." The General
Electric Company, for example, is at present expanding a
global data-information network whereby individual of-
ficers will have a direct telephone tie-in to a central computer on a time-sharing basis. Through such a network,
offices around the world will have immediate and simul-
taneous access to any information deposited in the central
"super computer."

It remains to be seen what the eventual impact on global
society will be of the electronic revolution. We do know
that the printing press had a revolutionary impact on society, giving man access to a much broader range of both
ancient learning and contemporary scientific thinking. The
invention of printing immeasurably expanded the capacity
for accumulating knowledge and for transmitting it from

generation to generation. The size of the library rather than the capacity of the human mind has become the limiting factor. Once printed material became widely available, it also altered the relationship between generations, greatly reducing the dependence of youth on their elders.

The electronic revolution, which is now in full flower, is further transforming the world in which we live. Over time it will no doubt eliminate differences among societies in much the same way as advances in communications and transportation have greatly reduced rural-urban and regional differences in the United States. It also means that in the modern world, information is becoming a central economic resource, much as coal was in the early industrial era.

The electronic communications revolution affects not only the storage and transmission of information, but it impinges upon traditional concepts of national sovereignty as well. International mail can be blocked or censored, but obstructing the flow of information crossing national boundaries by radio requires costly and sophisticated jamming equipment. Radio and TV signals from communications satellites may soon be captured by individual communities without passing through national relay networks. At this point national boundaries begin to lose their significance.

Not everyone feels comfortable with the new communications technologies and the emerging global system of electronic communications. For many, this global system represents a potential means of political influence and control, especially given the new possibility of broadcasting TV signals directly from a satellite to home receivers. It represents a particular threat to receiving countries if they are not permitted to participate in the programing. Overcoming this concern requires, at a minimum, the internationalization of communications and broadcasting entities operating internationally, as has recently occurred with

INTELSAT. But even this may not suffice for those countries zealously guarding their sovereignty, whether it be against another country or a supranational institution.

World Community and Communications

Advancing communications technology expands the optimum size of both economic and political organization. In the words of Norman Cousins: "The significance of communications has seldom been more pithily expressed than in Aristotle's comment that the size of a political unit is determined by the range of a single man's voice. He was thinking of the Greek world of course where all the citizens of a city state such as Athens could assemble in one place and attend to their common affairs.

"According to this yardstick the entire world today is a potential single community. There is no part of the globe that is not within range of a single man's voice. Hence the ultimate significance of the marriage of electronics to words is that it sets a stage for government on a world scale. The questions that now have to be asked are—what kinds of forces will shape it, what will be the philosophy behind it, will it ennoble or diminish the individual?"

The emergence of a global communications system is in and of itself a notable achievement in international relations. It required a willingness on the part of the United States, the country possessing the technology to make it available to other countries. Indeed, the legislation establishing COMSAT instructed it to make new technology available "to all countries of the world without discrimination." Beyond this, a high level of cooperation was required among scores of countries in order to bring the INTELSAT system into existence.

Almost as significant as the emergence of a global system is the rate of growth in its use. International communications traffic is now increasing at a phenomenal 20 percent yearly, more than *doubling every four years.* Television transmission via the satellite system during the first six months of 1970 totaled 1,322 hours of transmission and reception time, double the volume for the same period the preceding year. Some of this spectacular increase was spurred by such events as the World Cup Soccer matches in Mexico and the perilous return of the Apollo 13 astronauts.

The Apollo 11 mission, culminating in man's first step on the moon, was seen live by several hundred million viewers, making it the most widely shared event in human history. Other events, such as the 1972 Olympic games held in Munich, Germany, the investiture of the Prince of Wales, and the American political conventions, have been televised globally. Indeed, the number of viewers of the American political conventions outside the United States exceeded those within.

Man is now creating a central nervous system for the entire world, linking its diverse and distant parts directly to one another. The INTELSAT system makes possible instantaneous contact between any two points on earth. Heretofore many countries, particularly poorer ones, had only indirect means of communicating with one another. For example, before Chile and Argentina leased satellite circuits, there was virtually no direct communication between the two countries, even though they have a thousand-mile common boundary and their capital cities are less than an hour apart by jet. The Andes were simply an insuperable barrier to communications. Chile and Argentina now lease between them a total of 56 full-time INTELSAT circuits. With this new technique for communicating, contact between the two neighboring countries is much more frequent.

When visiting Latin America in 1968, President Lyndon Johnson pinpointed the implications of new satellite communications technologies for the poor countries. "We support the development of a global system of communications satellites to make modern communications available to all nations. A telephone call from Rangoon to Djakarta must still go through Tokyo; a call from Dakar, Senegal to Lagos, Nigeria is routed through Paris and London. During the recent Punta del Este Conference I discovered that it usually costs Latin American journalists more than their American colleagues to phone in their stories because most of their calls had to be routed through New York." This archaic and inefficient system of communication is no longer necessary. New communications capabilities are bringing even the poor countries close to one another, facilitating both economic integration and political cooperation. The communications satellite does not recognize geographic boundaries, is not dependent on a cable and owes no allegiance to a particular political philosophy; it is truly a product of the technetronic era.

Improvement in telephonic communications among countries brings with it a closeness which will become evident as more and more people begin to change their thinking, consciously or otherwise, about their proximity to one another. Increased communications contact does not ensure peace and international political stability, but to be potentially in touch with everyone at least makes conflict more uncomfortable. Once all men are equidistant from each other in terms of communications time, national boundaries will become even less meaningful. This will be so on both the personal and business levels. Countries are becoming increasingly dependent on one another for information in diverse areas ranging from economics to meteorology.

The instant communication which now exists is resulting in a much more intensive involvement of people in global affairs. This is true not only in terms of exposure of the individual to news events but also in terms of the increasing number and variety of events which are external to a given country, and which, because of growing interdependence among nations, affect the individual. Zbigniew Brzezinski describes this well: "Television has joined newspapers in expanding the immediate horizons of the viewer or reader to the point where local increasingly means national, and global affairs compete for attention on an unprecedented scale. Physical and moral immunity to 'foreign' events cannot be very effectively maintained under circumstances in which there are both a growing intellectual awareness of global interdependence and the electronic intrusion of global events into the home."

In an age when the atrocities of war penetrate into one's living room, attitudes toward war are certain to be affected. This must in part account for the revulsion shown by growing numbers toward the conflict in Vietnam. For the first time in history we are beginning to witness the formation of global public opinion on a wide range of issues. Governments cannot remain indifferent to it. As 1970 was drawing to a close, three distinct events dramatically illustrated this trend. The Soviet Union, faced with critical public opinion world-wide, chose to reverse the death sentences of several Soviet Jews associated with an attempted hijacking of an Aeroflot plane. At about the same time, the Franco regime in Spain commuted life sentences for a small group of Basque terrorists from death to life imprisonment. The indictment of Angela Davis in the United States came under fire from abroad, including a group of Soviet intellectuals. The U.S. government felt obligated to respond to this criticism and did so by inviting the Soviet critics to this country to witness the trial proceedings. Interestingly, none of these three governments has been noted for responsiveness to global public opinion in the past.

The communications revolution is bringing rich and poor into direct contact with one another. This has two interesting consequences. On the one hand it means that poor countries may have more ready access to information and technology than in the past. On the other hand it also means that penetration of remote regions by the transistor and TV tube will create new aspirations among the poor, generating demands to alleviate or eliminate hunger, poverty and discrimination. Exposure to extreme affluence is certain to raise the "dissatisfaction index" among the world's poor. As Henry Cassirer of UNESCO points out: "In the space age, communications media break through the traditional fragmentation of society and vividly bring to light outdated and frustrating limitations. Human rights and social aspirations, knowledge and information can no longer remain the monopoly of a privileged few. Broadcast signals may cross unhampered the artificial boundaries of sovereign nations underlining their artificiality. A stream of communications breaks down both the vertical stratification of society and the horizontal barriers of nationalism."

English: A Global Language?

Throughout most of history there has been little need for a global language, since interpersonal contacts, exchanges of information and communications seldom crossed linguistic lines. But this is not the case today, and in the years to come the need for a common global language will become even more acute as international travel and scientific, business, and academic relations of all kinds take on an ever broader scope. Society in rapid transformation is in need of communications channels which permit a continuing dialogue; the more rapid the transformation, the greater the need. Now that we have the hardware for a global communications network, we find that we lack the software—a common language.

Mario Pei, writing in *Saturday Review*, summarizes historical efforts to create a world-wide language: "Since the seventeenth century about 1,000 proposals of various kinds for a world language have been advanced. These include the worldwide use of an existing national language such as English or French and the international adoption of constructed languages such as Esperanto and Interlingua. Most of these have fallen by the wayside, but many still persist, notably the extension of an existing widespread language such as English, French, or Russian into a world tongue." Esperanto, most popular and widely known of the constructed languages, has been in existence since the 1880s when its creator, Dr. Lazarus Zamenhof, offered it to the world in the hope that it might reduce national antagonisms and promote the brotherhood of man.

Although there is a widely felt need for a global language, there is also much resistance to the adoption of any particular national language for this purpose, in part because of national rivalries. Margaret Mead thinks that a world tongue should not be a natural living language of a major power capable of threatening other states, since it would give them an even greater advantage. Using any of the half-dozen languages now widely spoken would divide the world into two classes of citizens: those for whom the language was the mother tongue and those for whom it was a second language. But, she feels, one shared second language used on a world-wide basis would tend to equalize the quality of communications and at the same time protect the local diversity of other languages. Only by keeping the world language as a second language is it possible to protect and ensure the diversity of thought which accompanies the use of different mother tongues. To this political argument by Miss Mead could be added a fundamental one, namely, that written English, not being a phonetic language, is difficult to learn.

Miss Mead's rationale, opposing the use of English, is not without merit. The one critical factor it does not take into account is the variation in time required to attain a functioning global language, depending upon whether a globally established natural language such as English is selected or some other lesser-known or constructed one such as Esperanto. If, as this book argues, our future well-being is contingent upon the achievement of a unified global community, then the great variation in time required may well become a decisive factor, arguing strongly for an established language such as English. But the issue may not be a live one today, given the predominance and momentum already achieved by English, whose contemporary predominance is due to two important factors: the central role of the British Isles in the British Commonwealth over a period of centuries and the more recent central role of the United States in world affairs.

There now exists an impressive array of arguments favoring the use of English as a global lingua franca. Perhaps most important, it is now *the* official language in 28 countries and *an* official language in 16 more, making 44 of the world's 160 countries entirely or partly English-speaking. It also utilizes the Roman script, as do Spanish, French, Turkish, Indonesian and many other languages.

Prior to World War II, French was the principal language of diplomacy, but it has since been displaced by English. Nowhere is this better demonstrated than in the United Nations, where 80 of the 126 country delegations currently receive their basic working documents in English. Another 15 delegations request some copies in English in addition to those received in one of the other official languages: French, Spanish, Russian or Chinese. All but a dozen or so of the permanent representatives in New York speak at least rudimentary English. The emergence of a widely used language within the United Nations greatly facilitates conduct of the world's affairs.

At the same time there is resistance to English in many poor countries where nationalists view it as the language of imperialism. Kenya and India are abandoning English as the official language and adopting Swahili and Hindi, respectively, but this is in fact little more than political window dressing in an attempt to capitalize on strong nationalistic feelings. English is the language of government and university instruction in both countries. In Zambia, a country with more than forty tribal languages and dialects, the government decided in 1965 to adopt English as the medium of instruction in the primary schools. In Nigeria, Africa's largest country with its more than 50 million people of diversified ethnic backgrounds, English is now the language of instruction in the schools. Here, and in many other countries which are linguistically diverse, it remains the only language of communication at the national level.

English is unquestionably and increasingly the language of science throughout the world. Half of the scientific literature published today is in English. With each passing year the gap between the size of the English scientific vocabulary and that of other languages widens. Advancing technology requires the continual, almost daily, coining of new terms, and in most fields this occurs first in English. The National Aeronautics and Space Administration, for example, has compiled a glossary of some 15,000 technical terms used in its day-to-day operations. Needless to say, few of these terms exist in Arabic, Hindi or Spanish.

Once a language is as well started toward becoming a global language as English now is, the trend can become self-perpetuating. Scientists wish to be read as widely as possible and can most easily achieve this goal by publishing in English. Every increase in the use of English for scientific articles and books puts more pressure on non-English-speaking scientists to learn to read and write in English.

With each passing year, English becomes increasingly the language of education. The "world library" is an English library. A person born Turkish or Thai who is literate only in his mother tongue does not have access to the library, since the resources required to translate the flood of material being published in English do not exist. These are the dimensions of our dilemma—how to communicate across the linguistic frontiers, how to give everyone access to the library.

The majority of the world's college and university graduates, the future political, corporate and academic leaders, are English-speaking. Then, too, English is receiving much attention in the Soviet Union, Japan and other non-Western countries. Linguist Dr. Hood Roberts estimates that there are 50 million students of English in the Soviet Union and 66,000 teachers of English in Japan. In order to open a window on the world, the linguistically isolated Japanese have been pursuing the mastery of English with great intensity. Viewing English primarily as a means of obtaining access to the "world library," they have emphasized reading proficiency, often neglecting its verbal mastery.

In Europe the study of English is spreading rapidly. English is the principal foreign language taught in French and German schools. Seventy-five percent of the secondary-school students in Austria study English. In Sweden it is compulsory from the fourth to the seventh grades. Thus we find that English is becoming the lingua franca of Western Europe, despite French efforts to make their language the official working language of the enlarged community.

In Latin America, English has become the second language in virtually every country within the region. But more important than its present status is the rising interest in and use of the language throughout the region. Technical publications and news magazines in English are growing steadily in popularity.

English is today the language of international business, the principal operating language of the great majority of multinational corporations, including many not based in English-speaking countries. For example, the Swedish-based ball-bearing corporation, SKF, uses English as its principal operational language. English is the language of international representatives of German and Japanese based multinational corporations, as well as those based in North America and Great Britain. As multinational corporations continue to increase in number and size, the trend toward the use of English in international business will be further reinforced.

Even while recognizing that English is well on its way to becoming a universal language, English-speaking people must not disregard other languages. If we who speak English as our first language profess an interest in other cultures, we too must make an effort to cross the language barrier, since language reveals much of the underlying values, attitudes and thought patterns of a people. Only by learning a language other than one's mother tongue can the cultural basis of the language barrier be fully appreciated.

Communications-Education Interface

The communications media have an enormous capacity to shape public opinion, to mobilize people and resources and to transform societies, a capacity far greater today than in the past. And it will be even greater in the future than at present. Given the growing influence of the communications media in modern society, their basic functions require reassessing. The circumstances in which we find ourselves indicate that the media must become an essential, central part of late-twentieth-century society, with responsibilities in education from preschool children to literate adults, from illiterate farmers in traditional societies to housewives in suburbia. The media can help the disadvantaged everywhere to improve their health, plan their families, prepare themselves for employment or to raise their children so that they can compete with those from more affluent societies and homes on a more equal footing. Awareness of the environmental crisis by adult Americans is largely the product of efforts by the communications media, since few Americans have been formally educated in ecological matters. Now that people are aware of the environmental crisis, the media must focus on how we can accommodate ourselves to a finite system by altering our individual behavior in such matters as childbearing, consumption habits and waste disposal. The media can also help overcome the disaffection of those whose cooperation is essential to the formation of a unified global society.

Traditionally, society has relied heavily on the formal-education system—the teacher with thirty children in a classroom—to prepare people for change. But the world in which today's youth will live out their lives is a dynamic, rapidly changing one. Never before has a generation of young people been confronted with a world in which population has projected to double in little more than a generation. Only recently has the division among nations of the earth's finite resources of marine protein, fresh water and energy fuels become a serious international issue. Traditional concepts of social justice and territorial discrimination must be modified to accommodate the new circumstances in which we find ourselves. These are urgent issues with which people must quickly become familiar, for they must be resolved in years rather than decades. This means the media must play a central education role, augmenting that of the traditional education system.

One segment of the communications media whose social and political importance is not adequately appreciated is the book-publishing industry. Public awareness of several critical issues has been raised measurably by popularly written books. Rachel Carson's *Silent Spring* triggered public concern over the adverse environmental effect of agricultural chemicals. The consumer movement in the United States was given a great boost by Ralph Nader's book *Unsafe at Any Speed*, attacking the automobile industry for its indifference to automobile safety. Jean-Jacques Servan-Schreiber's best seller, *The American Challenge*, dramatically highlighted the expanding role of American-based multinational corporations in Europe. British economist Ezra Mishan's *Costs of Economic Growth* drew attention to the negative effects of economic growth on the quality of life. Such books, which identify issues and the need for corrective political action, not only have a great impact in and of themselves if they are widely read, but they also provide material for journalists and radio and TV news commentators and programers. The relevance of the issues and the implied need for reform identified in each of the above four books—two written in the United States, one in the United Kingdom and one in France—extends far beyond the countries in which the books were written. As a result, each has been widely distributed, read and discussed internationally.

With the advent of INTELSAT, the world has an electronic global communications system which is internationally owned and controlled. In terms of hardware, it is superb. What is now needed is an institution capable of imaginative programing to provide TV programs for use in this system. At present, transnational TV broadcasting is centered on international news events such as moon landings or championship boxing bouts. International radio broadcasting is almost exclusively national in origin—Radio Cairo, Radio Moscow, BBC and Voice of America—and often heavily weighted with political propaganda. What is desperately needed is international programing which is less politically and more socially oriented, dealing with the global problems outlined in earlier chapters, such as our deteriorating environment, massive unplanned urbanization, hunger and the threat of uncontrolled population growth. Such programing could expand the awareness and understanding of these problems and eventually contribute to their solutions. If international TV programing is limited to the rebroadcasting of programs primarily of U.S. origin—Westerns, soap operas and talk shows—then it will fail to realize the potential of a remarkable new technology.

Since world society is slowly becoming a reality in technological and economic terms, furthering a sense of world citizenship should be one of the principal objectives of the communications media. With individual well-being and prospects for survival increasingly linked to the sum of our individual behavior, the media have a responsibility for informing everyone of this increasing interdependence on our shrinking planet. The media must educate the rich in the North to what life for the poor is like if the rich are to respond humanely to their plight. A dialogue of global dimensions must be initiated, encouraged and stimulated as to our mutual plight if a survival ethic and consequent new life style are to emerge.

14

A GLOBAL TRANSPORT SYSTEM

Advances in transportation technology along with those in communications are leading to global economic and social integration. Distance is losing much of its meaning. In the words of airline executive Najeeb Halaby, "Psychologically this new dominion over distance could lead toward a change in attitude about space and time. If there is less 'here' and 'there,' less 'we' versus 'they,' men will tend to find that 'we are all here,' interrelated, interdependent, and thereby compelled to cooperate to survive."

One of the most remarkable characteristics of the contemporary world is the mobility which modern man has achieved. Tens of millions of human beings today routinely travel at speeds only slightly slower than sound. A traveler catching an early-morning plane at sunrise in New Delhi can fly westward with the sun, arriving in New York on the far side of the globe before nightfall of the same day. Modern transport technology is converting oceans into lakes. American astronauts embark on trips to the moon with less trepidation than that experienced by Columbus and his small band of sailors embarking on their voyages to the New World.

The world is being woven together today with an incredibly complex web of transportation links. Advances in transport technology are affecting not merely man's mobility or the volume of goods which can be transported intercontinentally but the very organization of society itself. As people cross national borders more and more frequently, the significance of these artificial divisions in human society diminishes.

Transport and Economic Integration

Crucial to the gradual emergence of an integrated global economic system has been the steady decline in transportation costs over the past few decades. Distance is no longer the isolating factor it once was. With each advance in transportation technology, real costs per ton of freight and per passenger mile have declined, permitting vast increases in both freight and passenger volume.

Closely associated with, and indeed partly responsible for, the declining transportation costs is the increasing size of transport vehicles, particularly ships, trucks and planes. The Stanford Research Institute reports that "the revolution in ocean transportation is largely a consequence of the introduction of larger ships. Some tankers are hauling over 300,000 tons, and some dry-bulk carriers exceed 150,000 tons. Both vessel construction costs and operating costs per ton decrease with scale. Today ships carry as much as 10,000 tons of cargo per individual crewman. The standard liberty ship of the fifties carried a crew of 40 to 50 men for a 10,000 ton cargo." The early commercial airliners of the twenties were limited to a handful of passengers, but the jumbo jets of the seventies routinely carry 300 or more passengers.

Vast quantities of petroleum, grain, forest products and mineral ores now cross national boundaries. Each year 60 million tons of grain leave the North American breadbasket destined for more than a hundred countries throughout the world. Jumbo-jet freighters can now airlift a hundred tons of cargo several thousand miles at a speed of 600 miles per hour. By 1975 industrial complexes in northern Italy are scheduled to operate with natural gas piped from the distant Ural gas fields in the Soviet Union.

Advances in ocean transportation are affecting the global pattern of economic activity. Competitive positions of more efficient producers are strengthened by gains in transport efficiency. And it is no longer necessary for major industrial centers to be limited to sites where both coal and iron are located. Japan, which has exploited the new efficiency in ocean transportation as fully as any country in becoming a major industrial power, is a dramatic example of this. Though the lack of rich indigenous deposits of iron ore and coking coal forces Japan to import 88 and 64 percent of requirements, respectively, from sources an average of 5,500 miles away, it is now the world's third-ranking steel producer. The reduction in transport costs for Peruvian iron ore from $25 per ton in 1956 to $12 in 1969 illustrates the gains in transport efficiency which made this possible.

These technological advances are altering the concepts of who possesses raw materials, of who are the "have" and "have-not" nations in this respect. In political terms the Australians have vast reserves of iron ore in the northern part of the country. But in economic terms this ore belongs to Japan, since it is cheaper to haul it to Japan, using large new ore ships and Japanese deep-water ports, than to move the ore to steel-producing centers in southeastern Australia.

It is much cheaper to move many commodities between some coastal points in Brazil and New York than to other points in Brazil, especially if the latter involves inland transportation. West Virginia coal moving through Norfolk, Virginia, and to Japan by water is landed there at a cost comparable to that paid by some steel mills in neighboring Pennsylvania.

The pronounced reduction in ocean-transport costs and the introduction of jet air travel has dramatically shrunk the Pacific Ocean during the past fifteen years. Japan, for example, is geographically off the coast of Asia, but given its vast commerce with the United States and Canada, economically it is off the coast of North America.

One of the most rapidly expanding aspects of transportation in the seventies will be the air-cargo business, spurred by introduction of the jumbo-sized cargo jets and the streamlining of freight-handling facilities at air terminals throughout the world. Reduced freight costs mean that the huge new air freighters can routinely transport fresh Mexican and California produce, such as lettuce and strawberries, to major European cities via polar routes. U.S.-based electronics firms are air-freighting intricate electronics components to Indonesia, where unemployment is widespread and labor costs are low, for subassembly and return to the United States for final assembly and marketing. The list of items which can economically be shipped by air has lengthened immeasurably with introduction of the new technologies. Current projections indicate a global growth in air freight of *500 percent* during the seventies, much of it international.

The expanding international network of oil and gas pipelines receives little attention because pipelines are often underground and therefore much less conspicuous than other forms of transport. And yet this rapidly growing transport subsector provides the foundation for an exceedingly intimate form of international economic integration, linking oil and gas fields with consuming areas either directly or indirectly through coastal ports.

By the mid-seventies, a network of oil and gas pipelines will span the Eurasian land mass, extending from the North Sea to the Sea of Japan. These pipelines, totalling tens of thousands of miles and constituting a rather permanent linkage between suppliers and consumers, are scheduled to move enormous tonnages of petroleum plus vast quantities of natural gas each year.

The existing network of oil and gas pipelines in Western Europe is now being steadily expanded as import needs rise and as a result of natural gas discoveries in the Netherlands and in the North Sea. A new North–South pipeline, connecting the Rhône Valley in France with the Mediterranean and both North African and Middle Eastern oil is under construction. A pipeline from Trieste to Vienna gives Austria easy access to Middle East oil. Pipelines are thus being extended into the heart of Western Europe from several directions.

Construction is under way on two huge pipelines to carry Siberian oil to foreign consuming centers. The pipeline to the East, measuring 3,720 miles, will carry oil from the Soviet Union's huge Samatlor oil field in Western Siberia to Japan, the world's leading importer of oil. A pipeline to the West, which will link the same Soviet oilfield with East and West European industrial countries, will be 2,850 miles long. Still another pipeline will link the subarctic Medvezhye gas fields of the Soviet Union with industrial centers in West Germany, Italy and France. While plans to pipe Soviet oil and gas into Western Europe are progressing, Poland, Czechoslovakia and Hungary are considering with Yugoslavia the possibility of a large joint pipeline linking them with the Yugoslav port of Rijeka and with Middle Eastern oil.

In the Western Hemisphere new pipelines are being

constructed in both North and South America to link newly discovered oil and gas fields directly with areas of consumption or with transoceanic tanker routes. The proposed trans-Alaska petroleum pipeline, which will connect the rich reserves of Alaska's north slope with Pacific warm-water ports, represents a major new link in the global system. In addition, a Canadian firm proposes to build a pipeline to carry natural gas from Alaska across the Yukon, the Northwest territories and Alberta, connecting with trunk lines in the northcentral United States. A pipeline built by Gulf Oil across the Andes links Ecuador's newly discovered oil field on the eastern slopes of the Andes with the Pacific.

Advanced plans exist for a trans-Egyptian pipeline to link the Red Sea to the Mediterranean. This will augment existing pipelines which already connect Middle Eastern oil fields with the Mediterranean. One of these, the Trans-Arabian Pipeline (Tapline), carries Saudi Arabian oil across Jordan and Syria to a Lebanese seaside terminal on the Mediterranean. A line recently constructed by Israel carries oil from Elath on the Gulf of Aqaba to Ashkelon on the Israeli Mediterranean coast. Still another Middle Eastern pipeline carries Iraqi oil across Syria to the Mediterranean coast.

Pipeline construction projects are among the largest construction projects under way in the world today. The trans-Egyptian pipeline, for example, represents the largest construction effort in Egypt since the Aswan Dam. Soviet pipeline projects overshadow other construction projects in the current Five-Year Plan. The scale of financial and material resources required to construct many pipelines is such that several countries, several corporations, or some combination of the two, most often pool resources. For example, the trans-Egyptian pipeline is being financed by a consortium of eight European countries, two Arab countries and two American-based oil companies. Oil carried by it will come from several oil fields and will be utilized by several countries. Egypt, which initiated the project, expects to earn $180 million in transit fees each year once the pipeline reaches full capacity. Construction of the Soviet pipeline in the East is made possible by both Soviet and Japanese participation. Japanese steel firms will supply 1.7 million tons of steel pipe, the Japanese government will provide financing for the pipe and the Soviet Union will provide the construction crews. Not only are many of these undertakings transnational, but they involve both countries and corporations directly, including the larger steel producers in Europe and Japan, the larger international petroleum companies based in Europe and North America, and Western construction firms.

Transport and Social Integration

As incomes rise and transport costs decline, the share of humanity which can travel abroad rises. Even labor is becoming internationally mobile. The cost of travel from Ankara to Frankfurt relative to industrial wages in West Germany is such that it is feasible for 250,000 Turks to work in West Germany and return home for vacations and holidays. Not only do more people travel, but they do so for a variety of reasons, often traveling for pleasure and education as well as for business.

Man's increased mobility is clearly affecting his life style —where he lives, where he works and how he uses his leisure time. A high degree of mobility, particularly when it permits the crossing of national borders, is becoming routine and has profound psychological consequences, with a cosmopolitan world view often replacing a provincial one.

Technetronic man frequently travels hundreds and even thousands of miles in a given day. His routine commuting distance from home to office is not very different from that of industrial man, but the nature of his activities frequently takes him far from home and office. Located in Washington, he may commute to New York for an occasional business dinner and return the same evening on the hourly air shuttle. Working in New York, he may attend monthly staff meetings of a subsidiary headquartered in Brussels. In extreme situations, he may even hold teaching posts in Europe and the United States simultaneously, splitting each week between the two locations.

Transatlantic air travel continues to grow by leaps and bounds, drawing Europe and North America closer together. Passenger crossings by air alone now average 20,000 daily. Despite this growth in transatlantic travel, the most rapid growth in overseas visitors to the United States is coming from Asia. Indeed, in 1971 Japan was the principal source of overseas visitors, displacing Britain, the traditional leader. Travelers from abroad are no longer coming solely from high-income groups but from all walks of life, aided by special charter fares.

The combination of urbanization and advancing transport technology is profoundly altering the pattern of human mobility. Throughout most of recorded history, travel has been largely rural-urban in orientation. Rural people occasionally traveled to the nearest urban center but seldom elsewhere. As global society urbanizes, the importance of the rapidly evolving global transport system increases. Cities become the focal point of social activity, the nodes in the global system. Travel among the world's cities becomes relatively much more important, and that between rural and urban areas much less so. Intercity transport is more and more transnational. Indeed, airline tickets often do not bear the country of destination or the origin, only the respective cities. One goes to Athens, not to Greece, to Bangkok, not to Thailand, to London, not to England. In the technetronic era, both ocean shipping and air transport are geared to connecting urban centers. As air freight and travel increase at an explosive rate during the seventies with the advent of the jumbo jets, the importance of urban centers will be emphasized even further.

Growth in Tourism

One form of social integration facilitated by the growing ease with which one can travel among countries is international tourism, a form of integration made special by its vast size. Indeed, it has now emerged as one of the most rapidly growing areas within the expanding service component of the world economy. In 1969, 106 million tourists from more than a hundred countries traveled abroad, leaving behind a whopping $20.5 billion, a sum approaching the combined gross national products of Colombia, Nigeria and Thailand.

The importance of this "industry without smokestacks" was recognized in the early fall of 1970 by an extraordinary assembly of the International Union of Official Travel Organizations (IUOTO), a group including among its membership 105 of the world's leading tourist countries. This assembly was convened for the specific purpose of transforming the Union, a collection of government tourist offices, into a new supranational institution, the World Tourist Organization. Its purpose was to "lift the growth scale of world tourism to an entirely new dimension of development." Conversion of the Union into an organization officially affiliated with the United Nations would give it access to large sources of funds for developing the infrastructure needed to facilitate a massive expansion of tourism in the poor countries.

Over the past several years the barriers to the international movement of people, both political and economic, have been steadily reduced. Governments have been simplifying procedures for obtaining passports and visas, and for clearing customs in many countries. The economics of travel are also becoming much more favorable as incomes rise and the efficiency of transportation increases. The share of a person's annual income required for a transatlantic trip has declined markedly over the past decade as incomes have risen steadily on both sides of the Atlantic and as air fares have either remained steady or declined. In addition, the expanding availability of group charter flights and of credit for travel have given international travel an added boost.

In 1969, 4.6 million Americans traveled abroad, spending $5.4 billion, up 20 percent from 1968. For many poor countries, tourism is a principal source of foreign exchange earnings. Countries along the northern shore of the Mediterranean, particularly Spain and Greece, obtain a large share of their foreign exchange through tourism. In Israel, which now receives nearly half a million visitors yearly, tourism is the principal source of foreign exchange. Iceland today earns 10 percent of its foreign exchange from tourism. If the astronomic rate of increase in tourists visiting Iceland continues, government officials predict that within a few years the number of tourists will equal the country's population. The number of tourists visiting Spain is expected to exceed its population by 1975.

The potential of tourism as a source of foreign exchange is indicated in the vigorous attempts by the centrally planned economies to attract tourists. Strong incentives are provided for tourists to visit East European countries and the Soviet Union, including exceedingly favorable currency exchange rates for any hard currencies such as the dollar or the deutsche mark.

Hungary is literally reforming its economy in its campaign for the tourist dollar, with firms soliciting and servicing tourists competing with one another. If these firms make a profit the manager gets a salary increase and employees get a profit-sharing bonus. If the firm does not make a profit they get neither, and may even be faced with dismissal.

Tourist facilities are becoming recognized as a profitable area of investment by private financiers, multinational corporations and international lending institutions. The United Nations Development Program and Yugoslavia have jointly devised a $2 billion master plan for the development of tourist facilities along Yugoslavia's southern Adriatic coast, a plan which includes investment in new hotels, roads, water pipelines, harbors and airports.

Given the projected growth of international tourism and its potential as a source of foreign exchange, it must figure prominently in the development strategies of poor countries. In addition to earning much-needed foreign exchange, tourism is a labor-intensive industry and thus a means of alleviating the rising unemployment plaguing most poor countries. Many poor countries have great potential for attracting tourists with their scenic attractions, abundant wildlife and recreation facilities. Properly managed, these natural amenities can be converted into foreign exchange, jobs and a higher standard of living.

But with a few exceptions, most poor countries have not begun to exploit the tourist potential. At present, South America not only has failed to exploit this potential, but it has a tourism balance-of-payments deficit of $100 million annually. Malawi, a small country in southern Africa, is making a determined bid to expand its tourist industry, capitalizing on the 355 miles of Lake Malawi's beaches. Although it had only 25,000 visitors in 1969, it hopes to quadruple this within a few years, greatly augmenting the country's meager foreign exchange reserves.

The expansion of international tourism has benefits other than purely economic ones. This vast human enterprise can be a source of cultural enrichment not otherwise attainable. In addition, it is another of many strong integrating forces, a potential means of bridging geographic, political and ideological barriers. However, one must also add that tourism can cause friction between travelers and local populations, particularly if the former overload local transport, recreation or other facilities or are condescending and demanding.

Weaknesses in the System

There are few areas in which man has mismanaged technology so badly as in transportation. The gap between a carefully designed transport system and existing ones in terms of reliability, convenience and cost is enormous, as is evidenced by the alarming rates of air pollution, sound pollution, accidental deaths and injuries. Transport systems seem to be shaped not so much by society's needs as by the nature of technological advance and the profit motive.

Primary reliance on the automobile for mobility in the United States has resulted in an enormous consumption of the earth's natural resources of energy and metal. In the words of Najeeb Halaby: "The average 150 pound driver tooling down a million dollar highway here or abroad in two tons of expensive and rapidly deteriorating machinery bound for a destination where it may cost him the price of his day's food to park—this is surely what we mean when we speak of conspicuous consumption." In the United States, the world's most mobile society, there are enough automobiles to permit everyone to go for a ride on Sunday afternoon without anyone sitting in the back seat. Despite its evident popularity and the extraordinary individual mobility it provides, the automobile is on the defensive in the rich countries.

To most Americans the automobile is both a source of great pleasure and frustration, as when one is in a traffic jam or searching unsuccessfully for a parking spot. The *New York Times* entitled an article concerning the Long Island Expressway the highway connecting the Long Island suburbs with Manhattan, "The World's Largest Parking Lot."

With the rise of affluence elsewhere, other societies are being plagued by the automobile. A satirical piece by an Italian writer describes the decline of modern Rome as beginning with a monumental traffic jam resulting from the steadily growing number of cars trying to enter the city. The traffic jam spreads until eventually there is total paralysis with no one able to move, whereupon the city slowly dies, its streets jammed with automobiles.

Heavy investment in individual private transport has often deprived public transportation systems of the funds they needed. Tokyo's subway is so inadequate that the Tokyo city government has on its payrolls 300 *oshia*, or "pushers," whose job it is to push and stuff as many commuters as possible into the crowded subway cars during rush hours. These robust young men often succeed in stuffing three times as many people on board as the engineers designing the cars reckoned for.

Not only is the transportation system frustrating, inefficient and disfiguring the environment in advanced countries such as the United States, but the debilitation and fatalities from emphysema and other air-pollution-induced diseases are mounting alarmingly, perhaps even exceeding the already horrendous number of direct traffic fatalities occurring on the highways. Traffic congestion is commonplace in virtually every major city in the United States. Passenger-handling facilities at all but a few major airports are being strained to the utmost. This unfortunate state of affairs led the United States to belatedly organize a Cabinet-level Department of Transportation.

Most societies are devoting too much to private transportation and not enough to efficient and comfortable mass public transportation. According to the editors of *Business Week*, "Eventually it will dawn on a sufficient majority of the voters that a faltering transportation industry, one that is falling far behind what is technologically possible and not truly serving the public interest because a disproportionate amount of money and space is being devoted to individual private movement is becoming too serious a drag on the overall welfare." Both growing central control of transportation facilities, whether public or private, and a steadily expanding share of resources devoted to public transportation will be required to extract us from our present situation in the United States and elsewhere.

Among the worst defects in transportation are the ties between air and ground transport. It is possible to zoom from Paris to New York at an average speed of 550 miles per hour, only to find a system of ground transportation that averages less than 30 miles per hour in getting to one's destination in downtown Manhattan. This seems to be a common dilemma. Two Soviet journalists conducting an extensive three-week survey of air transportation in the Soviet Union observed that while the planes they flew in traveled at 500 miles per hour, delays on the ground reduced their average travel speed to only 120 miles per hour. Writing in *Literaturnaya Gazeta*, they pointed out that "passengers were flying this fast in the mid-1920's."

A Transport Research Institute

A smoothly functioning global transport system for people and for industrial raw materials, energy fuels, foodstuffs and manufactures is an essential part of a global society. Such a system should perform two important functions: the integration of various forms of transport—airlines, railways, subways and automobiles—and the integration of national systems into a single, smoothly functioning global network.

Foremost among the fuctions would be that of a global transport research center and information clearing house. Governments everywhere, both national and local, are plagued with transport problems. Urban governments in particular are being overwhelmed with traffic congestion. Solutions to the transport problems of Tokyo or Budapest, Caracas or Philadelphia or any other major city are often applicable elsewhere. All require detailed analyses of existing transportation systems in terms of efficiency, comfort, reliability, safety and speed. Projections of future transport needs and means of fulfilling them are very much in demand. Growth is so rapid that a failure to anticipate needs by even a few years can result in insufferable inconveniences.

The coordination of literally hundreds if not thousands of relatively independent public agencies and private firms engaged in transport to create an alternative to the existing amalgam of rather independent transport systems is a challenge to the systems analysis profession. A much greater effort must be made, for instance, to ensure that investment in transport is more evenly balanced between, for example, jumbo jets on the one hand and ground facilities for handling passengers and baggage on the other. If Trans World Airlines adopts superjets that disgorge 350 passengers at a time, then the airports in Madrid and Singapore must simultaneously make the necessary adjustments for handling passengers on this scale, lest many of the gains in efficiency be lost.

Similar situations exist with transport linkages elsewhere. The proposed tunnel between England and France, linking the British Isles with the Continent, will be of optimum use only if transport planning in the United Kingdom and on the Continent is designed to take full advantage of it. Its ties with numerous transport systems and subsystems throughout Europe must be carefully worked out.

The more various transport firms and agencies are welded into larger units, the easier it will be to attain coordinated transport. Within Japan, for instance, the government is attempting to improve the economic efficiency of air travel by encouraging domestic airlines to merge. This policy, adopted in 1966, has already reduced the number of airlines from ten to four. By the mid-seventies the number is expected to decline to two. A similar trend is under way in the United States. The greater the centralization at the national level, the easier it usually is to plan and operate a smoothly functioning global transport system. Traditional notions of the need to maintain competitive conditions between a number of carriers may not always be compatible with the maximum exploitation of modern technologies to meet the needs of society. Circumstances now call for a careful examination of the trade-off between bigness and the frequently associated monopoly powers on the one hand, and the inefficiency, duplication of services, and higher costs of many small independent carriers, on the other.

Transportation planners must become more concerned with the efficiency of the system in environmental and aesthetic terms. The automobile-centered society may allow a much greater role for carefully conceived public transport and perhaps even for bicycles. The steady reduction in the world's petroleum reserves and the increasing congestion and pollution caused by private transportation underline the need to design more efficient public-transport systems in all societies. Interestingly, bicycle sales surged in the United States in the early seventies, actually exceeding the number of automobiles sold in 1971. Residents of uptown Manhattan may in the future rely almost entirely on subways, buses and bicycles to reach downtown offices if the automobile is banned in much of the downtown area. The city government of Cairo recently issued a request that its residents rely more on bicycles for commuting and less on the overcrowded and dilapidated public buses.

Investments in research and development in the transportation field have so far been concentrated on conveyances themselves, such as automobiles or supersonic transports. Very little has been devoted to researching transport systems as such. As a result, transportation systems are shaped largely by the nature of the conveyances produced. For example, the automobile has been the dominant influence in shaping the U.S. transport system. What has not been done, even on a national level, is to take transport requirements in terms of the volume of passengers and freight needed to be moved in a system and then, applying modern technology, to design a system which would do that with the greatest comfort and efficiency.

At present, poor countries are patterning their transportation systems after those of the rich countries with heavy emphasis on individual mobility in the form of the automobile for the few who can afford it, while generally ignoring the needs of the bulk of their people. But transportation systems in the less developed countries need not, and in fact cannot, evolve through exactly the same stages as those in the rich countries. Planners in the poor countries have the advantage of seeing problems confronting urban centers in the rich countries and can act to avoid similar ones. Overpopulation, which poses an even greater problem to these countries than to the more affluent countries, limits the capacity of urban centers to cope with individual mobility and may force many to ban private transport in favor of expanded and improved public transportation.

In order to make public transport more acceptable, priorities must shift from mere quantitative expansion to qualitative improvement. Only when our trains, buses, undergrounds and stations are cleaner, more comfortable and efficient will people be willing to relinquish the much-cherished convenience and independence of private transportation. And only when we are prepared to allocate resources for designing better public transport on the scale comparable to those spent on designing the supersonic transport is this likely to become a reality.

The three efforts to build a supersonic plane undertaken by the Soviet Union (Tupolev 144), the United Kingdom and France together (Concorde), and the now defunct U.S. effort (SST), illustrate both the weaknesses of the existing competitive international system and the need for an international transport research center. Goaded by the potentially adverse balance-of-payment impact and the loss of prestige associated with failing to be the first with a commercially successful supersonic transport, these three enormously costly efforts were undertaken with little knowledge of either the ultimate costs or feasibility.

In retrospect, it appears that the supersonic plane may fail to be practical in economic, ecological and social terms. Estimates for both the U.S. and U.K.-French models indicate that fares would be perhaps 50 percent above existing first-class fares, thus sharply limiting the number of potential users. This covers only operational costs, since the R&D costs are borne by government, or more accurately, by the taxpayers. In ecological terms, the supersonic plane fails by an even wider margin. The sonic boom alone ruled it out for many, but potentially even more serious was the possible effect the exhaust would have on the upper atmosphere's capacity to filter out harmful radiation from outer space.

On the third count, the supersonic plane fails miserably. The enormous financing required to develop it—$1.34 billion for the SST and nearly $2 billion for the Concorde —amounts to a vast redistribution of income from poor to rich. The tax funds used come from all levels of society, while the costs of supersonic travel are such that only the elite jet set could ever afford to fly at twice the speed of sound. At the international level, it is even more difficult to justify this enormous expenditure of the world's scarce public resources to benefit a minute fraction of mankind, when much of mankind cannot yet afford a bicycle. As awareness of the gap between rich and poor in the world rises, it will become more and more difficult to use public resources in such a wasteful and cavalier fashion.

Sadly, much of the waste, duplication and inefficiency might have been avoided if the feasibility of the supersonic transport had been systematically examined on all counts by an objective interdisciplinary, international group. Now that the SST has been abandoned, it is questionable whether the British-French Concorde will ever be acceptable for widespread commercial service. Difficulties with the Soviet Tupolev 144 are evident in the postponement of the projected operational date from 1970 to 1975. Even more telling was the recent uncovering of an attempt by Soviet agents to steal design information from the British on the Concorde.

Attitudes and institutions relating to transportation are lagging far behind technology. Nowhere is this more true than with international travel. Waiting in line for two or three hours to obtain the necessary travel documents to cross national borders may have been tolerable at a time when a transatlantic trip required a week, but when it takes only a matter of hours, such waits become intolerable. Except for a few areas, as in Western Europe, where border crossing has become a rather simple matter, procedures for crossing national boundaries are still based on a world organized into a collection of independent nation-states rather than on an increasingly integrated global society.

The technology now exists for providing each international traveler with a computerized plastic card which would contain all essential data including identification, citizenship, health data (including inoculations), visas granted, etc. Each point of entry into a country would then be equipped with a computer terminal linked to a global computer center. Inserting the traveler's card into the terminal and comparing the information it contained with that in the memory of the central computer would determine in a fraction of a second whether the traveler met entrance requirements. Although some might object to the idea of computerized identification because of the loss of privacy, such a device would save an enormous amount of time and could make international travel infinitely more pleasurable.

Future Trends

As indicated earlier, the combination of rising incomes and the declining cost of international air transport is steadily expanding the group which can afford to travel internationally. Not too many years ago those who could afford to travel internationally were part of a small elite, but today mechanics, secretaries and factory workers are traveling abroad. Specific economic and social trends, such as the internationalization of production and education, the emergence of literally thousands of groups organized functionally across national boundaries, an expanding web of diplomatic ties among countries, especially between East and West, and the emergence of regional economic groupings, not to mention the expansion of international tourism, all contribute to the growth in international travel.

To cope with the future flood of international travelers, we will need passenger transport systems which are fast, reliable and capable of rapid expansion. Short-distance hauls up to 200 miles, whether domestic or international, are likely to be primarily the province of light-weight, high-speed rail lines, similar to the Trans-Europ-Express network, which provides first-class rail service on twenty-nine routes connecting nearly a hundred West European cities. Even speedier and more modern rail lines link Japan's major cities. In the United States, the Metroliner train, serving New York and Washington with speeds up to 122 miles an hour, is an early prototype of this form of rail service. Ultimately these express trains may approach a speed of 200 miles an hour.

Over the longer distances, commercial jet aircraft will continue to be pre-eminent, with the combination of economy and speed exerting a strong attraction on a growing number of travelers. Air transport, once the privilege of a global elite, will become more a form of mass transport, especially within the richer countries.

A global transport system capable of moving the vast quantities of goods needed to support modern living standards is easily disrupted and quite vulnerable to sabotage. One of the world's major petroleum arteries, a pipeline carrying nearly a million barrels daily of Saudi Arabian crude oil across Syria and Lebanon to the Mediterranean, was severed by a "tractor accident" in Syria. It remained out of use for nine months while Syria negotiated for a proper reimbursement for the damage caused by the leaking oil and for higher transit fees. Only after Syria's demand for an undisclosed hike in the transit fee was met was the line restored to operation. Syria had earlier shut off the flow of Iraqi oil to the Mediterranean through a pipeline owned by the International Petroleum Consortium, a firm jointly owned by American, British, French and Dutch interests. After a three-month interruption, oil began to flow through the pipeline, that is, when IPC agreed to raise annual transit royalties from $28 million to $40 million per year.

Some of the most important threads in the global transport system are the most vulnerable—witness closure of the Suez Canal with a few sunken ships. This product of the six-day Arab-Israeli war created a shipping shortage which affected ocean-freight rates for a wide variety of goods. Higher transport costs and scarcities of fuel affected living costs in virtually every country in Western Europe. Another portion of the global transport system which is easily disrupted is international airlines. Jet passenger lines, vulnerable to hijacking and bomb threats, have required heavy expenditures by both governments and airlines in elaborate procedures for passenger security checks, higher insurance rates on planes, and the employment of thousands of sky marshals and other security personnel. These economic outlays do not include the psychic costs to passengers fearful of being hijacked or to those thousands of passengers whose lives were imperiled when their plane was hijacked.

If the global transport system is to function efficiently, there must be a high level of international cooperation. One country can shut off enough of the oil flowing into the world market to affect the supply and price measurably. One country can plug the Suez Canal, creating an acute shortage of supertankers. A few countries refusing to ratify an anti-hijacking pact whose terms call for immediate return of the hijacker, as well as those hijacked, can effectively nullify the usefulness of such a pact, though it be signed by 140 other countries. Technological interdependence is now a reality of everyday life, but political cooperation lags far behind. With time, perhaps our state of mind will catch up with our state of technology.

Scarcely a day passes without news of a new thread in the fabric of the global transportation infrastructure. Air France recently inaugurated a new trans-Siberian flight linking Japan directly with Europe. Canadian Pacific Airlines expects to link mainland China to North America with flights from Shanghai. A new bridge to span the Dardanelles over the Bosporus will provide a direct link between Asia and continental Europe. Bell Aerospace is designing a 200-ton Hovercraft capable of crossing the Atlantic in two days. With each of these new threads, the world becomes less a collection of independent nation-states and more an integrated global society. As the mobility of man continues to increase, the significance of location in human affairs will decline. The psychological impact of increasing mobility will be far-reaching, creating an awareness by the individual that he is part of a global as well as a national society.

15

NEW SUPRANATIONAL INSTITUTIONS

As countries become more integrated economically and more interdependent ecologically and socially, the list of problems which cannot be solved at the national level lengthens. Some problems can be handled by a few countries working together, but others can be dealt with successfully only at the global level. Pollution in the Great Lakes can be controlled by the United States and Canada. The adoption of many modern technologies is feasible only with the economies of scale attainable at the regional level, as in the European Economic Community or the Andean trade group. But such things as effective weather-monitoring and forecasting systems, pacts to prevent aerial hijacking, and the orderly exploitation of oceanic resources require cooperation of virtually all the world's countries.

Recognition of the need for new supranational institutions is slowly spreading, but the political complexities and obstacles to the creation of these institutions are enormous. Effective supranational institutions capable of coping with the technologies man has developed in fields ranging from nuclear weapons to weather modification invariably require that countries sacrifice a measure of sovereignty, something which most countries are very reluctant to do. Unless the existing nation-state system is augmented with the needed supranational institutions, all of mankind could suffer. The real issue in every case is whether global public opinion is sufficiently enlightened to support creation of the institutions needed in the absence of a catastrophe of some sort. We know from bitter experience that supranational institutions are not created easily. The League of Nations failed during the 1920s, but beginning in 1930 the world went through a traumatic decade and a half, starting with a world-wide economic depression and ending with a world war. These two events, not entirely unrelated, were a clear signal that the world could no longer function satisfactorily as a collection of sovereign nation-states acting independently. The international monetary system had collapsed, sparking a wave of economic protectionism that brought international trade to a virtual standstill in all but the most essential commodities. Unemployment in the United States reached alarming levels. Desperation in both the United States and Europe led many to seek radical solutions, leaving them susceptible to demagogues like Hitler in Germany. A senseless global holocaust claimed 30 million lives within a five-year span.

Thoughtful men everywhere asked why. The consensus was that man's institutions had failed him. An international economic system was emerging, but there were no institutions to coordinate monetary and trade policies of nation-states which were tempted to act in their own narrow interests. National leaders agreed that the bitter experiences of the 1930–1945 period could not be repeated. Efforts to avoid a repeat of these experiences led to the creation of the United Nations and its several constituent agencies following World War II.

The United Nations After Twenty-five Years

The United Nations was initially conceived as a global community of nations, the first stage of a world government. After twenty-five years, most observers agree the United Nations has not yet lived up to its expectations. The cooperative international ethos that began to emerge following World War II was soon replaced by the Cold War and the divergence of East-West interests. More than any other single factor this has hobbled the United Nations, draining it of the resources, unanimity and strength needed to perform effectively in many of its capacities, particularly peace keeping.

Despite these inherent difficulties, the UN agencies have served mankind well in some areas. The International Monetary Fund was designed to bring order out of chaos in the international monetary system. The General Agreement on Tariffs and Trade (GATT) was charged with reviving international trade by reducing the barriers thrown up during the 1930s. The United Nations' specialized agencies—FAO, WHO, ILO, UNESCO—were designed to deal with some of humanity's pressing problems of hunger, disease and illiteracy. The International Bank for Reconstruction and Development (IBRD), or World Bank, was set up to provide capital for development of the infrastructure—highways, dams, power, communications—needed for the poor countries to modernize.

Today, nearly a generation later, some of these problems seem reasonably well in hand. The international monetary system, not without serious problems, has thus far weathered various crises en route to establishing a truly international system. Member countries sacrificed a measure of economic sovereignty in exchange for greater stability in the monetary system. The International Monetary Fund has been strengthened further with the responsibility given it in 1967, to create and administer the Special Drawing Rights, the new international currency intended to supplement and eventually replace the dollar.

International trade is ending its second decade of vigorous expansion, an expansion due in large measure to a series of five rounds of negotiations among 62 member nations of GATT to reduce tariffs. The liquidity crisis resulting from the rapid growth in international trade during the sixties, which at the time inhibited growth in trade, seems to be resolved, at least for the time being. The IBRD, firmly established in its role as a mobilizer of funds in capital markets of the rich countries for lending to developing countries, is planning to double its lending capacity within a five-year period. The United Nations itself, not nearly as successful as many of its founders hoped, is nonetheless a forum for discussion of international issues, a place where nations can come together to talk.

After the specialized agencies were established in the burst of internationalism during the immediate postwar years, the process essentially came to a halt, but the emergence of problems requiring supranational solutions did not. The circumstances in which we now find ourselves demand that we begin working toward creation of a second generation of supranational institutions.

Among the problems requiring attention by the entire community of nations are the need to regulate the exploitation of oceanic resources, the growing threat to the environment, and the troubled interface between nation-states and multinational corporations. Each of these problems can be solved only within new global political structures.

International Oceanic Regime

As land-based reserves of minerals and fossil fuels, particularly petroleum and natural gas, are depleted, and as fresh-water inland fish supplies are diminished by pollution, the resources of the oceans escalate in importance. Rapidly rising demand for these commodities and technological advances permitting exploitation of oceanic resources are generating conflicting claims. The search for oil and other mineral resources, once confined to shallow coastal waters, is now moving into international waters. Drilling for oil, limited to water less than 70 feet deep twenty years ago, is now taking place in several hundred feet of water; the feasible drilling depth is becoming greater year by year as new technologies evolve. Dredging for minerals, limited to 30 feet at the time the UN was established, is now feasible at 200 feet, greatly expanding the potential area to be exploited for mining purposes.

As technologies permit the exploitation of energy and mineral resources in international and ungoverned areas, the competition among nations is, in some instances, becoming fierce. The seizure of dozens of American tuna boats off the west coast of Latin America by the Ecuadorian navy illustrates the competition for oceanic resources which can arise.

Even more disturbing are the conflicting claims of jurisdiction over newly discovered underwater oil reserves in the South China Sea by Taiwan, China, Japan and South Korea, all but China heavily dependent on petroleum imports. Concentrated in a 210,000-square-mile region around the Senkaku Islands, these underwater petroleum reserves are believed to be among the most extensive in the world. Each of these countries, except mainland China, is parceling out overlapping concessions and counterconcessions to a total of nine multinational corporations engaged in petroleum exploration and drilling.

Conflicts over fishing rights off the west coast of Latin America and over oil exploration and pumping rights in the South China Sea are but two illustrations of a phenomenon which is certain to occur more and more frequently. Desirous of avoiding these potentially hazardous situations, Malta's Ambassador to the United Nations, Arvid Pardo, proposed that an international oceanic regime be established after appropriate study under the aegis of the UN to "ensure that national activities undertaken in the deep seas and on the ocean floor will conform to the principles and provisions incorporated in the proposed treaty [the treaty creating the regime]." The Ambassador also recommended that the UN refuse to recognize any national claims of sovereignty over the oceans not now in existence and that poor countries be given preference when considering the use of possible financial proceeds from regulating the oceans' exploitation.

The United States indicated its support for an international authority governing the exploitation of the world's oceanic resources in a White House statement issued in the summer of 1970. It further stated that the resources of the oceans were the common property of all mankind and should be made available to all nations, large and small, marine or landlocked.

As of December 1970, the forty-two-member UN Seabed Committee has made considerable progress in formulating the guidelines for regulating exploitation of the ocean. The General Assembly Political Committee adopted on December 15, by a vote of 90 to 0, a statement of principles "placing the seabed beyond the reach of national sovereignties, linking benefits from peaceful use to the needs of developing countries and looking forward toward conservation and anti-pollution measures."

Should an international oceanic regime come into being, organized along the lines now being considered, it would have a profound impact on the way the global community is organized, greatly strengthening the case for international sovereignty and collective approaches to meeting mankind's needs, vis-à-vis that of national sovereignty and independent national approaches. It would establish UN sovereignty over two thirds of the earth's surface in much the same manner that the 160 nation-states have sovereign rights over the remaining one third. Revenue from licensing governments or corporations interested in exploiting the ocean's potential would provide an independent source of income, giving the UN a certain independence it does not now enjoy, dependent as it is on financial contributions of member countries. This in turn would establish a precedent for the taxing of multinational corporations by a supranational institution along the lines advocated by Barbara Ward, where the proceeds could be used for development purposes. In these and other ways, establishment of an international oceanic regime could immeasurably strengthen the United Nations, greatly enhancing its capacity to serve mankind.

It is clear that there is no practical alternative to establishment of an international oceanic authority, but we must not for a moment underestimate the great hurdles to be overcome before such an authority can become a reality. For example, all nations agree that each nation should control its territorial waters, but even agreeing to a definition of territorial limits is fraught with difficulty. Some propose a 3-mile limit, others 12 miles, and some Latin American nations are claiming 200 miles. Still another approach involves establishing offshore limits to a certain depth of water, the commonly proposed 200-meter level. Other matters, such as the structure of the international authority over the oceans and the form of political control, are far more complex. One of the great achievements of the 25th General Assembly was agreement on a declaration of principles on the seabed. A UN Conference on the Sea is now scheduled for 1973, but the work preparatory to such a conference, so essential to its success, has scarcely begun.

World Environmental Agency

Arresting the deterioration of the environment does not seem possible within the existing framework of independent nation-states. Many dimensions of the environmental crisis extend beyond national boundaries. Rain in Sweden contains sulfuric acid as a result of burning high-sulfur fuels in the Ruhr Valley. The oceans serve as a common dumping place for a swelling flow of waste of all kinds. One could easily fill a volume with an inventory of environmental threats which can be coped with only through multinational or global cooperation.

In a competitive international economy it may be almost impossible to control some forms of pollution without establishing standards or at least guidelines at the global level. Those firms adopting costly pollution-control measures in one country may find themselves unable to compete in world markets with firms domiciled in countries with less stringent requirements.

A world environmental agency would have several functions. First, it would have a monitoring function, gathering a vast amount of data on environmental variables on a world-wide basis. Using the information accumulated over time, it would need to assess the impact of man's various interventions in the environment, whether they be turning a river around, speeding up the nitrogen cycle, or emptying mercuric wastes into rivers which feed into the ocean. This in itself is a massive undertaking requiring an enormous amount of manpower and financial resources, considering that man is now discharging some 500,000 compounds into the biosphere. But the next step, determining the precise effect on the ecosystem of these interventions, is a far more complex, time-consuming process of research and analysis. The knowledge gap must be filled, however, if the earth's ecosystem is to be preserved. Once the necessary information and analysis is complete, tolerance levels can be established and translated into the necessary regulations of human economic activity. No doubt ensuring compliance with these regulations will be exceedingly difficult. Nowhere does the gap between advancing technology and the institutions to cope with it so imperil the human condition as in the relationship between man and the environment.

This brings us to the key question of whether the world environmental agency should be part of the United Nations family or entirely independent of it. Those urging the latter include George Kennan, who in an article in *Foreign Affairs* proposed that a small group, perhaps ten, of the leading industrial powers band together and form an international environmental agency. He argued that the United Nations is too slow in its political and bureaucratic maneuvering to cope effectively with the urgent need for such an agency. Further, he implied that it would be difficult to create a UN agency with enough muscle to be effective. What Kennan overlooked is that some of the more serious global stresses on the ecosystem originate with the poor countries, particularly those deriving from the use of pesticides and from the increasingly extensive wind erosion and associated rise in particulate matter in the upper atmosphere.

Those who are for including a world environmental agency in the United Nations family feel that if it were not included, the United Nations would be weakened and undermined. They would argue further that man's future well-being and survival is too closely linked to a strengthened United Nations to risk undermining it in the short run. Hopefully, the foundations for a world environmental agency will be laid at the UN Conference on the Environment to be held in Stockholm in 1972.

If the UN Conference on the Environment should fail to create an effective environmental agency at the global level, the Kennan proposal might turn out to be a feasible alternative. Once a group of key countries established the needed agency, then it would be relatively easy to expand membership over time as other countries decided to join.

A National-Corporate Authority

The internationalization of production has, as was discussed earlier, brought with it many new problems along the national-corporate interface. The lack of a consistent set of rules regulating the relationship between national governments and corporations, particularly in areas such as antitrust regulations, ownership rights, capital repatriation, labor relations, tax laws and the issuance of securities has been costly, particularly for poor countries, because of apprehension and mistrust. No two nation-states have identical rules governing all aspects of a multinational corporation's activities. This results in overlapping, conflicting and inconsistent regulations in some instances and in others no regulation at all. Leaders in the poor countries have feared the power of some of the corporate giants, while at the same time every instance of expropriation by governments has contributed to a hesitation if not actual pulling back of corporations investing in these countries. The net effect has been to inhibit the flow of capital, and perhaps more important, technology from the rich to the poor countries.

Part of the difficulty in this relationship arises from governments attempting to deal with multinational institutions with what are essentially national policies. The anachronistic character of this approach was recognized in the method of patenting new technologies. In order to avoid the repeated patenting procedures for individual nations, thirty-five had signed a Patent Cooperation Treaty as of early 1971. The treaty established a standardized international patent application to be centrally filed.

International tax regulations of global corporations could clear up some of the existing problems confronting home and host countries. If handled by an international organization such as the United Nations, this new source of global revenue might be better distributed to areas where the need is greatest. Although many poor countries are exercising their increased leverage in demanding a greater share of the profits derived from subsidiaries located in their country, many corporations are still profiting from ill-defined or liberal tax laws.

There is a pressing need for a supranational institution to regulate the interface between global corporations and nation-states, particularly as far as the poorer nation-states are concerned. The sooner these corporations and national governments can find ways to cooperate, the greater will be the chance that the new technology will bring the poor countries into equal association with the industrial countries. Dr. Melville Watkins, who headed a Canadian commission to examine foreign investment in Canada, described this need as follows: "The major policy concern of the government surrounded by corporations should be to create an environment within which the corporations function for the public good. Since the operations of the multinational firm transcend the jurisdiction of any single nation, a case can be made that it should be subject to international or supranational control and, indeed, will not otherwise be effectively controlled in all respects. Multinational corporations have substantial economic power and political influence and their operations are far too important to many people for a nation-state to ignore them."

The need for established international arbitration procedures to solve disputes between national governments and multinational corporations is evidenced by the fact that two efforts have already been made. One was an effort by the World Bank to establish an International

Center for the Settlement of Investment Disputes. The second was the Court of Arbitration, organized by the International Chamber of Commerce. These two embryonic institutions might be considered as vehicles for development in this connection. It would seem, however, that association with either the World Bank or the International Chamber of Commerce would hamper the presumed objectivity and effectiveness of such an arbitrating institution, since both are identified so much more with corporate than with national interests.

Beyond the need to arbitrate disputes there remains the problem that few multinational corporations are truly multinational; most identify with the nation-state in which they are domiciled. This has led Orville Freeman, former Secretary of Agriculture and now president of Business International, and Arnold Toynbee, British historian, to suggest that the exclusive authority to grant charters to all corporations wishing to operate across national borders should be granted to a neutral authority, perhaps one situated on a small island. This would have the effect of divorcing or at least greatly weakening ties between nation-states and corporations, reducing the extent to which one could use the other to help further its basic political or economic objectives.

Supranational Research Institutes

As the magnitude of problems facing mankind become increasingly global in scale, they call for a new form of research institution, one which is supranational or global in outlook and purpose. Even where technologies exist, there is an enormous need for institutions capable of exploiting them for the benefit of all humanity. Only in a few specific areas, such as in space telecommunications with INTELSAT and in cereal production with IRRI and the International Center for the Improvement of Wheat and Corn, do such institutions exist. Otherwise there is little effort to systematically apply modern technologies to mankind's pressing problems at the global level.

Two problems which would lend themselves readily to this approach are population stabilization and waste disposal, the latter largely a matter of recycling. The population issue requires a major research effort, ranging from reproductive biology and more effective contraceptive methods to social motivation research analyzing factors influencing childbearing decisions. Governments now support family planning efforts in countries containing a great majority of the world's people, but are handicapped by a lack of successful experience to draw upon in organizing their own programs.

The waste-disposal question needs attention for two reasons: existing methods of disposal are exceeding the ecosystem's capacity to absorb waste, and recycling is also the key to conserving scarce raw materials. If methods of recycling can be perfected, progress will be made on two critical fronts. The waste-disposal problem, though affecting virtually every country, is one which few individual governments can afford to research adequately. Technologies evolved to facilitate recycling, however, are often universally applicable.

Not all research needs are global; some are regional or affect only those countries in a certain ecological area or at a certain stage of development. The locust threat which emerges periodically and affects countries of East Africa and the Middle East is an example of the latter. Other institutes might focus on specific diseases such as the cholera institute in East Pakistan, now Bangla Desh.

These institutes would both conduct action-oriented research and serve as information clearing houses. Perhaps the nearest thing to an existing model would be the International Rice Research Institute, located at Los Baños in the Philippines. Source of the "miracle rices" now revolutionizing rice production in Asia, it has become the undisputed world-wide source of advanced rice production technologies. The enormous contribution of this institute in the form of the new high-yielding rices was achieved with a small staff of less than fifteen professionals.

These proposed institutes would be mission-oriented with specific social objectives. The boards of directors and staffs would be both interdisciplinary and international in composition, and independent of any national government or international organization. Long-term funding should be assured, perhaps through an initial endowment supplied by an individual country such as the United States, which is in the process of shifting some of its aid resources from bilateral to multilateral channels. Or perhaps better yet, the U.S. and Soviet or Japanese governments could combine resources, jointly launching such an institute. An institute on population or any other subject relating most directly to the poor countries should be located within the poor countries themselves. For social technologies such as family planning or waste recycling, these institutions would play much the same role in disseminating technology across national borders as multinational corporations now do for industrial technologies.

United Nations Disaster Relief Force

As the world has become smaller by virtue of advances in transportation and communication, it has become feasible to consider a single disaster relief force for the entire world. The economic advantages of maintaining a single force to serve all nations is that with a given investment of resources in men, equipment, food stores and medical supplies, a much more effective job can be done with a single force covering the entire world than with numerous smaller forces of varying degrees of effectiveness serving individual countries.

Poised to respond whenever called to national disasters —storms, floods, hurricanes, earthquakes and volcanic eruptions—such a group would be manned by professionals with the most modern equipment. Given the hourly weather information now available through the global system of meteorological satellites, potential weather-induced disasters could be identified as they arose, and with continuous monitoring, relief could be moved into position on the basis of a severe threat, not even waiting for the disaster itself. Such a disaster relief force should have a sizable medical contingent, including doctors, nurses, paramedical personnel trained in the immediate care of the injured, and portable hospitals and power-generating equipment. It would be able to provide food and temporary shelter for large numbers of people. It would also have a well-developed logistical capability in the form of planes, helicopters, jeeps and a sophisticated airdrop capacity.

Although most of the personnel and equipment would be headquartered in one spot, three or four strategically situated continental offices would shorten the response time to unanticipated local disasters. The loss of life and suffering which could have been prevented during the past year or two with the existence of such a force is impressive, particularly considering that the global loss of life from national disasters in many recent years has exceeded that from armed conflict. To be fully effective, a UN relief force would need to establish early its impartial, nonpolitical character. By so doing, it would make it difficult for a national government to avoid inviting it in whenever the lives and well-being of its citizens were endangered.

The earthquake in Peru, the catastrophic typhoon in East Pakistan, the floods in Italy, the earthquake in Turkey, and a number of mine disasters, all come to mind. None of these individual countries, with the possible exception of Italy, possessed the resources to respond to disaster on the scale experienced. All welcomed external assistance. Once a UN disaster relief force were established and operational, it would be called upon at the first sign of a natural disaster, as automatically as calling the local fire department in case of fire. It would be a source of comfort to all and a source of aid to those caught up in a natural disaster. Not only would this provide a sense of security but it would also create a sense of mutual dependence, a sense of community among nations. In addition to reducing the loss of life and alleviating suffering among those in disaster areas, it would give the United Nations a much-needed psychological shot in the arm.

A Full Agenda

Bringing into existence the supranational institutions discussed above is an enormous, complex undertaking. But this is only a beginning. This chapter is not intended to provide an exhaustive listing of the many supranational institutions needed, but rather to select, for illustrative purposes a few of those most urgently needed.

The need for the United Nations itself is much greater today than it was a generation ago when the organization was created. And more, public recognition of the need for a United Nations is much greater than ever before. But despite some landmark achievements, such as assisting with the decolonization of territories containing nearly a billion people, ratification of the partial test ban treaty, peace-keeping activities in Zaire (the Congo) and Cyprus, the nuclear weapons nonproliferation treaty, the declaration of principles governing the seabed and other important accomplishments, most people are disillusioned with it. The problem is not that a global institution cannot function effectively. What is lacking in the United Nations is the political desire among many of its members for it to assume an effective role.

There are several specific actions which can be undertaken to strengthen the United Nations. Foremost among these is the need for universality. The recent admission of mainland China, resulting in part from relaxation of U.S. opposition and the U.S. initiative to re-establish the dialogue with mainland China, is a giant step in the right direction. If a way could be found—perhaps a package deal, as Richard Gardner, professor of international law at Columbia University, has suggested—to bring East and West Germany, North and South Korea and North and South Vietnam into membership, the credentials of the United Nations would be much more credible.

Unless the United Nations can be strengthened within the next few years, the organization's future and perhaps that of mankind is not very bright. Former UN Secretary General U. Thant has publicly stated that he feels the United Nations has ten years to become effective or disappear. Lester Pearson, former Prime Minister of Canada, has said: "If the United Nations is indeed the last great hope of mankind which must succeed, then it is time the nations of the world resolve to do something about it—by action and not merely by talk."

One effort under way to increase the effectiveness of the United Nations is that of eight countries from Latin America and Asia to revise the charter of the United Nations. So far this group has succeeded only in getting General Assembly support for a review of the charter, but this could eventually lead to its revision. Among the changes sought are a suspension of the Security Council veto in matters of common world concern, an upgrading of the entire UN peace-keeping machinery and giving the World Court of Justice the power to decide cases, even when governments involved are unwilling to submit to the courts adjudication.

Given the difficulties in establishing new supranational institutions, it might be desirable in tactical terms to concentrate on establishing those global institutions which are easiest to establish, such as in the research field. Some could even be launched unilaterally, as with the U.S. initiative in the creation of INTELSAT, or that of the Canadians with the International Development Research Center, an institution funded by the Canadian government but managed by an international board of directors.

In many situations it may be necessary to start with something less than a global organization. Indeed, many supranational institutions now including most of the world's nations in their membership, such as the GATT, IMF and INTELSAT, started with a relatively limited number of participants. The UN itself began with only two fifths of the members it now has.

Building new supranational institutions which are effective and have authority will not be easy. Nations are still torn between wanting both the benefits of autonomy and those of cooperation. Only with public recognition that the balance of benefits is shifting toward the latter can we expect significant adjustments to occur. And this in turn requires an educational effort designed to provide a better understanding of the relationship between various problems confronting people at the local or national level— such as rising seafood prices, threatened species, polluted beaches, drug addiction, aerial hijacking, urban deterioration and rising unemployment—and the cooperative supranational efforts needed to solve these problems.

Shaping the Future

16

IMPROVING THE QUALITY OF LIFE

We began this book with a discussion of the quality of life and three important factors affecting it—increasing per capita goods and services, decreasing per capita natural amenities, and the negative effects of expanding economic activity. In order to take positive steps to improve the quality of life one must understand not only these dynamic physical forces and trends affecting it but also the principal sources of human suffering in the world today. In terms of both the intensity of suffering and the number of people affected, one would have to point first to the symptoms of poverty—hunger, malnutrition, disease and ignorance. Hunger and malnutrition still affect a majority of the world's people. Half of mankind receives no health care at all.

For the 2 billion people with yearly incomes of less than $100, one fortieth that of the average American or one twentieth that of the average European, the quality of life must be measured primarily on a physical scale. A lack of the basic amenities of life is the greatest source of suffering for more than half of humanity. Reduction in poverty on a global scale can be viewed either as a narrowing of the gap between rich and poor nations, or in terms of providing a minimum level of living for all people. Over the shorter term, the latter is a more realistic goal both because it is more easily attainable and because it focuses more directly on the critical human needs.

A Global Minimum Living Standard

The advance of technology, the growth in human productivity and the accumulation of wealth in global terms have now evolved to the point where it becomes difficult to argue against providing a minimum level of living for all mankind. Such a level is best expressed in social rather than economic terms, including particularly the availability of food, housing, education and health services.

A minimum nutritional objective for 1980 should be not only enough food to fulfill caloric needs of all people but also the right kinds to prevent malnutrition and to ensure full physical and mental development. Neither the intellectual development of children nor the productivity of adults should be constrained by inadequate food supplies.

Virtually every national government has adopted a goal of compulsory elementary education, but many in Asia, Africa and Latin America lack the financial means to achieve this goal. Though the cost of this is substantial when compared with the present investments in education, the social cost to global society of continuing widespread illiteracy and ignorance is certainly far greater. Global society has now evolved to the point where we can and must begin thinking in terms of universal literacy for all mankind. This entails adult literacy programs as well as universal compulsory primary education. The prospect of large numbers of today's youth remaining illiterate is simply too costly, both in terms of foregone productivity and in terms of their capacity to comprehend and cope with the rapidly changing circumstances in which they find themselves.

The third component of a minimum standard of living is a provision of at least rudimentary health services to everyone. At a minimum this would include protection against infectious diseases through vaccinations, provision of safe water supplies, and family planning services, free upon request, as outlined in Chapter 8. Providing the latter both reduces the number of induced abortions, with the frighteningly high maternal mortality in the poor countries, and the number of unwanted children, an unnecessary burden on both the family and society. The United States, with passage of the Family Planning Services and Population Research Act of 1970, and India, with the country-wide free distribution of condoms, are now beginning to move toward this objective.

By defining development objectives in social terms, we go a long way toward coping with the question of how wealth and the benefits of external assistance are distributed within the recipient countries. Traditional methods of establishing objectives in terms of economic growth rates do not take into account income distribution, often permitting the further concentration of wealth among elite groups. If the focus is on providing the basic necessities as outlined above, then by definition the focus of development efforts is on the less fortunate members of a society.

Expressing development objectives in human terms contrasts with the more commonly used technique of establishing a target rate of annual economic growth, such as the 6 percent target set for the poor countries by the United Nations for Development Decade II. The latter method has a certain usefulness in that it gives countries a goal to strive for, but is not directly related to the needs of people, and that, after all, is the purpose of development.

The one thing that distinguishes the current era is that we have the means to achieve a minimum living standard for all of mankind. The gross world product of nearly $3 trillion now expands by about $120 billion per year, with the increase concentrated among affluent societies in North America, Europe, the U.S.S.R. and Japan. Shifting a sizable fraction of this annual gain in productivity and wealth from the rich countries to investment in the poor, along with a concerted effort to reduce birth rates, could raise productivity and eliminate much of the world's poverty in a matter of years.

We should note that it costs much less to obtain an acceptable standard of living in a poor country than in a rich one. An American consumes wheat in the form of bread costing 30 cents per loaf, although the wheat used costs only 2 cents. Consumers in the poor countries either produce their own wheat or buy it at a fraction of the cost of the same wheat in bread form in the United States. Costs are correspondingly lower for many other basic goods and services as well. A haircut costing 3 dollars in Boston may be available for 15 cents in a Pakistani village.

However we view it, the fact is that we can no longer argue that there are not enough resources to provide a universal minimum living standard. For most of mankind, this objective is attainable within this decade. It is just as much within the reach of global society as was the U.S. goal of journeying to the moon during the sixties. Not only is it now possible to think in the terms outlined above, but even more important, it is in the short- and long-term interest of mankind to do so. As man attempts to come to terms with his finite environment—to prevent disruption and impairment of the earth's life-support systems—the pressing need to stabilize global population acquires a new urgency. History tells us that high birth rates are not voluntarily reduced until populations reach a certain socioeconomic threshold. Reductions in fertility levels are closely related to improvements in food supply, declines in infant mortality, rising literacy and old-age security. Coping with the environmental crisis in the long run requires that man seek to eliminate global poverty in the short run. Thus are the destinies of the world's rich and poor now intertwined.

Technology for Human Needs

Recent years have witnessed a growing tendency to question man's capacity to manage technology effectively. Symptomatic of this is the antitechnology mood among youth, the technology-assessment movement in Congress, and the loss of public confidence in the relationship between technological advance and improvements in the quality of life. It would be a mistake, however, to view the questioning and uncertain attitude toward technology as limited to technology itself. Rather, it is part of a more profound questioning of the goals of society. It is within this context that we examine the need for new technologies to meet social needs.

The contrast between the actual uses of the global research and development (R&D) expenditures totaling $70 billion in 1970 and the needs of mankind does not inspire confidence in man's ability to manage technology. If one constructs a list of the ranking R&D expenditures in 1970 and a second list of mankind's most pressing technological needs, one finds distressingly little relationship between the two. A breakdown of the global R&D budget shows weapons research claiming the lion's share, followed by nuclear and space research. Indeed, the more pressing social needs, such as the need for a better contraceptive, a high-protein rice variety, an efficient cure for schisto-somiasis, improved literacy-training techniques or a pollution-free internal-combustion engine, still claim only an infinitesimal share of the total expenditures.

A closer examination of global R&D activity shows two sets of institutions—nation-states and multinational corporations—controlling expenditures for all but a small fraction of the total, most of which is accounted for by nonprofit groups, principally private foundations. R&D expenditures by the nation-state are heavily weighted by "national security" considerations, hence the massive expenditures on new weapons systems. The multinational corporation's outlay is directed largely at R&D activities which can potentially yield a profit. National security and the profit motive are the principal forces shaping the worldwide R&D program. Human or social needs are dealt with indirectly or only insofar as they coincide with the security objective or profit motive, which is all too infrequently. The specific development of technology to meet human needs as such is often left to private foundations such as Rockefeller, Ford and Carnegie in the United States, or Volkswagen in West Germany.

The real challenge now before mankind is to develop more efficient technologies for use by the world's poor, technologies which will permit attainment of a higher level of living at a much lower cost. A properly designed development strategy using appropriate technologies may make it possible to achieve a level of living now available at a per capita income of $500 per year while still at a $200 level. In part this is a matter of developing and using more efficient technologies, and in part a matter of more egalitarian national socioeconomic models.

What has been lacking to date is a mobilization of sci entific resources to focus on pressing social needs. Where efforts have been made, they have been extraordinarily successful. The notion of starting with a human need and utilizing existing technology to attempt to alleviate it can pay enormous dividends, as the work of Nobel Peace Prize-winner Norman Borlaug illustrates. His award for breeding the new high-yielding wheats resulting in the Green Revolution was not so much for the discovery of new knowledge as for the application of the backlog of existing knowledge to the problem of hunger in the poor countries.

Now that a good start has been made on raising cereal output, efforts are turning to breeding a high-protein rice, a feat which has thus far eluded the world's rice breeders. New techniques to convert the large unused supplies of oilseed protein into commercially successful food products could eradicate much protein hunger. New possibilities for upgrading vegetable protein with biologically synthesized amino acids, raising their quality to a level approaching that of animal protein, hold out the hope of providing nutritionally adequate diets at a fraction of the cost of consuming large quantities of livestock products as in the West.

Close on the heels of the agronomic breakthrough by Borlaug was the U.S. advance in the use of TV for educational purposes in the form of *Sesame Street*. This imaginative achievement may, if properly exploited on a global scale, make attainment of near-universal literacy through the use of village television a much more likely prospect than would otherwise be the case.

These strategic investments to exploit basic technologies, in the one case the existing storehouse of genetic knowledge and in the other the basic hardware of television, may dramatically improve the human condition on a global scale. Significantly, each of these two revolutionary advances was achieved with an expenditure measured in millions of dollars, in each case less than one hundredth of 1 percent of the global R&D investment—or stated differently, for less than 1 percent of the American R&D investment in the now defunct SST. This is not to imply that all investments in technologies for social betterment will reap enormous returns, but it does demonstrate that selected investments in social technologies can greatly improve the human condition on a world-wide scale.

Rising unemployment and massive urbanization represent socioeconomic problems which few countries are well equipped to handle. We need to know much more, for example, about how to distribute employment within a society with a given level of economic activity, about the relationships between both the agricultural and industrial technologies used and their impact on employment levels, and about how to deal with the complex of socioeconomic problems associated with rapid urbanization. Each is deserving of an international institute which could focus the interdisciplinary resources of the global community.

Using a more efficient combination of transport technologies selected from the panoply now available could permit a society at a low stage of economic development to satisfy the transportation needs of its people far more fully than is possible with the current approach of adopting what is essentially the American model. An automobile-centered transport system absorbs limited budgetary and foreign exchange resources of a poor country for the benefit of the small urban elite which can afford an automobile. A more socially equitable system, using the same resources but relying heavily on public transport, combined with the mass manufacture of simply designed, low-cost bicycles and motor scooters, would both provide a far greater mobility for the population as a whole and also distribute the benefits much more widely.

Attaining a higher level of living with a low investment of resources may be much easier with the adoption of one development model than with another. It might be appropriate to emulate one country in one sector and a different country in another sector. A country might do well to adopt the Japanese system of agriculture, the Chinese approach to providing health services with paramedical personnel, and the U.S. system of education. Taiwan, for example, has modeled its farm sector closely after that of the Japanese, but it has formulated a distinctly Taiwanese approach to foreign investment, and closely paralleled the American approach to family planning rather than the Japanese, by emphasizing contraception rather than abortion. By carefully selecting the technologies imported from abroad, by devising indigenous Taiwanese approaches where necessary and by stressing the redistribution of income, the Taiwanese have achieved a remarkably high standard of living at a low level of income, one comparing favorably with, say, Mexico, where average incomes are twice as high.

A quick examination of the scale of resources devoted to the development of technology versus those devoted to its dissemination at the global level indicate a heavy, seemingly inordinate emphasis on the former at the expense of the latter. The total expenditures both by government and by international agencies to disseminate the results of research are negligible compared with the annual investment. Indeed, as we noted in Chapter 10, the principal technological flows are those between rich countries, not between rich countries and poor. Available evidence indicates that human well-being would be greatly enhanced by a shift in expenditures from the development of new technology to dissemination of existing technology among the world's poor.

One reason why technology is not disseminated more readily from rich to poor is that so much of it is not relevant to the needs of the world's poor. Scientists, residing preponderantly in wealthy countries, have been unresponsive to human needs elsewhere in the world. In order for science to improve the quality of life, global R&D expenditures must be guided much more by improved knowledge of prevailing social conditions throughout the world and by a social vision, a vision of what society should and could be like, than by narrow national security or profit motives. The new technological frontier is not outer space or nuclear physics, but rather socially oriented technology, technology designed to meet the needs of the people. National priorities must be reordered so as to reorient the scientific establishment, mobilizing at least part of it to work on technologies to meet pressing human needs.

There are in the United States a few encouraging signs indicating an interest in managing technology and in focusing on human needs. One of these is the technology-assessment movement mentioned earlier. Perhaps the most encouraging action to date was the refusal by Congress to provide funds for further development of the supersonic transport in early 1971. This decision was significant not only because it prevented a major source of noise pollution from coming into being in the United States, but probably far more important because it represented the abandonment by the American people of the pursuit of technology for technology's sake.

At MIT, where most of the annual $92 million research budget has previously come from the Department of Defense, a student-inspired movement is under way to convert the country's largest university research complex to socially oriented purposes. Should future events show that abandonment of the SST and the science reform movement at MIT are early indications of a new trend in American society to assess carefully the social value of new technologies, it will bode well for all of mankind.

Interdependence and Well-being

Only when one inventories the many forms of interdependence which now exist among nations is it possible to appreciate how much our quality of life depends on the resources and cooperation of other nations. As incomes rise, dependence on imported foodstuffs, manufactures and raw materials grows, and the share of global output crossing national borders increases. Closely related to this growth in international trade is the growth in international production, resulting from the spread of the multinational corporation. This institution, with its capacity to develop and disseminate technology and to achieve the most efficient combination of capital, management, labor, technology and raw materials drawn from throughout the world, contributes importantly to our rising material affluence. Growing at double the rate of the world economy, international production is weaving the world together in ways quite without precedent, rapidly integrating national economies into a single global economy.

As technology becomes progressively more sophisticated, it becomes virtually impossible for any single country to conduct research in all areas. Thus, countries are beginning to specialize in various fields of scientific research, as has long been the case in production, making countries dependent on one another for new scientific knowledge. Increasingly, we look beyond our borders for new technologies to raise our living levels and to solve our problems.

As the level of global economic activity reaches the point where it is beginning to exert stress on the ecosystem, a new dimension of international cooperation to preserve the functioning of the ecosystem is called for. International controls are badly needed on the discharge into the ecosystem of toxic waste products such as mercury, lead and cadmium. Our capacity to alter rainfall patterns is progressing rapidly, but we lack a global institution to regulate these interventions, holding out the prospect that countries may soon use advanced technologies to compete for available rainfall.

Even the security of our food supply is becoming dependent on international cooperation. As inland lakes such as the Great Lakes of North America and the Caspian and

Aral seas of the Soviet Union become more and more polluted, and either produce no fish or fish unsafe for human consumption, individual countries are forced to rely more on the great oceanic commons for their supply of marine protein. Even the oceans, however, have reached the point where supplies of some commercial species are being diminished in many areas, including the Baltic Sea, the Mediterranean and the North Atlantic. Maintaining our supply of marine protein requires international cooperation to control overfishing and pollution of the oceans.

In the early seventies, serious social ills are emerging in many countries which cannot be solved by individual countries acting unilaterally. For the rich countries, growing addiction to hard drugs, and the associated rise in crime, greatly diminishes the quality of life. The United States, unable to intercept the inflow of hard drugs at the border, must turn to the poor countries where the heroin originates, asking them to alter their agricultural production patterns, prohibiting production of the opium poppy among their farmers. At the same time, the poor countries are experiencing great difficulty in coping with the rising unemployment without economic adjustments by the rich countries, principally in agriculture and light industry. Thus are the rich and the poor countries becoming increasingly dependent on one another for solutions to their respective social problems.

Given the advances in modern transportation, diseases now spread rapidly among countries making it essential that countries cooperate to control the spread of communicable diseases, whether they be human diseases such as cholera, animal diseases such as hoof-and-mouth disease, or plant diseases such as wheat rust or corn blight. An outbreak of hoof-and-mouth disease in England forced the destruction of tens of thousands of prized cattle in order to bring the disease under control. Failure to control corn blight in 1970 through internal measures forced the United

States to turn to other countries for assistance. Substantial seed imports of resistant corn strains produced in Guatemala and Yugoslavia lessened the threat of crop disaster considerably in 1971.

With the advent of long-range passenger jets, aerial hijacking has become a serious threat to the safety of air travelers, but an effective aerial antihijacking pact depends on near-universal cooperation. If even a few strategically situated countries hold out, such as Cuba or Algeria, there is little possibility of an effective pact.

The world is so interdependent and so interwoven today that economic, political or scientific decisions made within one country may affect far more people outside that country than within. Decisions by a multinational corporation may affect the well-being of the people in a given country more than those made by the government of that country itself. In many cases, those who are adversely affected have no political recourse to those responsible for their plight. Decisions by a U.S. congressional committee allocating sugar import quotas may have a greater impact on the well-being of rural laborers in northeastern Brazil than almost anything the Brazilian government itself can do. Permission by the government of Afghanistan to its hard-pressed farmers to produce opium for sale to illicit drug handlers could negate efforts to arrest the spread of drug addiction in the United States. A decision by an African government to expropriate holdings of a U.S. mining company can affect the retirement income of an elderly couple in Minneapolis. A decision by the U.S. government in August of 1971 to devalue the dollar relative to other major currencies caused a precipitous drop in the value of common stocks on the Tokyo stock exchange, a drop that the Japanese government was powerless to prevent.

Economic actions have social consequences extending far beyond national borders. So, too, do ecological forces. Deforestation in Nepal increases the severity of flooding in the Indus and Gangetic plains in India and Pakistan. The discharge of waste mercury by Japanese and Taiwanese industrialists can cause swordfish to be taken off menus in the United States. Oil spills from Norwegian tankers affect beaches in Florida. The discharge of industrial smokestacks in the Ruhr and Great Britain blackens snowfall in Scandinavia, chemically contaminating rivers and streams.

With each passing year the economic, ecological and social interdependence among countries increases. As it does, people find their personal well-being affected more and more by decisions and actions over which they have no control.

Global Social Issues

Thus far in this chapter we have focused on the physical factors affecting our well-being, but now we turn to the social factors. In the United States the key words in the field of human rights over the past several years have been freedom, equality and participation. Emergence of the social issues of the sixties represents the culmination of centuries of evolution in human rights. In the United States this evolution was marked by the Declaration of Independence, the abolition of slavery, and the granting of universal suffrage to women. The pace of social revolution has accelerated sharply since 1950 and is now reflected in a long list of executive decisions, Supreme Court rulings and new legislation.

The quest for human rights outside the United States was reflected in the dismantling of nearly all the colonial empires since World War II. Once under way in the immediate postwar period, it proceeded rapidly with the British, Dutch, French and Belgians divesting themselves of their colonies all within a matter of years. Only Portugal continues to maintain colonies.

In many ways the United States is a social frontier. The social issues that surfaced within it during the sixties are those now surfacing eleswhere in the world. Among these are racial and sexual equality, the peace movement and the eradication of poverty. Struggles for racial equality in the United States during the sixties were greater than at any time since the Civil War period. Blatant racial discrimination abroad, particularly in the Republic of South Africa, in Rhodesia and in Portuguese Africa, is under attack from many sides. Although the United States is far from achieving racial equality, the fact that the issue has come to an explosive head is an indication of the progress made. It is generally not until a certain degree of freedom is won that a minority becomes aware of its plight or feels that it can affect a change in its condition. In much of the world this awakening is just beginning, and the social upheaval and violence are yet to come.

Efforts by women to attain equal rights with men, traditionally focused on suffrage, gained momentum in the United States during the late sixties and early seventies. This struggle ranged across a broad front including equal educational and job opportunities, equal pay, abortion on demand, property rights, and a more equitable sharing of homemaking and child rearing responsibilities. This movement is now becoming world-wide, spreading rapidly to Canada, Australia, the United Kingdom, continental Europe, Brazil, among Arab women in the Middle East, and in Asia. Women everywhere are beginning to question and resist their traditional, sexually defined roles. The combination of reduced opportunities for childbearing in the years ahead and the search by women for alternative means of self-fulfillment is certain to alter the role of women in society. Indeed, as John Cool of the Ford Foundation has pointed out, "It contains within it the seeds of a fundamental restructuring of society."

The sixties witnessed the emergence of what eventually

became a broad-based antiwar movement in the United States. Significantly, opposition to U.S. involvement in Vietnam was probably far stronger at home than in any other country. Initially limited to the United States and focused on the Vietnam conflict, the antiwar movement is spreading to many other countries and now beginning to focus on the need to disarm and to reduce military spending.

As the Vietnam war subsides, it is quite possible that the immorality of continuing abject poverty in the world is going to disturb people in much the same way as did the immorality of the Vietnam war during the sixties. Poverty became an issue in the United States when people became aware of it, at a time when its continued existence was inexcusable. The same is likely to be true with global poverty. When poverty was the common and inevitable lot of man, it was quite tolerable. Now that it is no longer necessary, it is neither tolerable nor moral. As the tragedy and injustice of global poverty become clear, efforts to redistribute wealth and eliminate poverty will attain greater urgency.

Another sociopolitical factor which is very much influencing the quality of life in the world today is political repression. The extent to which it influences the quality of life is perhaps best indicated by the rate of immigration from the centrally planned economies of Eastern Europe and Cuba. Hundreds of thousands of East Germans migrating to West Germany during the late fifties and early sixties were so decimating the ranks of skilled laborers and professionals within East Germany that the government, in desperation, erected a wall separating East Berlin from West. East Germans were leaving their homeland not for want of material goods—they were adequately fed, clothed and sheltered—but because they bitterly resented the political repression and the absence of freedom. The desperate measures employed by those fleeing the centrally planned economies indicate how highly political freedom is prized by those who lack it. Thousands have risked and sacrificed their lives seeking it.

In some situations, social disintegration is greatly diminishing the quality of life. Often this is associated with poverty and extreme crowding, creating a near-desperate situation as in Calcutta and Bangla Desh. The United States, long considered the land of opportunity and a haven for the oppressed, has accepted tens of millions of migrants from other countries. But in recent years it has begun to lose some of its attraction, and a growing number of Americans are now migrating elsewhere because they are disturbed by social disintegration. An estimated 40,000 Americans quit the United States in 1970, most of them leaving for English-speaking Commonwealth countries, Western Europe and Israel. Many cited social disintegration and the lack of security and political repression as the reason for leaving. A commercial photographer now living in Toronto described what life in New York had been like. "It's like you're stuck behind bars; my wife and daughter couldn't go out at night." He voiced a concern now felt by millions of Americans, a lack of personal security that far exceeds fears of threats to national security from abroad.

The sixties witnessed a quickening of the social conscience of people in many parts of the world, but particularly among the young, and more particularly, the young people in the United States. This increase in social sensitivity took many forms—concern over racial discrimination, Vietnam, sexual discrimination, and poverty and hunger. In every case the issues became a matter of social concern and political action. New values were being formed, indeed a new ethic may be emerging.

A New Social Ethic

A social ethic is a set of principles, a code of behavior which enables society to function and, hopefully, survive. Today the social ethic which guides much of mankind in matters of childbearing, the production and distribution of wealth, and the relationship of man to nature, is one which has evolved over the millennia. By and large it has served us well. Not only have we survived as a species, but we have greatly multiplied our numbers and in some instances prospered as well. But now the old ethic is no longer adequate. Some values must be modified or abandoned, others strengthened, creating a new ethic, one dictated by the circumstances in which we find ourselves in the late twentieth century. However, the crucial factor may not be the required changes themselves but the limited time available for man to adapt successfully.

The values the new ethic embraces in turn define the new society which is just beginning to emerge. It is a society which is much less ideological and, hopefully, more humanitarian than those of the recent past, one whose essential character is determined by the desire to survive and to improve the human condition. It is even conceivable that the common crisis confronting all of us could draw mankind together, giving rise to a new humanism.

One of the most basic tenets underlying modern societies is that man should have dominion over nature, subjugating the environment to his needs. It is this tenet which is partly responsible for the worsening environmental crisis. The new ethic encompasses a new naturalism which places greater emphasis on man's harmony with nature and less on his dominance over it. The prevailing view of man as the center of the universe must be abandoned in favor of one which sees man as an integral part of the natural system rather than apart from it. The new ethic recognizes the finiteness of our biosphere, the only place in the entire universe known to be capable of supporting human life. In the words of Lester Pearson, "There is a need for a revolution in mankind's thinking as basic as the one introduced by Copernicus who first pointed out that the earth was not the center of the universe."

In seeking a more harmonious relationship with nature, our emerging global society needs to formulate a new child-bearing ethic. Throughout most of man's existence, large numbers of children were necessary to ensure survival of the species, given the high death rates, particularly for infants. Indeed, even with high birth rates, population growth was often scarcely perceptible within any given generation. But continuation of today's birth rates for many more years could threaten the very life-support systems on which man depends. Man must abandon the old "be fruitful and multiply" ethic, replacing it with one designed to stabilize population. Social mores must be geared to support such an ethic.

Another central component in the existing ethic is a near-exclusive emphasis on production and on the acquisition of wealth as an end in itself. A by-product of thousands of years of material scarcity, this must give way to a much greater emphasis on distribution and sharing. Poverty exists in the late twentieth century not because of a lack of technology to raise individual productivity above a minimal level, but because the diffusion of technology and wealth on a global scale have received so little attention. Modern man has excelled at production but failed at distribution.

The affirmative Biblical answer to the question "Am I my brother's keeper?" needs to be strengthened and broadened to encompass all of mankind. We are gradually accepting the idea of redistributing income systematically through progressive taxation in the rich societies, but still rely on alms giving at the international level. We recognize as socially necessary the provision of assistance for the disabled or elderly within our society, but often look upon capital assistance to the needy outside our borders, foreign aid, as wasteful. The new ethic must seek to eliminate territorial discrimination along with the more commonly recognized religious, racial and sexual discrimination. Superaffluence in a world with continuing abject poverty and associated suffering is coming to be considered immoral by many of today's youth.

The extreme emphasis on superaffluence has no place in an ecosystem already under great stress at existing levels of economic activity. For an economy not to be growing is now considered abnormal by economic planners and political leaders, something to be avoided at any cost. Within wealthy societies, we have come to equate progress with increases in material affluence. The growth ethic, which evolved in the West, has permeated the entire world. Virtually every national government in the world today is planning to expand its economy. Few have target rates of economic growth of less than 5 percent yearly. No nation has plans for reaching a given level of income and then stabilizing the size of its economy and improving the quality of life thereafter through other means. Rapid, sustained expansion of the gross global product, as we now know it, is necessarily a transitory phenomenon in historical terms, but governments, individuals and corporations are so growth-oriented that the attitudes, economic tools and policies for achieving a stable economy do not yet exist.

The new ethic must broaden the social scope of decision making. Modern societies encourage individuality and applaud individual initiative and action. But man's survival in a deteriorating biosphere requires that he be much more cooperative, acting in terms consistent with the collective welfare. Traditional loyalties to the nation must be expanded to include all mankind. Circumstances require that nations give up outdated notions of independence and sovereignty, replacing conflict and competition with cooperation.

The new ethic requires a new political man. Voting

regularly will not be enough. Individuals need to become actively involved in major political issues lest the special interests continue to prevail to the detriment of society. Unless the public—that is, you and I—can be mobilized to narrow the gap between special interests, whether they be powerful individuals, corporations or nation-states, and the global social interest, then it is quite likely that the quality of life for large segments of mankind will deteriorate in the years ahead. For many, self-realization can take the form of involvement in a cooperative effort to solve society's problems. The magnitude and urgency of the problems facing human society today are such that opting out, though a great temptation, is a luxury we cannot afford.

That there is a need for a new ethic there can be no doubt. It must not be a culturally biased ethic, but a universal one, a response to the circumstances in which late-twentieth-century man finds himself. Such an ethic has far-reaching implications for the behavior of both individuals and national governments. Its adoption would certainly result in new life styles and a new society, one far different from the one we now know.

17

CHANGING DIRECTION

Whether the quality of life for most of us improves or deteriorates during the remainder of this century will depend on how quickly we can reverse several global trends. The relationship between man and his natural environment is deteriorating despite sporadic efforts to reduce the adverse effects of expanding economic activity. The gap between rich countries and poor is widening in both absolute and relative terms. Continuously rising unemployment in poor countries is creating socio-political problems of enormous proportions. This in turn is fueling massive rural migration to urban areas. Widespread hunger saps the spirit and diminishes the humanity of a majority of mankind. With the possible exception of hunger, each of these problems is expected to worsen as this decade progresses.

Rapid population growth undermines efforts to cope with each of these threats. None can be solved without a major commitment of resources, a reordering of global priorities. None is likely to be solved by individual countries acting independently. If a cooperative global effort to deal with these threats to well-being is not launched soon, the political consequences may affect all of mankind. The aspirations unleashed among the world's poor by the communications revolution ensure that the seventies will not be a "business as usual" decade.

These threats to our future well-being are such that we cannot cope with them adequately in an international system dominated by either the bipolar power balance of the cold war era or a type of nineteenth century multipolar balance. Neither is consistent with the growing need for international cooperation and emerging concepts of social justice. The European power balance of Metternich during the early nineteenth century did minimize big power wars for decades, but was not relevant to the social problems of the time which overthrew nearly every throne in Europe by 1848. The nonmilitary problems of the late twentieth century are far more serious, and affect far more countries. We now need to work toward a new world order, a participatory world order, in which the role of individual countries is based on factors other than military power. Achieving the international cooperation needed to cope with existing and emerging threats to human well-being is dependent on creating a new concept of world order in which the basic emphasis is more on cooperation and a sense of community and less on conflict and competition.

The Need for Perspective

Perhaps the scarcest human attribute in the late twentieth century is perspective. There are two reasons for this—the accelerating rate of change and the growing complexity of the modern era. Change is now so rapid that it becomes difficult to see the world even as it is today, much less as it will be tomorrow.

The principal threat to our future well-being may not be the relationship of man to man, as global military expenditures of $204 billion per year would indicate, but rather the deteriorating relationship of man to nature. Some forms of economic activity are now beginning to approach the limits which the earth's ecosystem can accommodate without undergoing undesirable and perhaps irreversible changes. As yet we can only dimly perceive the revolutionary consequences of this fact, but we know it requires us to adjust our procreative and economic behavior to the carrying capacity of our planet.

Accommodating ourselves to the finite system of which we are a part will not be easy. The notion that we might need to examine existing life styles and abandon the pursuit of superaffluence is not a popular one. Many will refuse to believe it is necessary. In some ways the current situation is reminiscent of an earlier period in history when even though scientists were gathering evidence that the earth was round, many refused to accept the notion. Today, scientists are telling us the earth is finite, but it is not easy for us to accept the idea.

Many of mankind's most pressing problems are changing their dimensions and definition. During the sixties, population growth was viewed as a threat because it undermined progress in the poor countries. The need then was to slow population growth. During the seventies, rapid population growth is still undermining efforts to improve well-being, but the need now is to stabilize population in all countries. The principle is a simple one; with finite resources, the more there are of us, the less each of us can have. In an increasingly integrated global economy we must think of people versus resources in global terms. We all compete for the same supplies of petroleum, industrial raw materials and marine protein.

The need to redefine the hunger problem is influenced by similar considerations. It is no longer simply a matter of increasing food production more rapidly to get ahead of population. The challenge now is far more complex. It is still necessary to expand food production more rapidly, but it must be done at a time when existing levels of production are adversely affecting the ecosystem.

Throughout the modern era the principal economic issue has been how to produce more, but as we begin to press against the limits, the emphasis is beginning to shift from production to distribution. At this point, concepts of social justice governing distribution rather than economic techniques to expand production become the central focus.

The organization of global society itself has become incredibly complex over the past two decades. The major colonial empires had scarcely been dismantled, neatly organizing the world into a collection of sovereign nation-states, when this geographical delineation was complicated by the emergence of multinational corporations, a new type of economic entity overlaying the older political ones. These gigantic economic institutions, exceeding in economic size many of the nation-states in which they operate, make the world infinitely more complex, raising questions as to the respective roles of state and corporations. The latter have strengthened economic ties between many countries to the point where military conflict becomes highly unlikely, but their multinational character poses a problem because they elude the capacity of any nation-state to regulate their behavior to ensure that they act in the broader social interest.

The U.S. Stake

Confronted with the massive poverty afflicting much of mankind, discouraged by the seemingly futile involvement of Vietnam, and disillusioned with foreign aid, Americans are tempted by isolationism. Comforting though this retreat from reality might seem, it is not a very realistic possibility and with each passing year it becomes less so. Few of our problems can be solved, few of our material needs met in isolation from the rest of the world. As the enormous consumption of raw materials in the United States expands exponentially, indigenous reserves of petroleum, natural gas and many industrial raw materials are being exhausted. With projected import needs of petroleum and industrial raw materials in the year 2000 costing $64 billion (an eightfold increase over the 1970 level), the United States is acquiring an enormous stake in a liberal international trading system which will assure access both to the needed raw materials and to overseas markets where it can earn the necessary foreign exchange.

The rich countries are also acquiring a direct stake in eliminating global poverty. Given the need to eventually stabilize the global level of economic activity, there is now a new urgency to help raise living levels among the world's poor to the point where birth rates will begin to voluntarily decline.

The list of national problems which have only global solutions is increasing. As indicated earlier, one of America's most troublesome social problems is the spreading addiction to hard drugs. At least a quarter of a million Americans are addicts. This is a serious matter per se, but in addition, a majority of these addicts cannot finance their habit from their own incomes, thus contributing to rising crime rates in virtually every city in the United States.

The prospects of dealing with this problem through internal measures alone are not good. We have offered the Turkish government $35 million to assist with an agricultural adjustment program designed to replace opium with other cash crops. What we must realize is that there is a whole string of countries which produce opium, stretching from Turkey through Iraq, Afghanistan, Pakistan, India, Burma, Thailand and Laos, any one of which can easily supply the entire addict population of the United States. Eventually it might be necessary to secure the cooperation of all these countries to shut off the inflow of heroin.

There are other more critical matters where cooperation among countries is needed. One essential area is the orderly exploitation and management of the ocean's resources, both animate and inanimate. Unless we can agree soon on management of fish stocks, we face the prospect of diminishing supplies of several commercial species because of overfishing.

Concepts as to how the oceans should be developed vary widely. Rich countries rely on capital investments and advanced technology in fishing fleets to acquire a dominant share of the world fish catch. Poor countries, unable to compete in this way, are extending their offshore boundaries, often as much as 200 miles. Ecuador seized 51 U.S. fishing trawlers in 1971, levying more than $2 million in fines.

Still another area in which the rich countries are dependent on the poor for cooperation is in the setting of environmental standards which will regulate pollution emissions from various industries. To the extent that poor countries have less rigorous standards, they will have an advantage in attracting new investment and jobs away from the now industrialized countries. Because it will affect the distribution of jobs among countries, and in some instances, global pollution levels, it is a very sensitive issue.

Another troublesome internal problem for many rich countries is inflation. One factor aggravating this is the rising prices of energy fuels and industrial raw materials. As the competition among countries for the more scarce minerals increases and as those poor countries which control a major share of the reserves begin to organize and bargain collectively, as petroleum exporters are now doing, this could become an important source of inflationary pressure.

As acute poverty in the poor countries generates social and political unrest, social disintegration becomes a very real possibility in certain areas. Signs of this are already evident, for example, in parts of eastern India and the Philippines, where effective government no longer exists. Political assassinations may become commonplace as political stresses increase in many areas.

Those of us who are among the 6 percent of the world's people living in the United States must recognize how deeply our privileged position of great wealth is now resented among the 2 billion people who live on annual incomes of $100 or less per year and with whom we share this planet and its resources. As the pursuit of superaffluence continues in the United States while needs of the poor countries are virtually ignored, this attitude can only become more firmly entrenched. Technologically advanced societies are highly vulnerable, not only because they depend on imported energy supplies and industrial raw materials but also because computers, communications systems, petroleum pipelines, nuclear reactors, power plants and jet airliners are vulnerable to sabotage.

As social and political unrest worsens, the security of Americans traveling or working abroad may well diminish as they become the target of dissident groups. We are likely to witness the continual kidnapping not only of embassy personnel, ranging from ambassadors to agricultural technicians, but of others as well, such as business executives operating in poor countries. American tourists are also affected, since there are now many areas abroad where it is not safe for them to travel. The hijacking of airliners continues to be a major threat to safety, even though heavy investments have been made by governments and airlines in providing security personnel and adopting security measures.

Change and Complexity

Because of the accelerating pace of change, we find ourselves formulating policies and making decisions on the basis of a world that existed at some time in the past. Hans Morgenthau stresses this in the political area: "There is a great discrepancy between our conventional mode of thought and action on the one hand, and the unprecedented novelty of the objective conditions under which we live. We think and act in terms of the pre-atomic age, while we live in an entirely different age which has made those ideas of the past obsolete as earlier ideas were made obsolete by the previous industrial revolution. This concerns particularly the nation-state. I am convinced that the nation-state has been rendered obsolete by the nuclear revolution in the same way that feudalism was made obsolete 200 years ago by the first industrial revolution."

If we could devise an index to measure change, we might conclude that the next three decades will bring at least two centuries' worth of change, as measured in historical terms. Should this be the case, the consequences are profound, for whereas change in the past could occur between generations, it must now occur within a generation, putting a great deal more stress on the individual. Accelerating change is also putting an enormous burden on society, its values and institutions. In Alvin Toffler's words, "it puts us in collision with the future."

Many of mankind's pressing problems have mutually dependent solutions. Few can be addressed in their own right. Hunger is not likely to disappear unless we slow population growth. The ecological crisis has economic origins. Achieving a more equitable distribution of wealth in a society with rising unemployment is virtually impossible. The more we examine the principal problems facing mankind, the more clear it becomes that many have mutually dependent solutions.

In our increasingly complex world we have great difficulty distinguishing between the symptoms and causes of contemporary problems. Hundreds of billions of dollars are spent trying to cope with the consequences of the population explosion, but global expenditures to reduce birth rates are still infinitesimal.

We are severely handicapped by our educational system, which produces many highly trained specialists but few well-trained generalists. The world needs specialists, but it also needs generalists able to move between the natural and social sciences, between the academic and nonacademic worlds, and capable of seeing the forest as well as the trees. It very much needs policy advisers and political decision makers who can operate with confidence along the multifaceted interface created by the interaction of economic, ecological, demographic, social and political forces. It needs economists who can think like ecologists, and politicians who can behave like statesmen.

The future is going to be very demanding where leadership is concerned. The need is for leaders who will lead rather than follow, who are prepared to risk their political careers. The future will require both imagination of the kind demonstrated by Chancellor Willy Brandt of West Germany with his Ostpolitik, and the courage of New York State Assemblyman George M. Michaels, who reversed his vote on the abortion liberalization bill before the New York State Legislature in order to provide the one vote needed for it to pass, and in the process knowingly sacrificed his own political career.

A New World Order

Creating a new world order is a means to an end, not an end in itself. The end is an improvement in the human condition on a global scale. Measured in social terms, the cost of maintaining the existing system of independent nation-states is extremely high. It is largely responsible for spending more than $200 billion worth of the world's public resources for military purposes, and for the artificially high consumer prices for goods which are inefficiently produced behind the protection of national tariff walls. It is also responsible for a great deal of redundancy in scientific research.

If we are to reduce military expenditures greatly, then we must create an international system based on international law by which countries will abide. Within individual societies we have evolved extensive bodies of law. Without such laws, national societies as we know them could not function. What we must recognize is that the emergence of a global society, which is gradually becoming a technological and historical fact, requires a body of law and the means of enforcing the laws once they are established. Decisions by the Security Council or those rendered by the International Court of Justice in The Hague often cannot be implemented unless they are backed with sanctions, just as is the case within national societies.

As Phillip Jessup points out, "Unless the world achieves some form of international government in which a collective will takes precedence over the individual will of the sovereign state, the ultimate function of law, which is the elimination of force for the solution of human conflict, will not be fulfilled. The function of sovereignty was to protect the state in a world void of any alternative to self-protection." Jessup goes on to say that sovereignty in the sense of the unregulated will of states to do as they please is absolutely incompatible with international law. As we become more and more integrated economically, we begin to realize the futility and risk of attempting to maintain the current degree of national political autonomy. In fact, as argued earlier, economic integration among nations is gradually undermining traditional concepts of national political independence and militarism.

A unified global society must now be regarded not as a fiction or an ideal, but as the inevitable reality toward which we must move. The notion is not as far-fetched as it may at first seem. Human history is one of shifting loyalty from smaller to larger units. Personal allegiances and loyalties shifted from the clan to the tribe, from tribe to village, village to town, town to city-state, and in recent centuries, to the nation-state. Given the globe-spanning scale of technologies now being employed, the identification and loyalties of the individual must move beyond the nation-state, embracing all of mankind. Man has simply brought himself to the final step in the long progression extending throughgout his existence as a species.

The technological foundations for a global society—modern transport and communications technologies, and the capacity to organize global institutions—are already in hand. But the creation of a global society will not be either an easy or a smooth process. There are both centrifugal and centripetal forces at work in the world today, tending to bring us together and push us apart at the same time. The role of ideology is diminishing, but in some countries, particularly the poorer ones, nationalism is on the upswing, in part because of the inability of the existing global system to meet their needs.

The creation of a global society, a process of many dimensions, will often be a matter of two steps forward and one step backward. The building materials for this structure will take many forms—a joint annual meeting of U.S. and Japanese cabinets, trade preferences for poor countries' exports in the markets of the rich ones, an agreement by India and Pakistan to jointly develop the Indus River system, the formation of regional economic groupings, an exchange of landing rights between Aeroflot in

New York and Pan American in Moscow, the emergence of more and more global corporations, the interlocking of national electrical power grids in Western Europe, the liberalization of international trade and the formation of international professional associations.

An international monetary system, with the emergence of an embryonic global currency, the Special Drawing Rights, represents a strong unifying factor. Another is the formation of INTELSAT. With each of these developments the world becomes a bit smaller, a bit more closely knit, until eventually it will become more like a single community than a collection of sovereign, independent states.

A principal obstacle to the creation of a strong international community and a strong United Nations has been the limited financial support provided by the superpowers. The Ford Foundation's annual disbursements in 1970 exceeded the total budget of the United Nations, which totaled just over $200 million. Or, in national terms, the sum of all national contributions to the UN budget amounted to one fifth of 1 percent of the total military expenditures of its member countries. If we are serious about creating meaningful global institutions and a unified global community, mere tokenism will not suffice.

Needless to say, sovereign nation-states steadfastly resist the transfer of power necessary to create strong supranational institutions. Morgenthau recognizes this and says: "We can hardly expect the nation-state to make itself superfluous, at least not overnight. Rather what we must aim for is recognition in the minds of all responsible statesmen that they are really nothing more than caretakers of a bankrupt international machine which will have to be transformed slowly into a new one. The transition will not be dramatic, but a gradual one. People will still cling to national symbols."

Fortunately, there are some encouraging developments,

particularly among the young. The proposition "my country right or wrong" is no longer always accepted unquestioningly. Americans in particular have begun this questioning in earnest, as is evident in the lack of support for the Vietnam conflict. Unfortunately, in many countries this is not yet the case.

Some have expressed concern over the cultural homogenization and loss of individuality which might be associated with the creation of a global community. This is a matter of real concern but it is not inevitable. It is possible to create a global community which would protect diversity and preserve the different cultures which enrich the world. Furthermore, the emergence of a global community and individual participation in the political process need not be mutually exclusive. Robert Hutchins does not "believe it is necessary to emphasize these local [national] boundaries in order to achieve what is absolutely indispensable, individual participation in local life." Interestingly, we discover that as communications and transportation have improved over time, the fundamental structure of the intellectual world has become more decentralized and pluralistic. A few centuries ago a handful of universities, principally European ones, dominated world intellectual activity, but this is certainly no longer the case. The important thing is that we be conscious of the need to maintain diversity, pluralism and heterogeneity within a unified global society.

There is discussion from time to time on the need for a full-fledged world government. Realistically, this is not likely to come about in the short run. If we can build some of the supranational institutions that are needed in various areas, as indicated in Chapter 15, adding them to the International Monetary Fund, INTELSAT and the many others already in existence, these will eventually come to constitute an effective, though initially limited world government. The functions which these institutions undertake at the global level are essentially the functions of government within the nation-state.

Reordering Global Priorities

Our efforts to improve the quality of life are handicapped because although a global community is emerging technologically, we have not yet established a set of global priorities. And, as indicated earlier, the sum of national priorities does not add up to a rational set of global priorities. Indeed, there is little relationship between global needs and global priorities as measured by the current commitment of resources.

Circumstances in the early seventies call for a major shift in the use of public resources from military to social purposes. Global military expenditures in 1970 totaled an estimated $204 billion, a sum exceeding the total income of the poorest one-half of mankind. When military expenditures within a country are expressed as the percent of its GNP—7.8 percent for the United States in 1971, 4 for France, 11 for the Soviet Union—these figures usually appear rather small. But when they are expressed in terms of public expenditures—in many ways a more useful relationship, since military expenditures compete directly with social needs for these limited resources—they loom much larger. In the United States, a military budget of $78 billion currently consumes 37 percent of the federal budget, compared with only 1.5 percent for economic assistance to the poor countries.

As we enter the seventies, we find hopeful signs that the conditions influencing the global level of military expenditures are changing. Political leaders in both the United States and the Soviet Union are beginning to ask publicly whether war is becoming obsolete as an instrument of foreign policy. Traditional reasons for going to war—the acquisition of territory, the enslavement of people, expansion of spheres of influence, the prestige of successful military conquest—increasingly lack relevance and appeal today. Indeed, the distinction between victor and vanquished seemed largely to disappear with World War II and the advent of nuclear warfare. In the postwar reconstruction effort led by the United States, there was little differentiation between wartime allies, England and France, and enemies, Germany and Italy.

As economic and social ties between East and West increase, and as cooperation expands between the two major powers in space exploration, pollution control and other matters, conditions are being created for a major reassessment of military expenditures. The renewal of contacts between the United States and mainland China also enhances the prospect of reordering global priorities. Even a modest shift in resources from military expenditures to education, agriculture and family planning could make a great difference in efforts to improve living conditions for the world's poor.

A second major shift in resource use which the times call for is from the pursuit of superaffluence to the elimination of poverty. Superaffluence is the consumption of goods and services to the point where it has little bearing on individual well-being. An additional crust of bread for a man with only one crust greatly enhances his well-being, but an additional crust for a man who already has a loaf of bread only slightly improves his well-being.

A more sophisticated rendering of the same point is made by Charles Elliott in his book *The Development Debate*. Using a weighted index of twenty-four socioeconomic indicators, he points out that this index—which includes a variety of factors affecting well-being, such as life expectancy, protein intake, energy consumption, enrollment in elementary schools and newspaper circulation—rises rather rapidly with income until it passes $500 per person annually, whereupon the gains in the social index increase much less rapidly than income. Once incomes reach $1,500, each additional $100 has only a negligible impact on the overall index.

In the United States, where average incomes now exceed $4,000 per person yearly, further gains in income do not have much effect on well-being. Obtaining a second car, TV set or bathroom makes a rather small contribution to well-being compared with the first, but with the rise in affluence that now permits a third car, TV set, etc., improvement in the quality of life is scarcely perceptible.

As Americans, we must begin to ask ourselves what right we have to consume a third or more of the earth's resources in our pursuit of superaffluence though we constitute only 6 percent of its people. We must ask because others are beginning to do so and we must be prepared to respond.

An American Initiative

Creating a global community is a coin with two sides, one consisting of actions to encourage activities and build institutions of a supranational character, and the other consisting of actions designed to consciously denationalize the nation-state. Though contributing to the same end, these two means are distinctly different. Several examples of the former were cited above. An example of the latter was the decision by the United States government in the fall of 1969 to discontinue the policy of forcing foreign subsidiaries of U.S. firms to adhere to U.S. foreign policy in trade relations with the centrally planned economies. Another example was the shift in the U.S. role in INTELSAT associated with its reorganization in 1970, from a role of dominance and control to one of simply an important participant.

If a unified global society is to come into being in the near future, a strong initiative will be required. Although it may appear ethnocentric for an American to say so, one country—the United States—in many ways holds the key. It does so by virtue of the enormous economic and technological resources it commands. In economic terms, it accounts for more than one third of the world's total productive capacity. Its research and development budget represents nearly 40 percent of the global R&D budget. It is the first, and at this point the only truly global society in terms of its interests, contacts and involvements.

Because of its advanced technology and great wealth, the United States is free from many of the pressures and constraints confronting other societies. The United States is also unique in terms of the information it possesses. The information-gathering network of the U.S. government is enormous in scope, ranging from agricultural attachés in fifty-five posts throughout the world, reporting almost daily on crop and market conditions, to meteorological satellites transmitting an uninterrupted stream of information on global weather conditions.

Because of its enormous size and influence, the United States must consciously assume a low profile, denationalizing many of its international activities while still providing leadership and support. One specific way to denationalize is to shift resources from bilateral foreign aid programs into multilateral channels. This shift, endorsed in 1971 by the Presidential Task Force on Foreign Assistance, is constrained by the inability of the multinational institutions engaged in development, especially the United Nations Group, to use and administer a larger flow of resources effectively. Both this constraint and the rather successful U.S. bilateral programs argue for continuing a substantial bilateral program, capitalizing on its unique strengths in areas such as agriculture and family planning, and separating it institutionally from the State Depart ment and U.S. foreign policy. Another action which sug gests itself is the unilateral establishment and endowment of international research institutes along the lines discussed in Chapter 15.

The United States can also play a major role in strength ening the United Nations, especially in supporting a peace keeping force with enough muscle to be effective in enforc ing decisions of the United Nations. Much of the world would support and applaud such an initiative, since it may be the only hope for reducing appreciably the burgeoning military budget which helps keep so much of mankind in poverty.

The United States possesses far more information on the deteriorating state of the earth's ecosytem than any other country. Possession of such information brings with it a responsibility to both share the information and act upon it. One way of providing leadership is by example. In this sense, passage of the Family Planning Services and Popula tion Research Act of 1970 was most encouraging. So, too, are declining birth rates and the emergence of the strong Zero Population Growth movement in the United States. What we do in these matters will have far more impact on the remainder of mankind than what we say.

If we make family planning services available upon re quest to everyone in the United States, then the rest of the world may well follow. If we adopt a minimum standard of living at home and provide leadership in the same effort at the global level, then the remainder of the world will no doubt support such an initiative. This does not mean that we should wait until all our problems are solved at home before turning to those abroad. If we do, we will never turn to the global problems. More important, we cannot separate problems at home from those abroad.

We are the one nation controlling enough resources to

make a major and immediate dent in world poverty. Consider, for example, what the world would be like now if the $25 billion per year spent on the Vietnam military effort had been devoted to literacy programs, agricultural modernization and the provision of health and family planning services in poor countries. We must carefully examine the public-private distribution of our resources, asking with World Bank President Robert McNamara: "Which is ultimately more in a nation's interest: to funnel national resources into an endlessly spiraling consumer economy, in effect a pursuit of consumer gadgetry with all its senseless by-products of waste and pollution, or to dedicate a more reasonable share of those same resources to improving the fundamental quality of life, both at home and abroad." Narrowly defined, the issue is one of private opulence versus public responsibility. But in the longer run the former will not be possible without the latter.

Given the resources they command, Americans are in a unique position to help shape the world of the future if theirs is a vision of what that world could and should be like. But this role in shaping the future must be exercised more through example and less through influence than has previously been the case. The United States must be willing to use its economic and scientific resources in pursuit of global social objectives; we are reaching the point in the evolution of human society where it is becoming more and more difficult to defend our pursuit of superaffluence while much of the world still suffers from abject poverty.

You, Me and the Future

Any effort to reshape the future must begin with you and me. Being a taxpaying, law-abiding citizen who votes regularly is no longer enough to ensure our future. Our circumstances require that we become politically active, not in partisan Republican, Democrat, Christian Democrat or Communist terms, but in terms of our self-interest and that of our children. We begin with the formulation of a new ethic. At a minimum, this ethic must seek harmony between man and nature and encompass an ideology of global unification. It must seek to raise everyone above the subhuman conditions of life now prevailing for so much of mankind. Planned obsolescence, uncontrolled human fertility and nationalism are out of place in the late twentieth century. The politicians' distinction between the national interest and the global interest is diminishing in our increasingly interdependent world.

You and I must adopt and propagate this new ethic, translating it into political action. Our future well-being depends on how quickly the new ethic now emerging can be translated into a new, more humane set of global priorities, new global institutions and new levels of global cooperation. The future requires a commitment to society in its totality, and the number so committed must expand rapidly in order to reduce the damaging impact of special interest groups, whether they be the highway lobby in the United States, the military-industrial complexes in the United States and the Soviet Union, the beet-sugar interests in North America and Western Europe or the rice interests in Japan. Unless the gap between the broader social interest and these special interests can be narrowed, and soon, the prospects for a better world are dim indeed.

What specifically can you and I do to ensure that the quality of life for all mankind improves rather than deteriorates? In my opinion, we should focus on three specific and interrelated objectives: (1) the elimination of global poverty, (2) the stabilization of world population and (3) the reduction of global military expenditures.

How do we go about achieving these objectives? Fortunately, there are some forces working in our favor. Charles Reich has written eloquently, though sometimes overenthusiastically, of the transformation of values under way among American youth. Jean-François Revel, writing from the vantage point of a French philosopher, documents the evolution of a new American ethic in an even more persuasive manner. Many Americans, long content with the way things were going, are now becoming concerned and are beginning to work to consciously shape their future. One expression of this is Common Cause, the bipartisan organization established by former HEW Secretary John Gardner to focus public attention on the critical issues confronting our society. How successful this organization will be in the long run remains to be seen, but it is attempting to fill a major void in the American political system. In one year its membership climbed to 200,000.

The work of Ralph Nader with his Institute for Responsive Law is another important expression of the need to mitigate the influence of the special-interest groups. Nader and his staff, largely volunteers, have effectively entered the Washington political arena on behalf of the American consumer.

For perhaps the first time in history the American people have begun to assert themselves in the technology assessment area. In deciding not to support any futher government funding for development of the SST, the American people may have taken a second "giant step for mankind."

The recently established Coalition on National Priorities represents an impressive group of concerned organizations striving to reduce U.S. military expenditures. So, too, is the Urban Coalition with its carefully constructed counterbudget. It argues for sharply reduced defense expenditures and the shift of these resources to such pressing social needs as urban renewal and economic assistance to the poor countries.

These bipartisan political action efforts constitute a heartening trend in the evolution of our political system, holding out the hope that we can indeed narrow the gap between the special interests and the much larger common interest. These organizations deserve our support in terms of time and money.

Organizations involved in the critical effort to slow and stabilize population growth also deserve our strong support. Among these, three stand out. Zero Population Growth is a new but highly effective educational organization whose youthful membership after its first three years numbers 40,000 in 400 chapters throughout the United States. Another is the International Planned Parenthood Federation, an organization providing family planning services through its affiliates in some seventy countries around the world. IPPF needs both funds and volunteers. The Population Crisis Committee, which has successfully undertaken a major educational effort within the Washington political community, has measurably increased the amount of federal funds going into family planning services both at home and abroad.

Each of us must examine our own priorities in terms of how we use our time and money. There are endless numbers of useful causes and organizations, but we must distinguish between those which are critical and those which are merely useful. The former will measurably affect the world in which we and our children live. The three interrelated objectives outlined above—eliminating global poverty, stabilizing world population and reducing military expenditures—are truly critical, deserving of a total commitment by you and me.

If our society is to survive and progress in the seventies and eighties, we need a new ethic, a reordering of global priorities and fresh leadership. Continuing improvement in human well-being on a global scale is tied to the emergence of an increasingly unified global society. Forces at work are moving us inexorably toward a unified world or toward a deteriorating one. We can still exercise that choice, but not for much longer. The most urgent item on our agenda in the years immediately ahead is the creation of a world without borders, one which recognizes the common destiny of all mankind.

NOTES

2 *The Environmental Crisis*

PAGE	LINE	
18	2 fr. b.	Lave, Lester, and Seskin, Eugene, "Air Pollution and Human Health," *Science*, Vol. 169, No. 3947 (August 21, 1970).
19	31	Montague, Peter and Katherine, "Mercury: How Much Are We Eating?," *Saturday Review* (February 6, 1971), p. 51.
19	35	Washington *Star*, November 1, 1970.
20	16	*Sunday Times* (London), April 25, 1971.
20	19	Washington *Post*, May 28, 1971.
20	29	*Sunday Times* (London), April 25, 1971.
20	34	*New York Times*, July 11, 1971.
21	1	Washington *Post*, April 8, 1971.
23	1	*New York Times*, October 17, 1970.
23	5	U.S. Department of the Interior, Fish and Wildlife Service, Bureau of Sport Fisheries and Wildlife, "List of Extinct and Endangered Wildlife Species" (Washington, D.C., 1971).
23	14	*New York Times*, September 13, 1970

PAGE	LINE	
23	20	*Ibid.*, November 15, 1970.
23	32	*Ibid.*, April 27, 1970.
24	2	Washington *Star,* June 20, 1970.
25	36	*New York Times,* September 23, 1971.
26	3 fr. b.	Wurster, Charles F., "DDT in Mother's Milk," *Saturday Review* (May 2, 1970), p. 58.
37	16	*FAO Yearbook of Fishery Statistics, 1969* (Rome, Italy).
37	28	Sprague, Lucian M., and Arnold, John H., "Trend in Use and Prospects for the Future Harvest of World Fisheries Resources." International Center for Marine Resource Development (University of Rhode Island, Kingston, R.I., 1971).

3   The Widening Rich-Poor Gap

PAGE	LINE	
43	table	Population Reference Bureau, "World Population Data Sheet, April 1970" (Washington, D.C.).
46	13	Lewis, W. Arthur, *The Development Process.* Executive Briefing Paper No. 2, U.N. Centre for Economic and Social Information (New York, Praeger, 1970), p. 14.
46	23	Clifford, Juliet, and Osmond, Gavin, *World Development Handbook,* ODI, (London, Charles Knight, 1971), p. 59.
46	26	McNamara, Robert. Address to the Board of Governors, The World Bank, Washington, D.C., September 27, 1971.
47	14	Turnham, D. J., "Income Distribution: Measurement and Problems." Paper given at the SID 12th World Conference, Ottawa, May 16–19, 1971.
53	9	*New York Times,* September 20, 1971.
53	11	*The Economist* (May 29, 1971), p. 40.
53	16	*Ibid.*, p. 24.
53	31	Washington *Post,* June 15, 1970.
54	8	*The Economist* (February 6, 1971), p. 74.
54	12	Report of the Secretary of State, *U.S. Foreign Policy 1969–1970* (Washington, D.C.), pp. 247–48.

PAGE LINE

54   20   Washington *Post*, May 16, 1971.
56   29   Michanek, Ernst, *The World Development Plan:
           A Swedish Perspective* (Stockholm, Almqvist &
           Wiksell, 1971), p. 62.

           4 *Marginal Men*

59   17   Thorbecke, Erik, "What is Unemployment?,"
           Ceres, FAO Review, Vol. 3, No. 6 (November–
           December 1970), p. 24. (Rome, Italy)
59   26   Grant, James P., "Economic and Business Outlook
           for the Developing Countries in the 1970's."
           Development Issues Paper No. 1, Overseas
           Development Council (Washington, D.C.,
           1970).
59   29   *New York Times*, January 15, 1971.
60   8   *Towards Full Employment*, ILO Report (Geneva,
           1970), p. 13.
61   3   Thorbecke, Erik, "Unemployment and Underem-
           ployment in the Developing World." Paper
           given at Columbia University Conference on
           International Economic Development, February
           1970, p. 11.
61   28   ILO Report, *op. cit.*, p. 13.
63   25   *The Economist* (28 March–3 April, 1970).
63   31   *New York Times*, March 17, 1970.
64   34   *Ibid.*, January 18, 1971.
65   15   *Ibid.*, January 31, 1971.
65   26   ILO Report, *op. cit.*, p. 14.
66   3   Grant, *op. cit.*, p. 12.
66   36   *New York Times*, January 15, 1971, from OECD
           Study in the OECD "Observer."
67   25   Morse, David A., "Jobs—The New Challenge,"
           War On Hunger (Agency for International
           Development, Washington, D.C.), (March
           1970), p. 1.
68   6   Prebisch, Raul, Address to Eleventh Meeting of
           the Board of Governors of the Inter-American
           Development Bank, Punta del Este, April 1970.

5   *From Countryside to City*

PAGE	LINE	
74	29	Davis, Kingsley, "The Urbanization of the Human Population," in *Cities,* Scientific American Book (New York, Knopf, 1969), p. 8.
75	12	*Ibid.*
77	10	*Ibid.,* pp. 8–9.
78	35	*International Social Development Review,* No. 1, "Urbanization: Development Policies and Planning" (United Nations, 1968), p. 118.
79	14	Abrams, Charles, "The Uses of Land in Cities," in *Cities, op. cit.,* p. 125.
82	20	Hagmuller, Gotz, "A Noose Around the City," *Ceres* (FAO Review, Rome, Italy), Vol. 3, No. 6 (November–December 1970), pp. 46–47.
82	29	Jacoby, Erich H., "The Coming Backlash of Semi-Urbanization," *ibid.,* p. 51.
82	36	Dyckman, John, quoted in Hagmuller, *op. cit.,* p. 47.
86	23	*International Social Development Review, op. cit.,* p. 124.

6   *The Hungry Majority*

PAGE	LINE	
89	3	*The World Food Budget 1970,* FAER 19, U.S. Department of Agriculture, Economic Research Service.
89	31	Berg, Alan, cited in Lester R. Brown, *Seeds of Change* (New York, Praeger, 1969).
90	3	*New York Times,* May 17, 1970.
90	10	*Ibid.,* February 19, 1970.
91	32	"Weather Modification: A Technology Coming of Age," *Science,* Vol. 172 (May 7, 1971), p. 549.
93	11	Washington *Evening Star,* December 10, 1970.
97	26	Dalrymple, Dana G., *Imports and Plantings of High-Yielding Varieties of Wheat and Rice in the Less Developed Nations,* Foreign Economic Development Service, U.S. Department of Agriculture, January 1971.

PAGE	LINE	
97	last l.	Brown, *op. cit.*, p. 21.
101	20	Humphries, Robert, "The Imperiled Environment," *Vista* (March–April 1970).
105	23	Brown, Lester R., "Food Supplies and the Optimum Level of Population," in S. Fred Singer, ed., *Is There An Optimum Level of Population?* (New York, McGraw-Hill, 1971).
106	26	Altschul, Aaron M., *Proteins: Their Chemistry and Politics* (New York, Basic Books, 1965).
108	15	Anderson, Earl V., "Food: Preventing Hunger and Malnutrition," Foreign Economic Development Service Reprint 6, from *Chemical and Engineering News*, Vol. 49 (March 8, 1971), pp. 19–22.

7 The Educational Challenge

PAGE	LINE	
116	14	U.N. 1967 Report on the World Social Situation.
116	28	Jeffries, Charles, "Illiteracy, a World Problem," *Development Digest* U.S. AID, Vol. 8, No. 3 (July 1970), p. 87.
117	11	"A New Functional Approach to Literacy," *ibid.*, p. 96.
117	19	Jeffries, *op. cit.*, p. 89.
118	20	Jacoby, Neil H., "The Progress of Peoples." A Center Occasional Paper, Center for the Study of Democratic Institutions, June 1969. (Santa Barbara, Calif.)
120	3	Pearson Commission, *Partners in Development* (New York, Praeger, 1969), pp. 67–68.
121	10	Coombs, Phillip, *The World Educational Crisis— A Systems Analysis* (London, Oxford University Press, 1968).
122	7	Morrisett, Lloyd, "Sesame Street May Be Path for Other Technologies in Teaching," *New York Times*, January 11, 1971.
126	13	Coombs, *op. cit.*
127	7	*U.N. Statistical Yearbook, 1969.*
130	11	Lawrence, Robert de T., "Rural Mimeo Newspapers," *Development Digest*, U.S. AID, Vol. 8, No. 4 (October 1970).
130	18	*Ibid.*, Dr. D. J. Hays quoted.

8 *Stabilizing Human Population*

PAGE	LINE	
137	18	*Resources and Man,* National Academy of Sciences Study, Preston Cloud, chairman (San Francisco, W. H. Freeman, 1969), p. 5.
138	15	Wray, J. D., "Population Pressure on Families: Family Size and Child Spacing," in *Rapid Population Growth: Consequences and Policy Implications,* National Academy of Sciences (Baltimore, Johns Hopkins Press, 1971).
139	13	*New York Times,* March 14, 1971.
139	21	Campbell, Louise, "Running Against Growth in Hawaii," *Washington Monthly,* Vol. 2, No. 7 (September 1970).
142	11	"Population and Family Planning in the People's Republic of China," Population Crisis Committee, Washington, D.C. (Spring 1971).
142	26	Ravenholt, R. T., Piotrow, Phyllis T., and Speidel, J. Joseph, "Use of Oral Contraceptives," *International Journal of Gynaecology and Obstetrics,* Vol. 8, No. 6 (November 1970), p. 945.
142	34	Washington *Star,* August 31, 1971.
143	3	Hauser, Philip M., "World Population: Retrospect and Prospect," in *Rapid Population Growth, op. cit.*
147	25	Falk, Richard A., *This Endangered Planet: Prospects and Proposals for Human Survival* (New York, Random House, 1971), p. 78.
152	31	"Population . . . in . . . China," *op. cit.*
153	21	*Hindustan Times,* July 29, 1971.

9 *Building East-West Bridges*

156	9	Stockholm International Peace Research Institute (SIPRI), *Yearbook of Armaments and Disarmament 1969/70* (Stockholm, Almqvist & Wiksell, 1970).
156	25	Barnett, R., *The Economics of Death* (New York, Atheneum, 1970), p. 50.
157	22	McNamara, Robert S. Address to the Columbia University Conference on International Eco-

PAGE	LINE	
		nomic Development, New York, February 1970, p. 6.
161	16	Brzezinski, Zbigniew, "America and Europe," *Foreign Affairs,* Vol. 49, No. 1 (October 1970).
164	7	Scoville, Herbert, *Toward a Strategic Arms Limitation Agreement* (New York, Carnegie Endowment for International Peace, 1970).
165	10	*New York Times,* September 27, 1970.
167	12	Sakharov, Andrei D., *Progress, Coexistence and Intellectual Freedom* (New York, 1968), W. Norton, p. 143.
169	21	Washington *Post,* April 19, 1970.
169	33	*New York Times,* March 8, 1970.
170	12	Goldman, Marshall I., "The East Reaches for Markets," *Foreign Affairs,* Vol. 47, No. 4 (July 1969), p. 726.
170	35	*Business Week,* June 6, 1970.
171	4	*Ibid.*
171	29	Quinn, James Brian, "Technology Transfer by Multinational Companies," *Harvard Business Review* (November–December 1969), p. 150.
177	14	Pisar, Samuel, *Coexistence and Commerce* (New York, McGraw-Hill, 1970).

10 *The Growing Economic Interdependence*

PAGE	LINE	
184	14	Geiger, Theodore. Statement before Joint Economic Committee, U.S. Congress (Washington, D.C.), March 16, 1970, pp. 6–7.
186	12	Stanford Research Institute No. 9 (Menlo Park, Calif., 1968), p. 40.
187	36	Martin, William McChesney, "Toward a World Central Bank." Lecture at symposium sponsored by the Per Jacobsson Foundation, Basel, Switzerland, September 14, 1970, p. 5.
190	27	"Population and Family Planning in the People's Republic of China," Population Crisis Committee, Washington, D.C. (Spring 1971).
191	23	Oldham, C. H. G., *et al.,* "The Technological Balance of Payments," *Development Digest,* U.S. AID, Vol. 7 (January 1969).

PAGE	LINE	
191	34	*New York Times*, September 4, 1969.
192	31	*Ibid.*, October 11, 1971.
193	17	Cloud, Preston, "The Realities of Mineral Distribution," in Roger Revelle, *et al.*, *The Survival Equation* (Boston, Houghton Mifflin, 1971), p. 183.
195	17	*New York Times*, September 4, 1967.
195	21	Cloud, *op. cit.*
196	4	Bailey, Richard, *Problems of the World Economy* (Baltimore, Penguin Books, 1967), p. 40.
196	8	Park, Charles R., Jr., *Affluence in Jeopardy: Minerals and the Political Economy* (San Francisco, Freeman C, 1969).
196	23	Stanford Research Institute No. 14 (Menlo Park, Calif., 1969), p. 14.
197	2	Darmstadter, Joel, "International Energy Sources," Resources for the Future, Reprint No. 86, Washington, D.C. (July 1970), p. 68.
197	12	Barber, Richard, *The American Corporation* (New York, Dutton, 1970).
198	5	*Resources and Man*, National Academy of Sciences Study, Preston Cloud, chairman (San Francisco, W. H. Freeman, 1969).
199	6	"Five Year Oil Accord Is Reached in Iran by 23 Companies," *New York Times*, February 15, 1971.
199	26	Washington *Post*, September 21, 1971.
200	22	*New York Times*, July 5, 1971.
201	2	Martin, *op. cit.*, p. 1.
202	19	*Business Week*, December 6, 1969.
202	31	*New York Times*, December 28, 1969.
203	29	Stanford Research Institute Report No. 4 (Menlo Park, Calif., 1967), p. 16.

11 *The Multinational Corporation*

211	21	Polk, Judd, "World Companies and the New World Economy." Background Paper No. 1, Council on Foreign Relations, October 1970.

PAGE	LINE	
212	1	Watkins, Melville, ed., *The Battle for Control of Our Economy* (Toronto, New Press, 1970).
213	bottom l.	*OECD Main Economic Indicators*, May 1970, GNP 1968 at current prices and exchange rates.
		AID Economic Data Books, March 1970.
		IBRD International Financial Statistics, May 1970.
		World Bank Atlas, 1969.
		"Ranking the U.S. Corporations," *Fortune* (May 15, 1969).
		"The Top 200 Industrial Companies Outside the U.S.," *ibid.* (August 15, 1969).
216	6	Barber, Richard, *The American Corporation* (New York, Dutton, 1970), p. 20.
216	15	*New York Times*, March 30, 1970.
216	20	Lobb, John C., "Japan, Inc.—The Total Conglomerate," *Columbia Journal of World Business* (March–April 1971).
217	14	Barber, *op. cit.*, p. 264.
218	34	Sunday *Star*, September 26, 1971.
219	13	*New York Times*, February 27, 1972.
220	28	*Policy Aspects of Foreign Investment by U.S. Multinational Corporation*, U.S. Department of Commerce, Washington, D.C. (January 1972).
221	13	Rolfe, Sidney E., "The International Corporation in Perspective," *Atlantic Community Quarterly* (Summer 1969), p. 266.
224	10	*The Growth and Spread of Multinational Companies*, QER Special No. 5, The Economic Intelligence Unit (New York, October 1969), p. 27.
228	5	Quinn, Brian, "Technology Transfer by Multinational Companies," *Harvard Business Review* (November–December 1969).
229	2	*New York Times*, May 10, 1970.

12   Restructuring the Global Economy

234	29	Washington *Post*, November 29, 1970.
240	25	*Japan Times*, September 10, 1971.
241	27	Quinn, James Brian, "Technology Transfer by

PAGE	LINE	
		Multinational Companies," *Harvard Business Review* (November–December 1969), p. 149.
242	35	*Ibid.*, p. 152.
247	31	*The Economist* (September 26, 1970).
249	11	Terutomo Ozawa, "Japan Exports Technology to Asian LDC's," *Columbia Journal of World Business* (January–February 1971), p. 69.
250	8	Stockholm International Peace Research Institute (SIPRI), *Yearbook of Armaments and Disarmament 1969/70* (Stockholm, Almqvist & Wiksell, 1970).
250	18	*Ibid.*
250	32	*Ibid.*

13   *A Global Communications System*

261	7	Annual Report on Activities and Accomplishments under the Communications Satellite Act of 1962, Washington, D.C. (January/December 31, 1969).
263	11	Barber, Richard, *The American Corporation* (New York, Dutton, 1970), p. 146.
265	20	Cousins, Norman. Editorial in *Saturday Review* (October 24, 1970), p. 26.
267	10	Johnson, Lyndon B., quoted in "New Communications Era," COMSAT Corp., Washington, D.C. (November 1967).
268	11	Brzezinski, Zbigniew, *Between Two Ages* (New York, Viking, 1970), p. 19.
269	16	Cassirer, Henry, "Communications—Key to Man's Self-Awareness," *Environment and Society in Transition*, Vol. 184, New York Academy of Sciences (New York, 1971), p. 308.
270	9	Pei, Mario, "Prospects for a Global Language," *Saturday Review* (May 2, 1970), p. 24.
270	30	Mead, Margaret, "The Future As the Basis for Establishing a Shared Culture," *Daedalus*, Vol. 94, No. 1 (Winter 1965), pp. 148–53.
271	20	The British Council, English-Teaching Information Centre (personal correspondence), June 26, 1970.

PAGE	LINE	
271	31	English-Speaking Union of the United States (New York), *English Around the World,* No. 2 (May 1970), p. 1.
273	17	Dr. Hood Roberts, Georgetown Linguistics Center, Washington, D.C.
273	25	Council of Europe Special Conference: Curricula for the Teaching of English in European Secondary Schools (London, May 1969).

14 A Global Transport System

PAGE	LINE	
278	9	Halaby, Najeeb, "Transportation," in Foreign Policy Association, *Toward the Year 2018* (New York, Cowles, 1968), p. 46.
279	bottom l.	Stanford Research Institute Report No. 11 (Menlo Park, Calif., 1969), p. 25.
280	27	*Orbis* (Spring 1970).
281	30	Stanford Research Institute Report No. 5 (Menlo Park, Calif.).
282	28	Washington *Post,* June 14, 1971.
282	35	*Ibid.,* April 19, 1970.
285	12	*New York Times,* August 15, 1971.
285	16	Washington *Post,* August 11, 1971.
286	12	*Saturday Review,* October 24, 1970.
286	23	*Ibid.*
287	12	Washington *Star,* July 26, 1970.
287	24	Cultural Affairs Office, Embassy of Spain, Washington, D.C.
288	11	*Ceres,* FAO Review, Rome, Italy (January–February 1970), p. 64.
288	27	"Focus on South American Tourism and Air Travel," Market Research Group, Douglas Aircraft Co. (Long Beach, Calif., 1968).
288	32	*New York Times,* April 26, 1970.
289	24	Halaby, *op. cit.,* p. 39.
290	22	*Wall Street Journal,* August 26, 1970.
291	9	*Business Week* (October 17, 1970), p. 94.
291	26	"Aeroflot: Both Dream and Nightmare," *New York Times,* January 14, 1971.
293	11	*World Business,* No. 18 (First Quarter 1970).

PAGE	LINE	
		Special report on Japan, The Chase Manhattan Bank, N.A., New York.
297	12	Halaby, *op. cit.*, pp. 43–44.

15 *New Supranational Institutions*

PAGE	LINE	
305	14	Pardo, Arvid, "Who Will Control the Seabed?," *Foreign Affairs*, Vol. 47, No. 1 (October 1968), p. 125.
305	32	Washington *Post*, February 7, 1971.
306	8	*Ibid.*, p. 135.
306	29	*New York Times*, December 16, 1970.
309	20	Kennan, George F., "To Prevent a World Wasteland," *Foreign Affairs*, Vol. 48, No. 3 (April 1970).
311	32	Watkins, Melville, ed., *The Battle for Control of our Economy* (Toronto, New Press, 1970), p. 53.

16 *Improving the Quality of Life*

PAGE	LINE	
330	24	Washington *Post*, September 5, 1971.
335	35	Cool, John, "Population Growth and Social Services," AID Population Conferences, Kathmandu, Nepal, July 1971, p. 5.
337	15	Washington *Post*, October 19, 1970.
337	20	*Ibid.*
339	2	Pearson, Lester, quoted by R. J. Crooks, UN/UAW Paper.

17 *Changing Direction*

PAGE	LINE	
349	15	Morgenthau, Hans, "On the World Community," Center Occasional Paper, Center for the Study of Democratic Institutions, 1965, p. 23.
349	25	Toffler, Alvin, *Future Shock* (New York, Random House, 1970).
351	32	Jessup, Phillip, "On the World Community," Center Occasional Paper, CSDI, 1965, pp. 6, 12.

PAGE	LINE	
353	21	Ford Foundation Annual Report (1971), U.N. Budget Report (1971).
353	34	Morgenthau, *op. cit.*, p. 24.
354	18	Hutchins, Robert, Center Report, CSDI (April 1971), p. 3.
355	26	Washington *Post,* September 3, 1971.
356	30	Elliott, Charles, *The Development Debate* (London, SCM Press Ltd., 1971).
360	14	McNamara, Robert S. Address to the Columbia University Conference on International Economic Development, New York, February 1970, p. 4.
362	4	Reich, Charles A., *The Greening of America* (New York, Random House, 1970).
362	7	Revel, Jean-François, *Without Marx or Jesus* (New York, Doubleday, 1971).

FURTHER READING

Books

Barber, Richard, *The American Corporation*. New York, Dutton, 1970.

Barnet, Richard J., *The Economy of Death*. New York, Atheneum, 1970.

Boulding, Kenneth E., *The Meaning of the 20th Century: The Great Transition*. New York, Harper, 1965.

Brown, Lester R., *Seeds of Change: The Green Revolution and Development in the 1970's*. New York, Praeger, 1970.

―――― and Finsterbusch, Gail W., *Man and His Environment: Food*. New York, Harper and Row, 1972.

Bryant, John, *Health and the Developing World*. Ithaca, N.Y., Cornell University Press, 1969.

Brzezinski, Zbigniew, *Between Two Ages: America's Role in the Technetronic Era*. New York, Viking, 1970.

Carson, Rachel, *Silent Spring*. Boston, Houghton Mifflin, 1962.

Clifford, Juliet, and Osmond, Gavin, *World Development Handbook*. Overseas Development Institute. London, Charles Knight, 1971.

Ehrlich, Paul R. and Anne H., *Population, Resources, Environment:*

Issues in Human Ecology. San Francisco, W. H. Freeman, 1970.

Eichelberger, Clark M., *UN: The First Twenty-five Years*. New York, Harper, 1970.

Falk, Richard A., *This Endangered Planet*. New York, Random House, 1971.

Ferkiss, Victor C., *Technological Man*. New York, Braziller, 1969.

Foreign Policy Association, *Toward the Year 2018*. New York, Cowles, 1968.

Halle, Louis J., *The Society of Man*. New York, Dell, 1969.

Jungk, Robert, and Galtung, Johan, *Mankind 2000*. London, Allen & Unwin, 1969.

Keohane, Robert O., and Nye, Joseph S., Jr., eds., *International Organization* (Transnational Relations and World Politics), World Peace Foundation, Vol. XXV, No. 3, Summer 1971.

McHale, John, *The Future of the Future*. New York, Braziller, 1969.

Mead, Margaret, *Culture and Commitment: A Study of the Generation Gap*. Natural History Press. New York, Doubleday, 1970.

Meadows, Donella H. and Dennis L., Randers, Jorgen, and Behrens, William W., III, *The Limits to Growth: A Report for the Club of Rome's Project on the Predicament of Mankind*. New York, Universe Books, 1972.

Michanek, Ernst, *The World Development Plan: A Swedish Perspective*. Stockholm, Almqvist & Wiksell, 1971.

Mishan, Ezra J., *The Costs of Economic Growth*. New York, Praeger, 1967.

Myrdal, Gunnar, *The Challenge of World Poverty*. New York, Pantheon, 1970.

Owens, Edgar, and Shaw, Robert, *Development Reconsidered*. Lexington, Heath, 1972.

Pearson, Lester B., *The Crisis of Development*. New York, Praeger, 1970.

Perloff, Harvey S., ed., *The Future of the U.S. Government*. New York, Braziller, 1971.

Pisar, Samuel, *Coexistence and Commerce*. New York, McGraw-Hill, 1970.

Reich, Charles A., *The Greening of America*. New York, Random House, 1970.

Revel, Jean-François, *Without Marx or Jesus*. New York, Doubleday, 1971.

Rolfe, Sidney E., and Damm, Walter, eds., *The Multinational Corporation in the World Economy*. New York, Praeger, 1970.

Sakharov, Andrei D., *Progress, Coexistence and Intellectual Freedom*. New York, Norton, 1968.

Servan-Schreiber, J.-J., *The American Challenge*. New York, Atheneum, 1968.

Singer, S. Fred, ed., *Is There an Optimum Level of Population?* New York, McGraw-Hill, 1971.

Sprout, Harold and Margaret, *Toward a Politics of the Planet Earth*. New York, Van Nostrand Reinhold, 1971.

Toffler, Alvin, *Future Shock*. New York, Random House, 1970.

Vernon, Raymond, *Sovereignty at Bay: The Multinational Spread of U.S. Enterprises*. New York, Basic Books, 1971.

Wagar, W. Warren, *Building the City of Man: Outlines of a World Civilization*. New York, Grossman, 1971.

Wallia, C. S., ed., *Toward Century 21*. New York, Basic Books, 1970.

The Biosphere, A Scientific American Book. San Francisco, W. H. Freeman, 1971.

Cities, A Scientific American Book. New York, Knopf, 1969.

Resources and Man, National Academy of Sciences, National Research Council. San Francisco, W. H. Freeman, 1969.

Toward a Social Report, U.S. Department of Health, Education and Welfare, Washington, D.C., 1969.

Magazines, Pamphlets and Papers

Cassirer, Henry, "Communications—Key to Man's Self-Awareness." *Environment and Society in Transition*, New York Academy of Sciences, 1971.

Geiger, Theodore. Statement before the Joint Economic Committtee, March 16, 1970. (U.S. Congress, Washington, D.C.).

Goldman, Marshall I., "The East Reaches for Markets." *Foreign Affairs*, Vol. 47, No. 4. (July 1969).

Lave, Lester, and Seskin, Eugene, "Air Pollution and Human Health." *Science*, Vol. 169, No. 3947 (August 21, 1970).

Martin, William McChesney, "Toward a World Central Bank." Lecture at symposium sponsored by the Per Jacobsson Foundation, Basel, Switzerland, September 14, 1970.

Mason, Edward, "The Corporation in the Post-Industrial State." *California Management Review*, Vol. XII, No. 4 (Summer 1970).

Morgenthau, Hans, "On the World Community." Center Occasional Paper, Center for the Study of Democratic Institutions, 1965.

Oldham, C. H. G., *et al.*, "The Technological Balance of Payments." *Development Digest*, Vol. 7 (U.S. AID) (January, 1969).

Pardo, Arvid, "Who Will Control the Seabed?" *Foreign Affairs*, Vol. 47, No. 1 (October 1968).

Pecora, W. T., "Science and the Quality of Our Environment." *Bulletin of the Atomic Scientists*, Vol. XXVII, No. 8 (October 1970).

Pei, Mario, "Prospects for a Global Language." *Saturday Review*, (May 2, 1970).

Platt, John, "What We Must Do." *Science*, Vol. 166, No. 3909 (November 28, 1969).

Polk, Judd, "World Companies and the New World Economy." Background Paper No. 1, Council on Foreign Relations, October 1970.

Population Crisis Committee, "Population and Family Planning in the People's Republic of China." Spring 1971, Washington, D.C.

Powell, David E., "The Social Costs of Modernization: Ecological Problems in the USSR." *World Politics*.

Quinn, Brian, "Technology Transfer by Multinational Companies." *Harvard Business Review*, Vol. 47, No. 6 (November–December 1969).

Sprague, Lucian M., and Arnold, John H., "Trends in Use and Prospects for the Future Harvest of World Fisheries Resources." International Center for Marine Resource Development, University of Rhode Island, Kingston, R.I.

Turnham, D. J., "Income Distribution: Measurement and Problems." Paper presented at the Society for International Development 12th World Conference, Ottawa, Canada, May 16–19, 1971.

United Nations, "Urbanization: Development Policies and Planning," *International Social Development Review*, No. 1, 1968.

U.S. Department of Interior, "List of Extinct and Endangered Species." Fish and Wildlife Service, Bureau of Sport Fisheries and Wildlife (1971).

U.S. Department of State, *U.S. Foreign Policy 1969–70*, Report of the Secretary of State.

INDEX

ABOUT THE AUTHOR

LESTER R. BROWN is a Senior Fellow with the Overseas Development Council, a private, nonprofit organization located in Washington, D.C. He was formerly Administrator of the International Agricultural Development Service and served as policy adviser to the Secretary of Agriculture on world food needs and agricultural development abroad.

Recognized as a leading authority on the world food problem while still in his late twenties, he was awarded the Department of Agriculture's Superior Service Award in 1965. In 1966 Mr. Brown was selected by the U.S. Jaycees as one of the "Ten Outstanding Young Men of America." Especially commended was his work in anticipating the 1965 crop failure in India early enough to initiate a massive food rescue effort, thereby avoiding a famine.

Besides writing articles for scholarly and popular magazines, Mr. Brown is the author of *Man, Land and Food* (USDA, 1963) and *Seeds of Change: The Green Revolution and Development in the Seventies* (1970). He is a frequent guest lecturer on university campuses in this country and abroad, and also has served as a consultant to the United Nations and the Agency for International Development.

Mr. Brown lives in Chevy Chase, Maryland, with his wife and two children.